CHINESE PUBLISHING
—A Window to Chinese Civilization and Culture

张舍茹 顾曰国 编著

华夏文明之窗 WINDOWS TO CHINESE CIVILIZATION AND CULTURE

中国出版
追寻中华文明的字纸春秋

外语教学与研究出版社
FOREIGN LANGUAGE TEACHING AND RESEARCH PRESS
北京 BEIJING

图书在版编目 (CIP) 数据

中国出版：追寻中华文明的字纸春秋：英、汉／张舍茹, 顾曰国编著. ―― 北京：外语教学与研究出版社, 2016.11
（华夏文明之窗）
ISBN 978-7-5135-8333-6

Ⅰ.①中… Ⅱ.①张… ②顾… Ⅲ.①英语－阅读教学－高等学校－教材②出版事业－文化史－中国 Ⅳ.①H319.4；G

中国版本图书馆 CIP 数据核字（2016）第 280766 号

出 版 人　蔡剑峰
责任编辑　赵东岳
封面设计　郭　子
版式设计　涂　俐
出版发行　外语教学与研究出版社
社　　址　北京市西三环北路 19 号（100089）
网　　址　http://www.fltrp.com
印　　刷　北京盛通印刷股份有限公司
开　　本　787×1092　1/16
印　　张　17.5
版　　次　2016 年 11 月第 1 版 2016 年 11 月第 1 次印刷
书　　号　ISBN 978-7-5135-8333-6
定　　价　66.90 元

购书咨询：(010) 88819926　电子邮箱：club@fltrp.com
外研书店：https://waiyants.tmall.com/
凡印刷、装订质量问题，请联系我社印制部
联系电话：(010) 61207896　电子邮箱：zhijian@fltrp.com
凡侵权、盗版书籍线索，请联系我社法律事务部
举报电话：(010) 88817519　电子邮箱：banquan@fltrp.com
法律顾问：立方律师事务所　刘旭东律师
　　　　　中咨律师事务所　殷　斌律师
物料号：283330001

Chief Designer for this series of books: GU Yueguo
Chief Editor for this series of books: ZHANG Sheru

Chinese Publishing

Honorary Advisors

LIU Chaomei (Beijing Institute of Graphic Communication)

WANG Guanyi (Beijing Institute of Graphic Communication)

ZHANG Yangzhi (Beijing Institute of Graphic Communication)

Board of Advisors (in alphabetic order)

CAO Xiaoying (College English Reform Liaison — Office, Ministry of Education, China)

FANG Jizhong (Beijing Institute of Graphic Communication)

GUO Pingjian (Beijing Institute of Fashion Technology)

JIA Guodong (China Renmin University)

JIA Weiguo (Shandong University)

JIANG Xueqing (Beijing Jiaotong University)

LU Zhihong (Beijing University of Posts and Telecommunications)

SHI Jilong (Beijing Institute of Graphic Communication)

TANG Jinlan (Beijing Foreign Studies University)

TIAN Zhongli (Beijing Institute of Graphic Communication)

WANG Haixiao (Nanjing University)

XIE Fuzhi (Capital Normal University)

YU Weisheng (Chongqing University)

ZHANG Wenxia (Tsinghua University)

ZHOU Junying (Beijing University of Technology)

Board of Editors

Chief Editors: ZHANG Sheru, GU Yueguo (Beijing Institute of Graphic Communication)

Deputy Editors: Jason, Shaw (American), FANG Jizhong, LIU Xue (Beijing Institute of Graphic Communication)

English Copy Editors: Faulkner Graham Paul (British), Norman Pritchard (British), JIA Yuling (Central Compilation and Translation Brueau)

Web-based Courseware Production Team

General Director: GU Yueguo (Beijing Institute of Graphic Communication)

Team Leader: WANG Dejun (Beijing Foreign Studies University)

Scripts for Filming: LIU Yuhong (Beijing Foreign Studies University)

Camera Men: QI Yingji, ZHANG Shun, HU Yang (Beijing Foreign Studies University)

Make-up: LIU Yuhong (Beijing Foreign Studies University)

Post-editing: QI Yingji, ZHANG Shun (Beijing Foreign Studies University)

Presentation Team

Professor (Lecturer): Norman Pritchard (Beijing Foreign Studies University)

Philips (Advisor): XIE Fuzhi (Capital Normal University)

Irene: LIU Diandian (Beijing Institute of Graphic Communication)

Miriam: Pomi Assefa (Beijing Foreign Studies University)

Owen: Simon Sebastian Colipi (Beijing Institute of Graphic Communication)

《中国出版》课件制作群

顾　　问	顾曰国
文字作者	张舍茹
课程策划	唐锦兰
制作督导	王德军
责任编辑	刘育红
脚本设计	刘育红　齐英吉
导　　演	刘育红
演　　员	Norman Pritchard（英国）　谢福之　刘典典
	Simon Sebastian Colipi（澳大利亚）　Pomi Assefa（美国）
摄　　像	齐英吉　张　顺　胡　阳
剧　　务	孙　艳
视频剪辑	齐英吉　张　顺
场　　记	刘育红
化　　妆	刘育红
录　　音	Scott Powers Houston（美国）
	Johanna Christine Hemminger（美国）
声音剪辑	刘育红
美术设计	李双双　广博文
课件制作	靳伟峰
技术支持	曹新龙　王珠泉

Preface

Among human beings language is surely the most important and widely used method of communication. The entire range of human complexity, subtlety, ambiguity, anger, concern, confusion, a list too long to include here, is passed from one human to another through language. We acknowledge and appreciate the other forms of human interaction such as music, art, printing, acting, to name just a few, that are in this category. People who can command language are able to communicate with all other human beings, and we know that when the other forms of communication listed above are combined with human language, for example when we combine an artistic piece with a verbal explanation, the impact of the emotional and intellectual exchange is often especially profound.

Language helps to make more precise the idea being conveyed. We know that words and meanings regularly change within cultures and throughout different historical periods. The same can be true of appreciation for objects of art, the implications of music, the purpose of theatrical acting. As times change and social/cultural values and forms alter through the passage of centuries, language about art or music or theater allows us to record those changes and to reconstruct the values that originally brought forth the art, music, or theater. In those cases written language has the greatest potential to allow us to understand the people of different, earlier times.

Because human beings are so inventive, there are many, many spoken and written languages in the world today, as there have been over past times as well. The Chinese language is surely among these great accomplishments of human beings. Its historical, geographic, and cultural influence has been overwhelming, and continues to be so today. As China's role in the international community continues to expand, the Chinese language will take on even more influence in many corners of the world. All human beings should respect and celebrate the gifts given to mankind by the Chinese language.

The English language has a shorter history as a means of widespread communication, perhaps only a few hundred years. Its pedigree is longer than that, though because it traces its roots as a Germanic language with many influences from Latin, classical Greek and French, all links that preceded it by hundreds of years. Because of historical circumstances, especially the quest of the British people for exploration and world trade from the 16th century on, and because of the Industrial Revolution of the 18th century, English has come to be the single most widely used language in the world today. Many people who do not use English as their first language find it is convenient to communicate with others through the use of English. Indeed, the person who can communicate in English has instant access to fellow human beings all over the world. As stated in this series, English has become "the matter-of-fact *lingua franca*."

It is also the case that these days people all over the world have found new ways to communicate through language. This is so because of the blindingly fast advances in technology. We are able to see and hear each other instantaneously regardless of where we are in the geographic world. We can talk and laugh and share ideas quite easily through the Internet. It can store, examine, change and convey amazing amounts of information, all of it created by human beings and intended for other human beings. Through this technology we can speak and revise our statements, we can make friends and inform others, we can express our ideas and learn new information much more quickly and with greater ease than has ever been possible in the past.

Happily, the new technology does not mean we must abandon the human inventions of the past. The new technology employs all of the contributions of our inherited cultures, and provides them to us often in "real time," meaning we communicate with each other in a matter of seconds, regardless of where our friends are physically. Understanding and respecting our past is now more effortless, and maybe even more important, than it has ever been before. This is so because others around the world also have access to information about our inherited past, and they want to know about our past just as we show interest in their cultural roots.

This new series *Windows to Chinese Civilization and Culture* has been created in a way that maximizes the latest in technology. It is designed for a web-based delivery of courseware and allows for mobile delivery of these materials. Printed materials, which have been so vitally important in the history of mankind are also included. All of this material is organized to fit in perfectly with the latest effective technology-based teaching methods. What are those methods? They ask the learners to be active in designing the questions they ask. They allow all of the learners to communicate with each other through discussions and a back-and-forth give-and-take of communication so that any of the members pondering a question can contribute to the conversation. When people learn information in this manner, combined with the offerings of the printed texts they truly learn the subject, not in a passive but in an active and an interactive way. Their seminar room is a virtual seminar room because they communicate on-line.

At the same time, the series respects the traditional methods of time-tested education. There is a specialist professor to guide the learners, to offer perspective when it is needed, to keep learners on the right path. The series also continues to respect the use of written textual materials. Of course the subjects it introduces are from the rich, traditional past, as seen for example in the introductions to Chinese painting, printing, ink and paper-making techniques covered as part of this extensive series. The traditional past is used to instruct and encourage the students of the present day.

Moreover, in this series young students who themselves want to learn are ready to welcome new learners into their group. The young students do not pretend to have all of the answers. They don't even pretend to have all of the questions, since they ask their new friends to also provide questions. And they plan their group activities together, just as many students are encouraged to do these days. The series approaches its topics from the learner's point of view. This is an open and easy way to come to enjoy new material.

All of this is accomplished as a way to learn English. The English used in this series is standard, current-day language as it is used by students and professors throughout the world in English-speaking countries. The language level is relaxed, casual and conversational, just as young students would use it. The language spoken by the teachers and professors is more structured and professional, as it would be in real life. But these are modern day instructors, because they are relaxed about welcoming new learners into the discussion. They are the type of professors we always want to meet when we are trying to understand new material.

If you jump in to this material sincerely you will learn about China's past, maybe things you've heard before and maybe something you never fully understood before, and you will learn how to discuss the particular topic of each section. You will learn the necessary vocabulary in English and the sentence patterns that are most useful when talking about these important topics. Your reading comprehension will expand in a way useful to you and you'll find that other English language texts outside of this series will become easier to understand because of what you have learned from these lessons.

There is provision for translation practice, which is a fun way to demonstrate your English comprehension skills to yourself and to others. You will learn about how to attend a lecture in English and how to listen carefully when serious topics are being presented. You will learn how to write up a summary in English of the material that has been examined.

An unusually creative and forward-looking group of individuals has come together at the Beijing Institute of Graphic Communication to devise this series and present it to you. English language experts from the Foreign Language Teaching and Steering Committee of the Ministry of Education have examined portions of these materials and offered their guidance. The series is funded by the Beijing Institute of Graphic Communication (BIGC), and numerous distinguished faculty at the BIGC lent their expertise to the project. A number of native English speakers participated in the project. You will find a list of these scholars and advisors in the Acknowledgements section. Two professors at BIGC took the lead in organizing and producing this series and they deserve special thanks for their work: Professor Sheru Zhang and Professor Yueguo Gu.

It has been my pleasure to visit the BIGC campus on several occasions and to meet a number of the faculty and also some of the capable students there. In the summer of 2014 my university, Suffolk University in Boston, welcomed Professor Zhang and her delegation of faculty and students to our campus, where I was able to discuss this important series with her.

Ronald Suleski, PhD

Professor and Director
Rosenberg Institute for East Asian Studies
Suffolk University, Boston (Current position)
Fairbank Center for Chinese Studies
Harvard University (Former position)
December 2014

Contents

Acknowledgements I

A Note from the Author II

General Introduction III

Pre-Course Activity VII

Unit 1 Prerequisite of Chinese Publishing — the Origin and Development of Chinese Characters 01

Unit 2 The Emergence of Chinese Publishing from Signs to Characters to Books 31

Unit 3 Early Editing, Compilation and Publication in Ancient China 63

Unit 4 The Requirements of Publishing — Book-Sellers, Authors, Editors and Printers 95

Unit 5 Artistic Design and Book Collection of Ancient Chinese Publications 125

Unit 6 Major Accomplishments in the Chinese Publishing Industry 155

Unit 7 Published Output: From Rare Ancient Books to Modern Magazines 185

| Unit 8 | The Evolution and Diversification of Publishing in China in Modern Times | 215 |
| 主要参考文献 | | 253 |

Acknowledgements

The present work is part of the *Windows to Chinese Civilization and Culture* series funded by Beijing Institute of Graphic Communication. It has taken 3 years to complete *Chinese Publishing*. The series would have been impossible without the support both academically and financially from the Committee of Discipline Construction of Beijing Institute of Graphic Communication. Professor and Director ZHANG Yangzhi provided a lot of the cultural background for the subject construction, which served as the guideline, gradually forming the practical and BIGC-characteristic teaching material system. My thanks go to our president LIU Chaomei and Professor WANG Guanyi who offered not only great encouragement and help in overcoming many unexpected difficulties, but also in triggering my creation of this series of text books.

While researching and writing this series I incurred many debts. First to Professors FAN Jizhong and SHI Jilong who, as experts in the field of printing and publishing, offered a lot of valuable documents and reference materials, and answered many of my questions at length. PENG Junling, the librarian, managed to provide the videotaping site for network — based courseware. My deep gratitude and great appreciation also go to Professor JIA Yuling from the Central Compilation & Translation Bureau as well as foreign specialists Graham Paul Faulkner, Norman Pritchard and Richards Shaw who translated, refined and revised the English language to make sure the texts can be authentic, readable and fluent.

I was fortunate to collect many precious suggestions from English language experts from the Foreign Language Teaching Steering Committee of China's Ministry of Education. They include WANG Haixiao, ZHANG Wenxia, YU Weishen, JIA Guodong, LU Zhihong, JIANG Xueqing etc. Other professors such as XIE Fuzhi, SHEN Suping, JIA Weiguo also commented on draft chapters or sections.

During the probation period, many readers including my colleagues and students sent their questions or suggestions for improvements. Of these the most assiduous were SUN Yan, LIU Xue, LIU Diandian and XIA Qing, who over the course of 2 years sent me a lot of feedback.

My heartfelt thanks are given to Professor GU Yueguo and CAO Xiaoying. Being one of the chief editors, Professor GU designed the structure of the text books and introduced many advanced teaching notions into the text books. Being one of the administrators responsible for College English Teaching Innovation, CAO presented or made a lot of constructive suggestions from the perspective of macro-language teaching aspects.

Thanks also go to Ronald Suleski, professor and director of the Rosenburg Institute for East Asian Studies, who did a lot of proofreading and wrote the preface for this series of text books.

Thanks finally go to the Foreign Language Teaching and Research Press for their patience and advice. And lastly, I'm alone responsible for errors that may still remain.

ZHANG Sheru

July 16, 2014

A Note from the Author

All students, professors, advisors, some places, and exhibitions are fictitious. All the figures mentioned in the work are historically real, unless indicated otherwise. What should be especially declared is that some filmed locations are in the Chinese Printing Museum, some are in the library of Beijing Institute of Graphic Communication in order to simulate real-life activities.

General Introduction

The Package

Chinese Publishing: A Window to Chinese Civilization and Culture is a package consisting of

- Web-based delivery of the courseware bearing the same title;
- Mobile delivery of the same courseware materials;
- Printed materials traditionally known as a textbook.

The Web- courseware provides you with audio materials which you may listen to, and video-based lectures which you may watch and enjoy. Furthermore, the Web mode enables you to interact with fellow users, teachers and even with the authors via social media tools.

The mobile mode is somewhat less empowering than the Web mode due to the limitations of the mobile technology. However, it gives you an easier access while you are on the move. It enables you to make the most of your precious time!

The printed textbook reminds you of the "good old days", doesn't it? It never runs out of battery! You may lie snug on the sofa, reading! But unfortunately you cannot listen to, or watch a printed text, or send an instant message around by pressing it!

So the package as a whole has harvested all the advantages from its components while overcoming its separate disadvantages.

Readership

Chinese Publishing: A Window to Chinese Civilization and Culture is prepared for students with a higher English level, especially for students who major in related subjects; for Chinese readers who are keen on publishing and media in English; and for foreign readers who hope to understand Chinese publishing development. Chinese was among the earliest languages to have a writing system, whereby knowledge, wisdom and all experience could be preserved and disseminated, leading to the development of publishing. The foundation of publishing is writing, calligraphy, media, skills together with printing techniques. All these are worded in English together with Chinese equivalents. It is beneficial for the world to know the origin of Chinese publishing in English, since English is an important lingua franca in the world.

In its preparation, *Chinese Publishing* has been intentionally aimed at integrating English skills like listening, speaking, reading, writing and translation with professional knowledge so as to train the students' comprehensive ability. The texts do not assume that you are already well versed in English, or well-informed in the subject matter. This series of books has taken on an extra responsibility of upgrading students' or readers' existing English proficiency as well as knowledge of the subject matter, so all the materials have been prepared with these two broad objectives in mind.

Objectives

There are broad and specific objectives. The broad ones are described already in the *Readership*.

Here are specific objectives. By working through the *Package*, users should be able to talk especially, but also write about Chinese publishing from the following aspects:

- the historical outline, from the beginning of publishing to the present day
- the prerequisite of publishing: writing system, calligraphy, media and printing techniques
- the printing technologies from woodblock, woodcut to the invention of clay movable type, metal movable type and the introduction of lead movable type. Modern digital printing is also involved.
- a brief introduction to some masterpieces from each dynasty
- important figures who contributed greatly to the development of printing
- a clear explanation or description of some key concepts, terminologies etc.

Design

There are two fundamental principles guiding the *Package* design.

The first is the *Principle of 3-M Learning*, that is, the Principle of Learning via Multimodality, Multimedia and Multiple Environments. Natural learning involves multiple sensory organs working seamlessly and harmoniously together. In fact it takes a whole body to learn. This means that traditionally explicit cognitive-oriented learning is inadequate, and that the implicit, sub-conscious learning through immersion experiences must be given due appreciation. Learning via multimodality has become a default mode in the digital Internet Age. The era of orthographic only text-based presentation of learning materials has passed. The integration of printed texts, audio and video streams, still images and photographs, hypertext links, etc. has become the dominant model of the day.

Learning via multiple environments, a long-dreamed goal of human education is now a reality. The boundaries between class and out-of-class, between campus and off-campus, between learning time and work or leisure time, — all these traditional boundaries set up by man according to physical space and time, are rendered immaterial, thanks to digital mobile technology. Learning anywhere at anytime has become a matter of will — you can do it if you please! Nothing prevents you from doing so.

The second guiding principle is the *Principle of Learning by Doing*. The importance of this principle cannot be overemphasized. It is meant to counterbalance the habit of passive reading, and mechanical learning by rote. Passive reading can only lead you to shallow learning at best. Learning by doing leads to deep learning. The most distinctive feature of our design, as part of putting the Principle of Learning by Doing into practice, is the presentation of the materials from the user's perspective rather than from the teacher's. Traditionally the content is presented to the reader through the silent voice of an expert. Between the textbook and the reader/learner there is a teacher standing in the classroom acting like a bridge guiding the reader/learner to the textbook content. This Sage-on-Stage role of a teacher is no longer existent in our design. The materials are structured in such a way that they flow from learners themselves. There are a group of enthusiasts who are keen on getting Chinese Printing known to the outside world in English. The enthusiasts organize their own learning activities, e.g., reading groups, seeking advice, doing fieldwork, hands-on practicing, summarizing or commenting, organizing public lectures and forums, etc. The potential users of the *Package* are invited to join them and learn by doing things together with them. It's fun!

Task designs and instructions will convince you that the two guiding principles are fully implemented throughout the *Package*. Your adoption of the two principles as your learning guide will be richly rewarded.

Organization

The Package is organized into 8 units. Each unit consists of 8 tasks. The unit always begins with a warm-up exercise: It prepares everybody for the unit's workload. It also acts as an interface between units.

The first task is generally a *historical note* from the adviser. It is primarily intended for learners to obtain information or advice by listening to the adviser. The transcript is also provided for reading in print or on screen. The questions, answer activities and drag-match exercises, etc. can be either completed over the Internet or in the printed book.

The second task is the process of collating, comparing and commenting on information so far to prepare the students for the tasks ahead.

Tasks 3-6 center on reading tasks, covering the essential language training practice ranging from reading comprehension, vocabulary learning, translation to challenging discussions in a group. Some excerpts about Chinese publishing are taken from works written by native speakers of English. Editorial adaptation has been kept to a minimum. Others are written, re-written, and revised by both Chinese and native-speaker specialists. Most of the tasks are hands-on exercises involving exploring and reflecting to achieve progressive learning. In terms of the subject matter, these tasks are designed to promote deep learning about key concepts in Chinese publishing. In terms of language skills, they are intended for output training, that involves both oral and writing skills as well as thinking in English.

Task 7 is a public lecture delivered by a professor of publishing on a specific topic, which in general is also the theme of a given unit. In terms of content organization, the public lecture serves as a climax: The learners up to this point are guided and gently pushed by the speaker to reflect upon what they have learned, to do a bit of theorizing, as it were.

Task 8, the last one, is a follow-up forum. Learners are urged to organize an online debate discussing problems, issues and questions that have been raised in the public lecture. And finally they should summarize what they have grasped.

How to Use the Package

The *Package* is by design self-contained. It is suitable for independent users for self-study. Self-study does not mean studying it in solitude or isolation. On the contrary, independent users are urged to join online study groups, and actively participate in online forums.

It is, of course, suitable for campus learning and credit-bearing programmes. In this case, an integrated approach is recommended. Campus learners are encouraged to be first of all online learners, independently or in groups. All the online learning activities are automatically monitored and recorded for later inspection. Moreover, teachers are also empowered to be able to check learning progress and homework, give and mark assignments — all online, both synchronously and asynchronously. If the timetable permits, teachers are advised to use face-to-face contact hours specifically for reading tasks and public lectures, since these two could be somewhat demanding to some students.

The website for the Package is: http://waiyubu.bigc.edu.cn/.

Good luck in your studies!

Pre-Course Activity

Task 1 Organizing the Group

Introduction: This textbook is written from the students' perspective rather than from teachers'. A group of 3 students is assigned to probe the Chinese publishing from its history to its evolution or development assisted by two professors as their tutors or advisors. Such design aims at embodying two principles as mentioned in the above. One is the *Principle of 3-M Learning*, and the other is the *Principle of Learning by Doing*. This group will aim at exploring or discovering how Chinese publishing originated and progressed in content, binding, and media evolution, meanwhile they are trained to learn English by integrating listening, speaking, reading, writing and translating together so that five language skills can facilitate their language acquisition.

This learning group was initiated by 3 students. They are as follows:

Irene: Hello, I'm Irene, an undergraduate student majoring in press and publications here at BIGC (Beijing Institute of Graphic Communication). I specialize in publishing science, including the publication industry, editing, publication distribution, and the publication trade, though I'm more interested in the related history and culture. Together with two other visiting students — Owen and Miriam, we've formed a study group and aim rather ambitiously to share whatever we can obtain through our exploration with anyone else who shows interest. As I'm sure, you all know China is growing powerful both economically and militarily. It is our duty or mission to introduce Chinese culture and civilization developed over 5,000 years of history to the world. Ideologically, China is devoting itself to becoming not only culturally large, but also culturally powerful. Our group hopes to track Chinese publishing by following the principle of integrating the resources of government, industry, research and users. So a myriad of tasks will await us.

Owen: Hi, I'm Owen, an American exchange student in BIGC — a distinguished communication university. I'm happy to be one of the members doing on Chinese culture. I'm totally in agreement with Irene. The world needs to understand China. I'm eager to witness both the splendour and the mystery of Chinese culture myself. Here we're learning publishing by exploring or practicing it. Publishing is an important vehicle for the dissemination of Chinese culture, and therefore should have great significance attached to it. Hence, two classmates Irene, Miriam and I have grouped ourselves, hoping to probe Chinese publishing sources and sort out clearly out its path of development.

Miriam: Hello, I'm Miriam — one of the group members, and I'm from Australia. I'm here in pursuit of my goal of Digital publishing, Journalism, and Communication Science. What I really hope is to make friends with more students here and that our program can attract more learners to join us in studying how to transmit the ancient Chinese civilization to the world, how to peel away the mysterious oriental culture layer by layer chronologically. People outside China long to know more about what used to be here and what will be in future. Publishing just acts as a bridge to link China and the world. This is why I have taken out membership. Moreover, I'll be able to take advantage of easy access to the Chinese Museum to acquire first-hand information.

Irene:	In addition to the above members, we have specially invited two specialists as our supervisors. Let's roll out the red carpet for them. These are sinologist Richards, and Professor Philips.
Richards:	Hello, it's my pleasure to introduce this series of lectures exploring ancient Chinese publishing culture and civilization. Professor Philips and I, together with other sinologists, will be delivering online lectures in addition to offering assistance to students face to face.
Philips:	Hi, I'm honored to be the supervisor for this study group. I'll be offering historical notes and responses to student queries, and will help to design learning guidance materials for them to develop their autonomous studying ability.
Irene:	Okay, so much for our personal introductions. Now let's get down to business.

Task 2　Naming the group and setting up web connections

Irene:	Hello, everybody, from today on we begin our journey. Our key goal is to establish an accurate record of the history of publishing.
Owen:	Sure. I'm interested in getting to the root of the matter. But wouldn't it be better if we announced the name of our group first?
Miriam:	You're absolutely right, Owen. A really catchy name can attract more students to join.
Owen:	I think Professor Richards should be able to think of something appropriate and appealing.
Richards:	Hello everyone, so you want me to help with the name of this group. Normally names of groups or associations are based on combinations of family names, or group functions, or popular themes of the times. What do you hope to highlight with your group name?

Irene:	In my opinion, our group name should be associated with our goal and our majors.
Philips:	I agree with Irene. The name should be meaningful. I suggest the name should contain the reference to the people in your study group as well as your major. What do you think?
Richards:	I approve entirely of your idea. So how about PRIMO? Do you like it?
Owen:	But why PRIMO? What does it mean?
Miriam:	It means "the first" in Latin, doesn't it?
Richards:	Totally right. This name has an ancient flavor because you need to start researching from very ancient origins, don't you? I think Professor Philips can explain the rest.
Philips:	Well, I think you've all probably seen the explanation. I already pointed out that a group name can include the individual names.
Irene:	Oh, I see. I'm sorry to jump in.
Philips:	Not at all, you're welcome to air your point of view.
Irene:	P is a pun. It refers to both our key topic "publishing" and P for professor Philips. And…
Owen:	Oh I get it! Our group name is made up of the first letter of our names. R refers to Professor Richards, I means Irene, and M & O stand for Miriam and me.
Richards:	You have indeed got it. What do you think of the name?
Owen, Miriam & Irene:	Great. We love our group name. It implies that we are the first students to explore publishing history and civilization.
Philips:	Absolutely right. But I suggest you need to set up your own website.
Miriam:	Boys are usually good with the Internet. So Owen, why don't display your wonderful cyber talents?
Owen:	Ha-ha. To tell you the truth, I've already had a good idea.
Irene & Miriam:	Amazing! What is it?
Owen:	Here is our URL: www.primo.com.
Irene & Miriam:	Yeah, "Owen the Great"!

Owen: Now that I'm your webmaster, you all need to follow my advice to register first so that you can become a privileged user. There are a lot of extra benefits for privileged users. Please visit this website: www.primo.com for further information.

Miriam: And our motto is — PRIMO. Let's study together, everybody?

ALL: PRIMO! Let's study together!

Unit

Prerequisite of Chinese Publishing — the Origin and Development of Chinese Characters

TABLE OF CONTENTS

Warm-up:	Be proactive
Task 1	Listen to a historical note: Wang Yirong — the discoverer of Ancient Chinese characters
Task 2	Discuss the historical note
Task 3	Build up our vocabulary
Task 4	Reading activity: The Origin of Oracle Bone Script and Chinese Writing System
Task 5	Reading comprehension
Task 6	Translation practice
Task 7	Attend a public lecture: Unique Writing Mediums and the Development of Chinese Characters
Task 8	Join the online forum and write a summary
Appendix:	Vocabulary for Unit 1

Unit 1: Prerequisite of Chinese Publishing — the Origin and Development of Chinese Characters

WARM-UP: Be proactive

Irene: Hello everybody. The PRIMO group is now beginning its journey into the past to track the history of publishing in China. I'd like to start the discussion with an opinion: without Chinese pictographs and characters, there wouldn't have been any development in printing or publishing or even other social development.

Owen: Yes, it's pretty clear that you couldn't have any kind of printing or publishing without written characters.

Miriam: So that means the history of publishing begins with the earliest known attempts to create a writing system?

Owen: But why not go even farther back to the beginnings of language itself? You couldn't have a writing system if you didn't have a language. I was reading the other day about the proto-human language.

Irene: What, you mean the original human language from which all other languages are supposed to have developed? What do our Professors think about that?

Philips: Well, it's an interesting topic, but the proto-human language — if it existed — was tens of thousands of years ago. We simply can't go back that far. What do you think, Professor Richards?

Richards: I agree that it's a fascinating topic. There're all sorts of linguistic evidence for similarities between languages that point to some sort of common ancestor, but as you say, that would have been perhaps a hundred thousand years ago or even longer. What we have to concentrate on is the history

	of writing — and that's only four or five thousand years.
Owen:	I see what you mean, Professor — that was a pretty stupid idea of mine, huh?
Philips:	No no, not at all — that's exactly what PRIMO should do, question everything, throw up ideas. Some will be good, some not so good, but it's the discussion that matters.
Miriam:	I think PRIMO should construct a sort of tree-like structure in our exploration of Chinese publishing. There'll be the main trunk on which we all agree, but there'll also be many branches going off in different directions as well. This'll make our explorations more interesting and perhaps attract an increasing number of other learners.
Irene:	I share your view. I also think we should prepare pictures or slides to illustrate our points, because sometimes it's hard to express some ideas clearly without some sort of graphic support.
Owen:	You're right — some of this stuff is bound to be really abstract, so we'll need to be very well organized.
Miriam:	I agree — and that organization has to come from us sharing all our thoughts and opinions. We're an autonomous study group and should rely on ourselves, not just count on our supervisors to provide everything for us.
Irene:	I think you're both right, and all three of us are ready to accept the challenge. Having said that, I know we're all eager to hear the first talk, so let's give a warm welcome to Professor Philips' first systematic historical speech.

Task 1 ▶ Listen to a historical note: Wang Yirong — the discover of ancient Chinese characters

Philips: Hello, everybody, let me extend a very warm welcome to this historical note on the discovery of Chinese characters. It's very good to be with the group PRIMO and to see so many other faces. I'm quite surprised to know why such a big group is interested in this topic. It's a great pleasure to be here this morning to speak to you. I'd like to begin now by just giving you some idea of some of the things I'm going to be talking about in the lecture. In particular, I hope to begin with the point where you are most interested but have hardly any idea. I hope this historical note can actually leads the way to your main exploration in this regard. You may think it's a pretty sort of unilinear, fairly uninteresting account of what actually happened in very ancient times. But one of my suggestions is to keep the topic in mind and reflect on it. As well as that, here is a task for you: filling in the blanks with the words while you are listening to the introduction to Wang Yirong — the discover of ancient Chinese characters. (Here you are required to fill in the blanks with the words or phrases you hear while listening)

As I mentioned at the beginning, my topic will focus on "Wang Yirong who discovered Oracle Bone Script". In ancient China, 1) _____ were a traditional medicinal 2) _____ that was often mentioned in medical texts. The term "Dragon Bones" was used in a general sense to describe the 3) _____ of animals from ancient times, as well as other animal bones that 4) _____ them. However, scattered among these "Dragon Bones" were 5) _____ of turtle shells and animal bones that carried man-made inscriptions dating back to the Shang Dynasty. For centuries, these 6) _____ went almost totally unnoticed, with no one taking it upon themselves to study their origin.

This remained the case until the late nineteenth century, when an esteemed scholar by the name of Wang Yirong finally 7) _____ the mystery of the oracle bone script — an early form of Chinese characters that had been lost for thousands of years. A native of Yantai, Shandong, Wang

Yirong was a director at the Imperial Academy, an 8) _____, and a master book collector. After coming down with malaria in the summer of 1899, Wang Yirong had the good fortune of being treated by a royal doctor sent especially by the Guangxu Emperor, who held Wang in high regard. The royal doctor examined Wang Yirong and produced a 9) _____ that consisted of several kinds of medicine, one of which was "Dragon Bones." Wang Yirong had one of his servants procure the medicines from the West Heniantang Pharmacy in Caishikou. Upon inspecting the medicines that his servant had brought back for him, Wang Yirong discovered that the pieces of "Dragon Bone" were marked with strange symbols that did not appear to be 10) _____. Despite resembling seal script, they definitely were not seal script; and despite resembling bronze inscriptions, they definitely were not bronze inscriptions. Wang Yirong suspected that the symbols were most likely an unknown form of ancient characters. A master of epigraphy and ancient texts, Wang Yirong knew that he had come across something special. Despite his illness, he travelled to the West Heniantang Pharmacy the very next day to enquire about the origin of the bone pieces. There, he was told that most of the bones had come from a small village by the name of Xiaotun, which was located not far from the city of Anyang in Henan Province. The bones had been discovered accidently by a group of local farmers, who sold them off cheaply to an antiques dealer for use as medicinal materials. The Heniantang Pharmacy had procured the bones from an antiques dealer by the name of Fan. Overjoyed by his discovery, Wang Yirong had his servants purchase all of the inscribed "Dragon Bones" they could find in the nearby pharmacies. At the same time, he quickly tracked down the antiques dealer named Fan, and for a considerable amount of money procured a more complete set of inscribed turtle shells and animal bones. Hearing the news, a number of other antiques dealers also approached Wang Yirong, looking to sell him more "Dragon Bones." Before long, Wang Yirong had amassed a collection of more than one thousand pieces of shell and bone. As his collection grew, he began to study the inscriptions day and night, pondering where they had come from. The news that Wang had discovered a "mythical language" spread quickly to scholars and collectors both in the capital and elsewhere, causing the price of the shell and bone fragments on the market to rise sharply. A number of fellow epigraphers flocked to Wang Yirong, waiting with great enthusiasm and excitement for Wang to reveal more about the inscriptions.

  Drawing on his academic expertise and considerable experience as a collector, Wang Yirong came to his initial conclusion one day in the autumn:

the shell and bone inscriptions were produced from the middle to the later stages of the Shang Dynasty, and the beautiful yet mysterious symbols they carried were the earliest form of Chinese characters to have been discovered. Wang Yirong formally announced his findings at his home in the presence of his most distinguished friends. However, Wang Yirong and his friends never realized the full implications of that day, a day in which the history of Chinese pictographs was pushed back by at least another thousand years. The discovery of oracle bone script sent shockwaves throughout the world cultural community.

Unfortunately, Wang Yirong died just one year after discovering oracle bone script at the West Heniantang Pharmacy. As the 20th century dawned, the great scholar Wang Yirong led local militia in an unsuccessful attempt to resist the invading Eight-nation Alliance. Unable to come to terms with defeat, Wang Yirong and his family plunged themselves into a well, ending their lives in a tragic display of patriotism. Wang wrote his final words in a solemn and composed regular script, "When the ruler is distressed, the subject should be disgraced; when the ruler is disgraced, the subject should die." Following Wang's death, the study of oracle bone script was continued by scholars such as Liu E, Wang Guowei, Luo Zhenyu, Sun Yirang, Dong Zuobin, and Guo Moruo, becoming a multi-disciplinary subject spanning archeology, grammatology, history, and publishing. At present, only 2,000 of the 4,500 known oracle bone characters have been deciphered, which means there is still a great deal to be learned about this ancient form of writing discovered by Wang Yirong.

Task 2 ▶ Discuss the historical note
(Students are required to do role play in groups by imitating the PRIMO's dialogue)

Irene: Hello, PRIMO members — what did you think of Professor Philips's long note? I got so much information from it, but it's all tangled up. I need to disentangle some of my thoughts before we go on. Do you feel the same?

Owen: Not entirely, Irene. I thought the Professor's description of how Wang Yirong discovered Oracle Bone script was a straightforward narrative that enlightened me greatly on

	the relationship between Oracle Bone script and Chinese characters. I think our discussion should follow the narrative of the note.
Miriam:	Mm, I'll just sit on the fence for this one — I think both of you are right. I see some of the story quite clearly, but some of it still needs explanation. Why don't we start by making a list of any problems we have with the narrative?
Irene:	I agree with you, Miriam. I accept Owen's point about understanding the whole story, but I really do want to share my questions about individual points. What do you think?
Owen:	I'm always ready to do what you want, Irene, you know that.
Irene:	That's true, Owen, you're really easy to get on with — in fact both of you are so cooperative. Well then, let me raise my questions first, and then we'll go on to yours. First, I'd like an explanation of "Dragon Bones" and what the relationship is between dragon bones and turtle's shell.
Owen:	Yes, I've got a question about the early part of the narrative, too; I'd like to know more about Wang Yirong — where he lived, his personal background, and his contribution to Chinese calligraphy.
Miriam:	I wonder who's going to answer all these questions? It's easy enough to ask them, so here's mine. What was the main influence of Wang Yirong and his family on their time, and why?
Owen:	Don't worry too much about the answers yet. That's the whole point of our discussion and research. And anyway, we have our two supervisors to help us.
Irene:	You're always right, Owen. What I want to know is why the earliest writing characters were called oracle bone script instead of shell and bone script. Turtle shells were also used for early writing as well as bones.
Miriam:	Yes, but I think shell counts as bone, doesn't it? From my reading about the subject, I can answer most of your question, Irene. The majority of the oracle bones date from the late Shang dynasty, so oracle bone script essentially refers to a Shang script. People believed that the bones or the shells

	could show what the gods had in store for them, in other words they were an oracle — a prediction of what was going to happen.
Irene:	But aren't we getting away from the topic of the historical note?
Miriam:	Not really. The connection is that though the oracle bones were over three thousand years old, it was only in 1899 that Wang Yirong first recognized that the fragments of bone and shell that he originally bought as "dragon bones" to be ground into powder and used to stop bleeding, were in fact ancient writings.
Owen:	And that was Wang's great contribution, wasn't it? Another thing he did was to discourage fakes.
Irene:	Yes, I read about that. Almost as soon as his first book of rubbings of oracle bone inscriptions appeared in 1903, the number of collectors grew rapidly. Dealers began to exploit their ignorance by selling obvious fakes. Wang Yirong's research revealed that genuine oracle bones all came from the village of Xiaotun (小屯) near Anyang (安阳) in Henan Province. This allowed counterfeit goods to be controlled in relation to Oracle Bone Script.
Miriam:	So you mean some of the early collectors were fooled by forgeries.
Irene:	And even afterwards, but the Chinese Academy of Sciences have done a lot of archaeological at Xiaotun since 1928, and have established beyond doubt that the oracle bones were all part of the Shang royal archive, dating from the period between 1400 and 1200 BC.
Owen:	Well done, Irene — you've cleared up at least some of our questions. Shall we carry on then?
Miriam:	Yes, let's move ahead.

Task 3 ▸ Build up our vocabulary
(Drag and match exercises)

Match the English words in column A with the Chinese equivalents in column B.

	A		B
1	Pottery writing	A	正始石经
2	Oracle bone script	B	帛书
3	bronze inscriptions	C	草书
4	"Mao Gong Ding"	D	大篆
5	stone inscriptions	E	行书
6	Stone Drum inscription	F	侯马盟书
7	Houma Covenant	G	甲骨文
8	"Xi Ping Stone Classics"	H	金文
9	"Zengshi Stone Classics"	I	开成石经
10	"Kaicheng Stone Classics"	J	楷书
11	Silk manuscripts	K	隶书
12	Bamboo and wooden slips	L	毛公鼎
13	paper	M	石鼓文
14	Hand-copied paper manuscripts	N	石刻
15	great seal script	O	手抄本
16	small seal script	P	书法
17	official script	Q	陶文
18	running script	R	熹平石经
19	regular script	S	小篆
20	cursive script	T	纸张
21	calligraphy	U	竹木简牍

Task 4 ▸ Reading activity

*The following excerpt is recommended to PRIMO, some of which is from A Journey Through Time in China by Peter Hessler in 2007. It is about **The Origin of Oracle Bone Script and Chinese Writing System.** It will help PRIMO members to clarify how Chinese characters came into being.*

4.1 The Origin of Oracle Bone Script

Oracle Bone Script is an ancient form of Chinese writing. It has long been regarded as the earliest form of modern Chinese character. Actually, it is not the oldest form of writing in China or in the world. But it can be regarded as the best integrated writing system existing in China. Although other ancient languages may be older than Chinese Oracle Bone, for example, Sumerian (楔形文字), Egyptian, or Sanskrit (Figure 1.4.1), with the exception of the third they are no longer in use. The only European language that is still spoken today and can claim a continuous recorded history as long as Chinese or even longer is Greek, whose earliest traces, Mycenaean Linear B (1500-1200 BC) (Figure 1.4.2)— the most ancient attested form of the Greek language, may be older than the oracle-bone script of Shang China (ca. 1250-1050 BC). Why Chinese Oracle Bone Scripts have been given such close attention is because these "oracle bones" have remained the single most enduring icon of Chinese elite culture for most if not all of Chinese recorded history.

Figure 1.4.1: *Inscription of Sanskrit.*
(https://www.pinterest.com/cassiek4792/sanskrit/)

Figure 1.4.2: *Inscription of Mycenaean Greek* written in Linear B. Archaeological Museum of Mycenae (from Flickr upload bot).

Oracle Bone Script is thus one of the earliest surviving examples of writing in the world (Figure 1.4.3) dating back over 3,000 years ago. These "oracle bones" originated from the years as recordings of meteorological and astronomical data, including the early records of eclipses and comets, and divined answers to questions sought at the court of the royal house of Shang, which ruled central China between the 16th and 11th centuries BC.

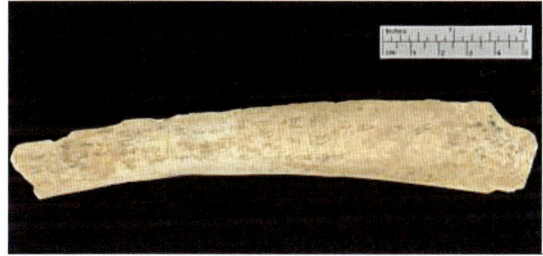

Figure 1.4.3: This inscribed ox shoulder-blade contains some of the earliest surviving Chinese writing in the world© Cambridge Digital Library.

Questions about crops, the weather or the royal family were engraved with a sharp object and the bone was then heated with metal rods. Because of the heat, the bones would crack and the answers would be given by the diviners who interpreted the different shapes and the patterns of the fractures. The response was also inscribed on the bone. Most of the cracks produced by the heat on the reverse side of the bones appeared on the front side with a distinctive shape (⼘) (Figure 1.4.4) from which comes the Chinese character for the verb "divine".

Figure 1.4.4: Shang Dynasty oracle bone (via British Library).

The script was accomplished by buffing the obverse of the bone or shell once it had been sawn onto shape and chiseling hollows onto the reverse. Questions were inscribed on the polished side. Then, heat was applied to the hollows with heated metal rods, creating the distinctive ⼘ shaped cracks. The inscribed ox shoulder-blades (Figure 1.4.5) and flat under-part of turtle shells also documented information on subjects like warfare, agriculture, hunting and medical problems, and these examples have never before been displayed (Figure 1.4.6).

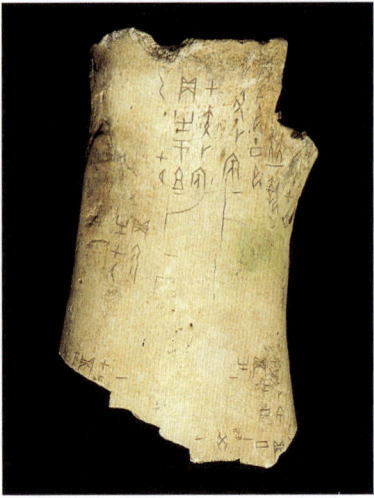

Figure 1.4.5: "Oracle bone" with shaped cracks ⊢ used for divination© Cambridge Digital Library.

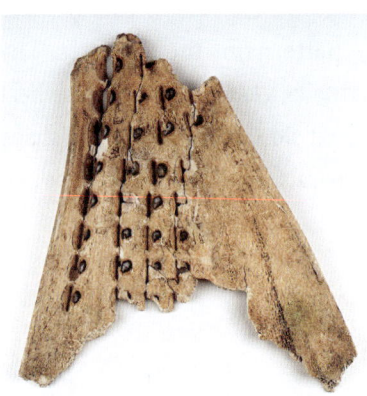

Figure 1.4.6: Shang Dynasty oracle bone (via British Library).

Excavated bones reveal that the Shang inquired about everything from warfare to childbirth, from weather to illness. They asked about the meaning of dreams. They negotiated with the dead: on one bone, an inscription proposes sacrificing three human prisoners to an ancestor, and then, presumably after an unsatisfactory crack, the next inscription offers up five prisoners. Sometimes the Shang sacrificed hundreds of people at once. Oracle bones provided access to the mysterious messages conjured from a spiritual fire, which are voices of the dead echoing through the evolution of language and its power.

Prior to the turn of the 20th century, oracle bones were regularly ground up for Chinese medicine. It was not until Wang Yirong, a collector and director of the Chinese Imperial Academy brought attention to this record of the Bronze

Age that their significance was recognized. Unfortunately, Wang's place in the Boxer Rebellion as a commander culminated in his suicide, and a friend named Liu E posthumously published the oracle bone inscriptions he had amassed.

4.2 The writing system goes a long way back

It is hard to imagine what China would be like without Chinese characters. China started its present day civilization from the second millennium BC. in the Shang Dynasty, which occurred during an era that also saw the destruction of Troy and the reign of Rameses, and King Tut, and the Hebrew patriarchs. As its contribution to civilization, the Shang era produced oracle bones (Figure 1.4.7) — shoulder blades and turtle shells inscribed with signs and symbols, many of which are recognizable today as Chinese characters.

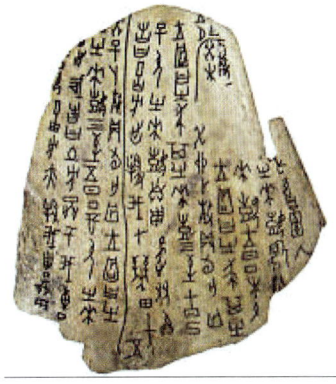

Figure 1.4.7: *Oracle-bone script.*
(http://www.ebay.com)

These long engravings or Chinese characters, used for divination and containing some 5,000 signs in total, represent a relatively mature system of Chinese writing. Intriguingly, pottery dating back several centuries earlier is painted with some of the same symbols, often grouped together as though forming a sentence. Even though many of the earliest characters may have been pictographs or ideograms, Chinese writing for the last two thousand years has been neither pictographic, phonographic, nor logographic (or morph graphic), but morphosyllabic and phonetic, the former suggesting the meaning and the latter the sound. In other words, most characters represent both morphemes (or words) and syllables (or phonemes).

The first special terms for the different scripts or graphic forms of Chinese characters (Figune 字形) date from the Later Han, notably those in the *Shuowen Jiezi* (说文解字) (Figure 1.4.8). These terms can now be elaborated and in some cases corrected using the writing on the oracle-bone and bronze inscriptions and on other excavated artifacts and texts. The history of Chinese scripts can be broadly divided into two stages: 1) ancient scripts (*guwen* 古文), which were in use from the Shang to Qin; 2) those that came later (called from the Han *jinwen* 今文 and today often referred to as *likai* 隶楷), from the Han to the present (the last four entries). The Late Warring States to the early Han marks a transitional stage between the two. Modern typefaces are based on standard script, *kaishu* (楷书).

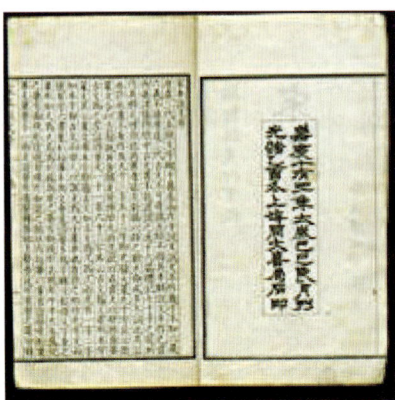

Figure 1.4.8: The *Eastern Han Dynasty XU Shen's Shuowen Jiezi* (A Dictionary written at Han Dynasty) including recordation of a good many cultural phenomena. (东汉 许慎《说文解字》) (http://image.haosou.com)

Needless to say, the different scripts did not follow one after the other in orderly fashion, each growing from the previous one in a linear progression. Rather they evolved over several centuries and often overlapped. A clear-cut profile of each of the main scripts was established only long afterwards when fine examples were taken as calligraphic models and later still, when the writers of textbooks in the twentieth century sought to present their readers with a simplified and orderly progression.

Hence, it was a script that was used to record words or parts of words, not directly things or ideas and that eventually evolved into the different ways of writing characters before they became standardized. Characters can be analyzed into variously defined constituent parts. They were well constructed in certain ways. And a huge number of them are classified into a surprisingly few semantic categories.

Task 5 ▶ Reading comprehension

(Students are required to launch a discussion to pose new questions and answer all the questions raised in the dialogue, and do the role play based on the following)

Irene: Well, how do you feel after reading that amazing stuff about

	the origins of Oracle Bone Script? I'm impressed by our ancient ancestors — they tried so hard to understand the future, didn't they?
Miriam:	I share your admiration, but I'm a bit confused. I need to get all this information into some kind of order. Can anybody help me?
Owen:	You mean just go back over what we've read? That's easy, I can do that!
Miriam:	I'm sure you can Owen, but I don't mean that. I think we need to review the material in order to gain new insights from it.
Irene:	I'm with you on this, Miriam. I think what we need to do is to challenge each other with questions that lead to discussions so that finally we solve the problems ourselves. What do you think?
Owen:	Yeah, I'll go for that. Okay, here's my first question: What are the earliest written languages in the world?
Irene:	That doesn't sound too tough, does it? I'm sure we can easily answer that one. But my question is a little more complicated: How did oracle bone script come into being, and why are historians and scholars so interested in it?
Miriam:	Those are actually two questions, aren't they Irene? But I know what you're getting at. My question may be a bit more challenging. I understand that the |— shaped crack is the origin of the word "bu" for divination, but did the people really believe that cracks in a bone could answer people's questions about the future?
Owen:	That's a big question, Miriam — you'd need a time machine to travel back 3000 years and ask the Shang people yourself.
Irene:	So you mean this is a question that the great Owen cannot answer? This must be a first!
Owen:	Not just for me, Irene — I don't think you could answer it either!
Miriam:	Now now children, don't squabble! Can I ask another question?

Irene:	Of course you can — try and find one Owen can answer!
Owen:	Let me ask another question first, just so I know I can answer at least one. Are Chinese characters pictographs or ideograms?
Miriam:	Good question. And my last question is: How should we understand the relationship between Guwen and Jinwen?
Irene:	Ooh, that's another big challenge. I think there are enough questions for now. Shall we start trying to find some answers?
Owen:	Yeah, how about starting with that big one about "bu" divination? Did they really believe it?
Miriam:	Good idea, let's get started!

Task 6 ▶ Translation practice

(Students are required to translate the following Chinese paragraph into English individually, in pairs or in group)

Irene:	So, we have done some research and discussed some concepts relating to the origin of Chinese characters. Are we ready now to set out on a new journey into the history of Chinese publishing?
Owen:	I think we are. We all know English and Chinese, so I'm sure we can do a good job of spreading the word about Chinese publishing to people outside China.
Miriam:	Oh sure, we're linguistically capable, but before we start spreading the word, hadn't we better elaborate a few more relevant concepts connected with publishing?
Irene:	You're quite right, Miriam. When people hear the word publishing, they can't help thinking about books. But books are only one sort of publishing. Before the invention of paper and printing, the ancient Chinese recorded what they knew on oracle bones, bronze, jade and stone. I think these inscriptions represent the very earliest forms of publication.
Owen:	Yes, I take your point. They come under the heading of

	publication because they recorded history in a form that could be accessed by later generations and understood by them. But weren't the earliest formal publications, that is, things that actually looked a bit like books, written on bamboo strips?
Miriam:	Oh yes, and not only on bamboo strips or slips. Formal publications on silk and wooden slats similar to bamboo strips date back to the Spring and Autumn and Warring States periods, that's…770 to 221 BCE.
Irene:	And of course Confucius contributed hugely to the development of early Chinese publishing. He was one of the first scholars to write and edit books privately, although it was the aristocracy and high officials who had the monopoly on ancient books and records.
Owen:	That's true, but didn't Confucius and his students produce a whole series of textbooks that became the basis for the education system? Publications like the *Book of Changes*, the *Book of Songs*, the *Book of Documents*….
Irene:	Yes, the 4 books and the 5 classics — these were some of the earliest Chinese publications.
Miriam:	So our research into the history of Chinese publishing is totally justified because it opens a door into the glories of Chinese civilization. Isn't that a wonderful thing? But now we have to get down to a more practical task — we've got to do this translation. Everybody ready?
Owen	Yes, let's go!

　　出版是人类社会的经济、政治、文化发展到一定阶段的产物。出版物凝结着人类的思想和智慧，集聚了科学技术的发明创造和社会实践活动的经验与成果，反映了社会生活的各个侧面。出版与印刷术的发明密切相关，一般来说，先有印刷术后有出版。所谓版，在中国古代，是指上面刻有文字或图形以供印刷的木片的称谓。用雕版印刷的书籍，称雕版书。史料查证，中国早在五代时就有刻印板、镂板，宋代有开板、刻板、雕版（板与版在古代意通）等词，但未曾出现出版一词。出版一词，英语为 publication，来源于古拉丁语 publ-icattus。我国最早的出版活动可以追溯到辽金两代，当然，也有学者认为，出版一词是19世纪末、20世纪初从日本传入的。但多数学者认为我国出版一词出现于近代。出版——意指图书、报纸、期刊、音像、软件等的编辑（制作）、印刷

(复录)和传播的统称。虽然出版一词在中国出现于近代,但书籍出版在中国有悠久的历史。原始书籍的产生,即帛书的出现,可以追溯到春秋战国时期。而中国古代书籍的流传,最初是由人们辗转抄录。以后有人抄书出卖,书籍开始成为商品。据记载,西汉时就出现了书肆。公元2世纪初,中国发明了纸张,使文字载体发生了巨大变化,为书籍出版的发展提供了重要的物质条件。公元7世纪,中国发明了雕版印刷术,有了印本书,开创了书籍出版的新时代,正式的出版业开始出现了。

Task 7 ▶ Attend Professor Richards's public lecture

Lecture 1

Unique Writing mediums and the Development of Chinese Characters

Professor Richards

Hello everyone. It is my privilege to introduce you to a fascinating subject — the history of publishing in ancient China. The Beijing Institute of Graphic Communication, in conjunction with various noted scholars and historians, has developed this series of lectures in order to inform and educate you concerning this topic. The study of publishing in China will not only open a historical window into the past, but will help you to better understand the development of Chinese civilization and culture leading up to today, and just maybe, give you a glimpse into the possibilities of what the future may bring.

Here, I'm going to present you the first in a series of eight lectures regarding the history of publishing in China from the formation of the very first Chinese characters written on clay, stones and bones to the corporate atmosphere of modern day publishing houses and the comparatively recent transition into the digital age. The history of publishing in China is as rich and storied as the very country in which printing and paper were invented.

It should come as no surprise to you that the art of publishing played an integral role in the formation, continuance and success of the country with the longest existing civilization in the world; through cycles of prosperity and decline, the publishing of books has been constant and has served not only as a barometer for social change, but also as a reminder of the cultural values and ideas which constitute the very foundations on which this country was built.

In order to gain a full understanding of modern publishing in China, it is first necessary to journey back in time and take note of the great strides, innovations and historical advances which took place. By allowing yourself to gain this historical perspective you will be better equipped to appreciate just how far Chinese men and women have advanced the art of publishing.

So where and when did publishing actually begin? Scholars and historians may disagree as to an exact date when publishing first began, but for our purposes we will begin with the use of the Chinese character, not only as a written form of communication, but also focusing on the various media to which the very first characters were applied.

The first lecture in our lecture series will cover the development of Chinese characters and the diverse surfaces on which they were written… from pottery to bones, stone to metal, bamboo and silk to paper, the reproduction of Chinese characters evolved over time and became very technically and artistically advanced.

One of the earliest media used for the writing of the Chinese language was pottery, including tiles. Pottery writing, the practice of writing characters and symbols on pottery, emerged during the latter stages of primitive society and embodied three very distinct methods of production. The three methods included: engraving on unpainted clay prior to firing, cast engraving, and the firing of clay followed by engraving. The earliest forms of pottery which have been discovered present evidence of the link between engraved symbols and the art of calligraphy, affording historians a glimpse into one of the earliest transitional stages in the evolution of Chinese characters.

Another form of engraving and perhaps one of the most interesting media used for the engraving of symbols and characters was bones. Oracle bone script was the practice of engraving characters and symbols into both bones and turtle shells. (Figure 1.7.1). This practice dates back to the Xia and Zhou Dynasties and was particularly prevalent during the Shang Dynasty. In Anyang City, located in Henan Province, a number of oracle or "dragon bone" fragments have been unearthed. To date, over 150,000 oracle bone fragments have been discovered.

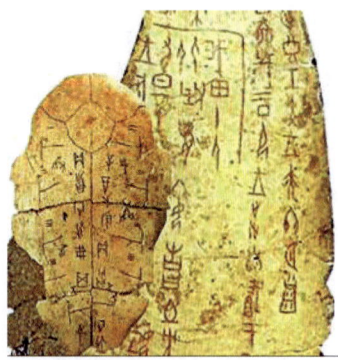

Figure 1.7.1: The characters on the Oracle Bone.（甲骨文上的汉字）

Dragon bones, as oracle bones are often referred to, once functioned as official documents and were used in large scale rituals. The bones were used in ceremonies which were held in order to divine the future; the ceremonies can be described as follows: first a question would be asked before a bone was ceremoniously placed into a fire (where the heat was applied by placing a heated metal rod into hollows carved into the reverse side of the bone). The fire would then burn the bone, drying and cracking it; the bone was then removed and the will of heaven interpreted through the various cracks and patterns which were formed by the heat, in turn, answering the previously asked question. The entire process would then be recorded onto the bone, providing a written record of the time, place and attendees present, the subject addressed, the prediction made and the subsequent results which would actually transpire. The bones would then be arranged in sequence and stored by category in a central location. Oracle bone script is considered to be the direct antecedent of Chinese characters and represents both an advanced writing and record keeping system.

The first characters to appear on metal objects are known as bronze inscriptions. Similar names for the art of inscribing characters onto metal are: bell inscriptions, cauldron inscriptions and law codes known as "Xingshu", which literally translates as "books of punishment". Bronze is a very soft metal combining copper with tin or lead and was prevalent during the Shang and Zhou Dynasties. At the time bronze ware was used by the noble classes for the production of ritual and also as household vessels which were exquisite and inscribed with carefully crafted patterns and designs.

Bronze inscriptions evolved during the Shang Dynasty and later rose to prominence in the Western Zhou, Spring and Autumn and Warring States periods. Over time the inscriptions became very ornate; the characters flowed much more naturally, were more standard in form and possessed more artistic flair.

Of the over 5,000 bronze ware pieces so far discovered, perhaps the most noteworthy example dates to the Western Zhou Dynasty and is referred to as the "Mao Gong Ding", or cauldron of the Duke of Mao (Figure 1.7.2). This cauldron contains 497 separate character inscriptions, more characters than any other bronze object yet discovered. Interestingly, the characters are inscribed on the inside of the cauldron and are noted for their simple, yet elegant form (Figure 1.7.3).

Figure 1.7.2: Duke Mao Tripot made in the Western Zhou Dynasty, unearthed in 1843, in Qishan, shaanxi Province. (西周毛公鼎)

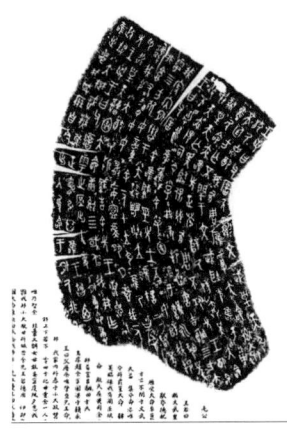

Figure 1.7.3: The epigraph from Duke Mao Tripot by rubbing. (毛公鼎铭文拓片)

Not surprisingly, characters inscribed into natural or altered stone are referred to as stone inscriptions (Figure 1.7.4). The precise origin of stone inscriptions is not known but they began to appear with some frequency during the Warring States period. The carvings consist of two types, cliff and individual inscriptions. Cliff inscriptions are those inscribed into a natural stone face, say in a cave or on the side of a mountain, while individual inscriptions refer to the practice of inscribing characters into altered stone pieces, either in the form of round or square tablets.

Figure 1.7.4: The big-seal style epigraph from the stone drum by rubbing. (石鼓文大篆拓片)

Stone inscriptions tended to be classical writings, such as scriptures or epitaphs, which were produced with the intention of being passed down to future generations. There are many well known examples of stone inscriptions from the ten-sided Stone Drum inscription from the state of Qin and dating to the Warring States period to the Houma Covenant from the state of Jin, which contains inscriptions carved into pieces of jade and also dates to the Warring States period. The "Xi Ping Stone Classics" dating to the Eastern Han Dynasty, the "Zengshi Stone Classics" dating to the Cao-Wei Dynasty and the "Kaicheng Stone Classics" of the Tang Dynasty are also very famous and represent the largest known inscriptions of Confucian scripture yet discovered.

Stone inscriptions by themselves are impressive, but they also serve as a historical link to the advent of calligraphy. For example, the Stone Drum inscriptions from Qin are typical examples of medium and large forms in seal script, while the "Zhengshi Stone Classics" include classical Chinese characters, seal script and official script.

Stone was a very unforgiving and hard surface compared to our next medium, which was both lightweight and flexible and ideal for writing, carrying and collecting. Of course I'm referring to silk, which when rolled or folded for the purpose of storage begins to resemble the form of a book. Silk manuscripts emerged during the Spring and Autumn period and were most prevalent during the Warring States and Three Kingdoms periods. Unlike stone, silk was expensive to produce. The considerable cost meant that manuscripts were generally only available to either royalty or the nobility.

To date, the largest discovery of silk manuscripts was made in Changsha, in 1973. While excavating a Han Dynasty tomb a number of silk manuscripts dating to the Warring States period were discovered; the collection is known as the Mawangdui Silk Manuscripts (Figure 1.7.5) and consists of 20 classic texts. These silk texts are hand-made copies, written in official script and are over 100,000 characters in length. In addition to their enormous historical value, included in the collection is the most complete version of *Laozi* ever discovered.

Figure 1.7.5: The silk scroll — the second part of *Laozi* unearthed in Mawangdui.（马王堆帛书《老子》乙本部分）

Bamboo and wooden strips date back as far as the Warring States period, although they truly reached their peak of use during the Qin and Han Dynasties. The long narrow strips of bamboo were easily obtained with each strip generally measuring as long as a chopstick and as wide as two. Characters would be brushed onto the bamboo or wood surface (Figure 1.7.6); for longer texts multiple strips would be bound together in sequence with thread. Small knives would also be employed to scrape away mistakes or make amendments to the slips and it became fashionable for government officials to carry decorative knives as a symbol of their office, displaying for all to see that they had the power to amend records. Many examples of bamboo strips have been discovered in royal tombs; the durable pieces have preserved many works in their original form throughout the centuries.

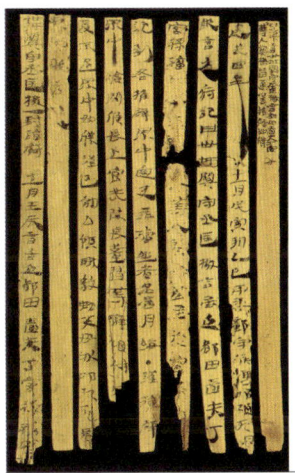

Figure 1.7.6: The Hexi Wood Tablet Document in the Eastern Han Dynasty.（东汉的河西简牍）

Last, but certainly not least, we have paper. Paper, one of the four great inventions of ancient China, first appeared during the Western Han Dynasty and with improvements made to the manufacturing process during the Eastern Han Dynasty, soon became the preferred of all writing media. The popularity of paper was due to the fact that as a writing medium it was not only flexible like silk, but also easy to obtain like bamboo. These qualities spurred the rapid spread of paper making across China and by the year 404, an official of the Eastern Jin Dynasty declared that paper would replace bamboo strips as the official writing medium for the country.

Hand-copied paper manuscripts were the primary form of book produced which started from the Eastern Jin Dynasty and continued until the Tang Dynasty. Books from this time period differed significantly in appearance due to the various methods by which they were bound, including scroll, accordion and butterfly bindings. Notably, both Chinese characters and calligraphy evolved during this age of hand-copying. Characters themselves evolved from oracle bone script, to great seal script, small seal script, official script, running script, regular script and then eventually to cursive script (Figure 1.7.6-1-4)… the ultimate script of calligraphy. It was also during this period of hand-copying that the art form of calligraphy reached its peak and gave rise to masters such as Wang Xizhi, Yan Zhenqing, Ouyang Xun and Liu Gongquan, whose regular script would eventually become the standard for woodblock carving.

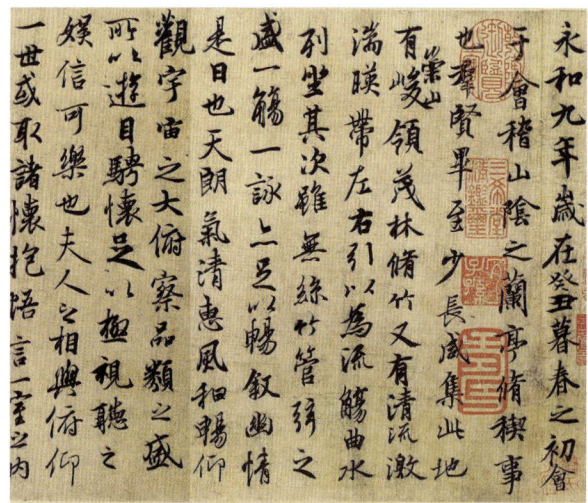

Figure 1.7.6-1: Wang Xizhi's Cursive handwriting. (王羲之行书)

Figure 1.7.6-2: The Small-Seal handwriting by Li Si in Qin Dynasty.（小篆书体，李斯书写）

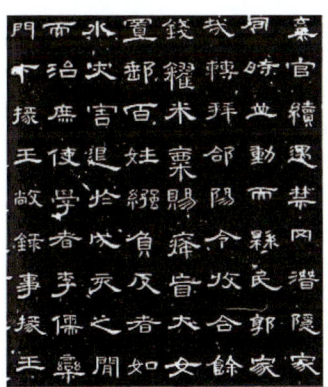

Figure 1.7.6-3: Li-Style form evolved from Seal-Style and further developed into regular form is one of the Chinese scripts.（隶书书体（汉代隶书））

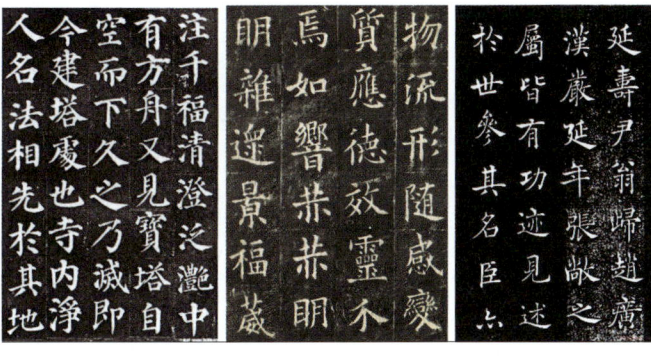

Figure 1.7.6-4: Several forms of regular scripts written by Yan Zhenqing, Ouyang Xun and Chu Suiliang)（唐代几种楷书书体 —— 颜真卿、欧阳询、褚遂良）

Conclusion

Eastern Asia, the birthplace of Chinese culture, is a vast expanse of land with various climates and some of the highest levels of diversity on the planet. For centuries, the ancient Chinese stood at the forefront of the world's civilizations in the invention and application of writing media. In turn, the use of the various media I have mentioned allowed for the emergence, usage and development of Chinese characters. The use of these unique and very different writing media and the evolution of Chinese characters were unique to the world and contributed directly to the inventions of both paper and printing, innovations which had a lasting effect on the world.

Task 8 ▶ Join the online forum and write a summary

(Students are required to have an instant and online post-talk discussion)

Irene:	What a wonderful talk, dear Professor Richards. On behalf of all three of us I want to express our sincere thanks for your lecture — we have all learned so much from it!
Richards:	You're very welcome, but perhaps your thanks are a little premature, since I have some tasks for you to carry out, and I believe Professor Philips also has some recommendations for you to consider.
Philips:	Indeed I have. As I'm sure you know, Professor Richards lectures will be a series, and they will define the focus for each unit. My suggestion is that you organize an online forum to discuss and elaborate further on the topic. I'm sure many other students will be interested in such a forum and join in, so that they too can reap the benefit of Professor Richards' lectures.
Miriam:	Oh, that'll be terrific! It's just what I'm hoping for — to meet a lot more people and make friends while we study.
Owen:	Me too! And I really want to make the most of our supervisors' valuable time, so I'm eager to find out what Professor Richards' assignments for us are.
Richards:	That's a good attitude, Owen. I'd like the PRIMO group to work on the following questions through discussion, even argumentation, and a lot of reflection.
Irene & Owen:	We'll do our best, Professor!

Richards:	I'm sure you will. Here are my questions or tasks. First, I want you to reflect on the correlation between bones used in ceremonies to divine the future and the birth of Oracle Bone Script. Second, I want you to practice talking in English about the earliest forms of writing in the Chinese language with examples and evidence for what you say. Third, try to chart the evolution of different media for writing before the advent of paper, and fourth talk about the different varieties and styles of Chinese calligraphy. Fifth and last, say what you know about the foundation of regular script for writing and the standard for woodblock carving.
Philips:	And I'd like to add a really final task: I think you would gain a great deal if you write a summary of the lecture.
Owen:	That'll be really interesting — I'll volunteer to help organize the forum.
Irene:	Thank you Owen, your contribution is always appreciated.
Miriam:	And will our dear Professors be able to join us on the forum?
Richards:	Certainly, we're always ready to help.
Philips:	Absolutely — any questions are welcome, and we have plenty of materials ready. So that's the end of the unit. See you soon!
Irene:	See you on the online forum!
Owen & Miriam	See you. Bye!

Appendix: Vocabulary for Unit 1

Historical Note

unilinear /ˈjuːnɪˈlɪnɪə/ adj. 始终遵循一条发展道路的，一条路线贯穿始终的；单线的

resemble /rɪˈzembəl/ vt. 相似

inscription /ɪnˈskrɪpʃ(ə)n/ n. 题词；铭文；刻印

prescription /prɪˈskrɪpʃ(ə)n/ n. 药方；指示；惯例

pharmacy /ˈfɑːməsɪ/ n. 药房；配药学，药剂学；制药业；备用药品

antique /ænˈtiːk/ n. 古董，古玩；古风，古希腊和古罗马艺术风格

inscribe /ɪnˈskraɪb/ vt. 题写；题献；铭记；雕
procure /prəˈkjʊə/ vt. 获得，取得；导致
pictograph /ˈpɪktəɡrɑːf/ n. [语] 象形文字；古代石壁画
archeology /ˌɑːkɪˈɒlədʒɪ/ n. 考古学；古物学；文化遗物；古迹
grammatology /ˌɡræməˈtɒlədʒɪ/ n. 写作学
decipher /dɪˈsaɪfə(r)/ vt. 解读；破译

Reading Activity

Oracle Bone Script 甲骨文
Sanskrit /ˈsænskrɪt/ n. 梵文
attest /əˈtest/ vt. & vi. 证明；证实；为……作证
icon /ˈaɪkɒn/ n. 图标；偶像；肖像，画像；圣像
meteorological /ˌmiːtɪərəˈlɒdʒɪkəl/ adj. 气象的；气象学的
astronomical /ˌæstrəˈnɒmɪk(ə)l/ adj. 天文的，天文学的；极大的
eclipse /ɪˈklɪps/ n. 日蚀，月蚀；黯然失色
diviner /dɪˈvaɪnə/ n. 预言者；占卜者；推测者
buff /bʌf/ vt. 用软皮摩擦；缓冲；擦亮，抛光某物
chisel /ˈtʃɪzl/ vt. 凿；雕
sacrifice /ˈsækrɪfaɪs/ vt. 牺牲；献祭；亏本出售
　　　　　　　　　　　vi. 献祭；奉献
conjure /ˈkʌndʒə/ vt. 念咒召唤；用魔法驱赶；提出，想象；恳求
　　　　　　　　　　vi. 施魔法；变魔术
culminate /ˈkʌlmɪneɪt/ vt. 使结束；使达到高潮
　　　　　　　　　　　　vi. 到绝顶；达到高潮；达到顶点
posthumously /ˈpɒstjʊməslɪ/ adv. 于死后，于身后
millennium /mɪˈlenɪəm/ n. 千年期，千禧年；一千年，千年纪念
Rameses /ˈræmɪsiːz/ n. 拉美西斯 (人名)
intriguing /ɪnˈtriːɡɪŋ/ adj. 引起好奇心的；令人感兴趣的
patriarch /ˈpeɪtrɪɑːk/ n. 家长；族长；元老；创始人
phonographic /ˌfəʊnəˈɡræfɪk/ adj. 留声机的；速记的
logographic /ˌlɒɡəʊˈɡræfɪk/ adj. 语标的；语素文字；意音文字
morph /mɔːf/ n. 词态；语素；变体
morpheme /ˈmɔːfiːm/ n. [语] 词素；形态素
typeface /ˈtaɪpfeɪs/ n. 字型；铅字样
calligraphic /ˌkælɪˈɡræfɪk/ adj. 书法的；缮写的

Lecture

integral /ˈɪntɪɡr(ə)l/ adj. 积分的；完整的；整体的

barometer /bəˈrɒmɪtə/ n. [气象] 气压计；睛雨表；变化的标志
innovation /ɪnəˈveɪʃ(ə)n/ n. 创新，革新；新方法
engrave /ɪnˈɡreɪv/ vt. 在……上雕刻；给……深刻的印象 (engrave的现在分词形式)
calligraphy /kəˈlɪɡrəfɪ/ n. 书法；笔迹
prevalent /ˈprev(ə)l(ə)nt/ adj. 流行的；普遍的，盛行的
fragment /ˈfræɡm(ə)nt/ n. 碎片；片断或不完整部分
transpire /trænˈspaɪə/ vt. 使蒸发；使排出
　　　　　　　　　　　　vi. 发生；蒸发；泄露
antecedent /ˈæntɪˈsiːd(ə)nt/ n. 前提；先行词；祖先
cauldron /ˈkɔːldr(ə)n/ n. 鼎；大锅
exquisite /ˈekskwɪzɪt/ adj. 精致的；细腻的；优美的，高雅的；异常的；剧烈的
prominence /ˈprɒmɪnəns/ n. 突出；显著；卓越
ornate /ɔːˈneɪt/ adj. 华丽的；装饰的；(文体) 绚丽的
flair /fleə/ n. 天资；天分；资质；鉴别力
tablets /ˈtæblɪt/ n. [药] 药片，匾 (tablet的复数形式)；便笺
epitaph /ˈepɪtɑːf/ n. 碑文，墓志铭
covenant /ˈkʌvənənt/ n. 契约，盟约；圣约；盖印合同
amendment /əˈmendmənt/ n. 修正案；修订；改正
strip /strɪp/ n. 带；条状

2 Unit

The Emergence of Chinese Publishing from Signs to Characters to Books

TABLE OF CONTENTS

Warm-up:	Be proactive
Task 1	Listen to a historical note: The Translator Kumārajīva: From Chinese to Indian
Task 2	Discuss the historical note
Task 3	Build up our vocabulary
Task 4	Reading activity: From the earliest signs and symbols to the construction of Chinese characters
Task 5	Reading comprehension
Task 6	Translation practice
Task 7	Attend a public lecture: The Early Publishing in Ancient China
Task 8	Join the online forum and write a summary
Appendix:	Vocabulary for Unit 2

Unit 2: The Emergence of Chinese Publishing from Signs to Characters to Books

WARM-UP: Be proactive

Irene: Hi, PRIMO team, are we all ready for today's discussion and lecture? I'm sure we can continue our exploration based on our discoveries from the last session. Where's Owen? I want to thank him for the online forum he organized for us — it was so enlightening!

Owen: Here I am, Irene — and you don't have to thank me, everybody was involved! I think online discussions are really awesome! You remember Professor Richards assigning us last week to reflect on the earliest forms of Chinese writing? Well, listening to you guys discussing it on the forum really helped me get a much clearer picture of the whole topic.

Miriam: Well, they say many hands make light work. I think we're going to attract many more members and have really great discussions.

Irene: The more the merrier! I think lots of people will want to discuss the origins and development of Chinese publishing. But are you guys totally clear now on the evolution of the media for Chinese characters? Professor Philips wanted us to summarize the whole progression.

Miriam: That's not such a tough question now, after all our discussion, is it? Chinese characters were inscribed on all sorts of different surfaces, starting with pottery and bone or shell, then cut into stone and metal, then brushed on to silk and finally printed on to paper.

Irene & Owen: Yes, that's exactly right!

Miriam: As you know, I really want to learn more about ancient Chinese characters. They're so fascinating! Every single word has its own wisdom and mystery!

Owen:	Yes, and they're all part of the origins of Chinese culture, too.
Irene:	I couldn't agree more — I'm a total fan of the ancient Chinese. They were so clever to create characters and then to find ways to spread them all over their land through different media.
Miriam:	I can't wait to get a more systematic understanding of the whole thing.
Owen:	So what're we supposed to discuss in class today?
Irene:	The first lecture's about the famous translator Kumārajīva. Professor Phillips will lead us through the topic.
Miriam:	Yes, I've already read a bit about him. Wasn't he born into a noble family, but still committed himself to the preaching of Buddhism? And he was very influential in the spread of Chinese Buddhism?
Irene:	That's right. Buddhism was introduced to China via the Silk Road by groups of monks, amongst whom Kumārajīva was one of the most outstanding.
Owen:	And I can see that there's probably a very close connection between the rapid spread of Buddhism and the development of Chinese printing and publishing.
Miriam:	Oh absolutely! The printing of Buddhist scriptures must have contributed enormously to the growth of the publishing industry in China. But where do we go from there in its evolution?
Irene:	Well, the foundation stones of publishing have to be characters and books, don't you agree?
Miriam:	Yes, of course.
Owen:	Oh sure!
Irene:	So today, Professor Phillips will take us through the story of Kumārajīva and his wonderful translations of Buddhist scriptures. After that, Professor Richards will give us a lecture on other book productions during the Qin-Han, Wei-Jin, and Sui-Tang Periods.
Miriam:	That's terrific! All our bits and pieces of knowledge will be brought together into a complete picture!
Owen:	I can't wait! Professor Phillips is on his way, right?
Miriam:	In fact he's here now — let us welcome our lecturer today, Professor Phillips, to continue our exploration into Chinese characters and publishing!

Task 1 ▶ Listen to a historical note: The Translator Kumārajīva: From Chinese to Indian

Philips: Hello there! I'm glad you could join us and to see you are interested in learning about Chinese characters and publishing. To study the construction of Chinese characters is not an easy task, but I have great confidence in you since each of you is so eager to learn and to exchange opinions and information. Owen, very well done on the online forum!

Owen: Thank you, Professor. The PRIMO group is honored to have you with us. You are so ready to help.

Miriam: You know, Professor, before I came to China, I just regarded Chinese characters as artistic calligraphy, but now I'm beginning to appreciate their profundity. I'll have a lot of questions to ask today.

Irene: Yes, so mysterious and so beautiful! Professor Philips, I'm really looking forward to your introduction to the construction of ancient Chinese characters. That will be fascinating.

Philips: It is, and I will come to that. But before I do, I want to discuss how we should understand **Publishing.** On a general basis, publishing is the process of production and dissemination of literature, music, or information — the activity of making information available to the general public. What do you think are the most indispensable elements?

Miriam: Language and graphics.

Owen: Yes, that's crystal clear. But surely, media and technology are equally essential.

Philips: They are indeed, but today I want to talk about how people with different languages communicate with each other. Being the first key element for publishing, language — and its translation into other languages — naturally falls into the top category of discussion. And of course, any questions and discussions will be very welcomed. Now I'd like to share some historical notes in this regard with you. (You are required to fill in the blanks with the words and phrases you hear while listening)

Exchange between languages was 1) _____ from the transmission of religion from very beginning. In China, the most 2) _____ translation activity can be 3) _____ the Southern and Northern Dynasties period, when the large-scale translation and transmission of Buddhist scriptures in the Central Plain was 4) _____. Despite being a task of 5) _____, the translation of Buddhist scriptures into Chinese was actually carried out by a small, multi-cultural group of translators. Among them was Kumārajīva (Figure 2.1.1), a 6) _____ of royal Kuchean descent hailing from India.

Figure 2.1.1: The Statue of Kumārajīva kept in the Cave of One-thousand Buddhist. [克孜尔千佛洞（在古龟兹国故地）前的鸠摩罗什铜像]
(http://spaceresource.dadunet.com/artweb/20090810134439924.jpg)

Born into a 7) _____ line of ministers from the country of Tianzhu (the word for India in ancient China), Kumārajīva never actually traveled to Tianzhu during his lifetime. Kumārajīva's initial Sanskrit education came from his father. He learned his Chinese in Kucha, where the influence of Han culture was heavily felt. Kumārajīva's father Kumārāyana had no interest in power, and 8) _____ his post as an official when he was still young. Traveling east, he eventually settled in Kucha (present day Kuqua, Xinjiang). The King of Kucha, noticing that his sister was fond of Kumārāyana, insisted that Kumārāyana take his sister's hand in marriage. The two soon welcomed a son, Kumārajīva, which in Chinese meant 9) "_____". Kumārajīva's mother was 10) _____. When Kumārajīva was just seven years old, his mother became a nun and took her son to live in a nunnery. Gifted from childhood, Kumārajīva first studied Hīnayāna Buddhism and later Mahayana Buddhism under the strict guidance of his mother and the scripture interpreters in the nunnery. Before long, he was able to recite 32,000 characters of Buddhist verses each day. When Kumārajīva was 12 years old, he traveled around the neighboring countries with his mother, studying and delivering sermons as they went. At the age of 20, he was brought back to Kucha. Kumārajīva's aptitude for the interpretation and translation of Buddhist scriptures placed him far above his peers. Gradually displaying the unrestrained character of a great talent, he became the subject of much criticism among his fellow followers of Buddhism. When his mother traveled to Tianzhu, Kumārajīva chose to remain in the western territories, where he translated and taught Buddhist scriptures. He eventually became an eminent monk, being held in great esteem throughout the various countries of the western territories. So great was his repute that kings would willingly leave their thrones and kneel down beside him when he delivered a sermon. Word of Kumārajīva's great talent eventually reached the Central China Plain, capturing the attention of King Fu Jian of the Former Qin, who had a strong desire to recruit men of virtue and talent. In the year 382, Fu Jian found a pretext for an attack on Kucha, ordering his general Lü Guang to bring Kumārajīva back to the Former Qin by force. However, when Lü Guang's (Figure 2.1.2) forces reached Liangzhou, word reached them of Fu Jian's defeat and death at the Battle of Fei River. Upon hearing the news, Lü Guang proclaimed the establishment of a new regime in Liangzhou, where Kumārajīva was forced to stay for 17 years. Yao Xing, the ruler of the Later Qin, had a deep respect for Buddhism despite being a devout Confucianist. In the year 401, Yao Xing captured Kumārajīva from the clutches of the Lü regime and brought him back to Chang'an, where he received the treatment of a Grand Master. Benefiting from the tranquility afforded by the West Bright Pavilion and Free Garden, Kumārajīva resumed his teaching and translation activities. This period would see him reach the pinnacle of his career as a scripture translator. In the last eleven years of his life, Kumārajīva, accompanied by his many apprentices, translated and revised a total of 384 scrolls from 74 scriptures of Mahayana Buddhism (See the *Kai Yuan Lu* (Figure 2.1.3)). Kumārajīva took the translation of Buddhist scriptures extremely seriously. Before starting a translation, he would contemplate the meaning of the text and try to grasp the overall style of its language. The translation process saw Kumārajīva first translate the scriptures from Sanskrit to Tokharian, following which he would translate them into Chinese orally while his apprentices wrote them down. Each sentence had to be checked a total of three times. After the translations were completed, Kumārajīva would check them personally. These expertly produced Chinese translations were gracefully worded and highly faithful to the original scriptures. Many of them would be passed on for generations to come.

Figure 2.1.2: Lv Guang — the Founder of Hou Liang Dynasty. (后凉的建立者吕光)
(http://p0.so.qhimg.com/t013ca57f9e5e90d830.jpg)

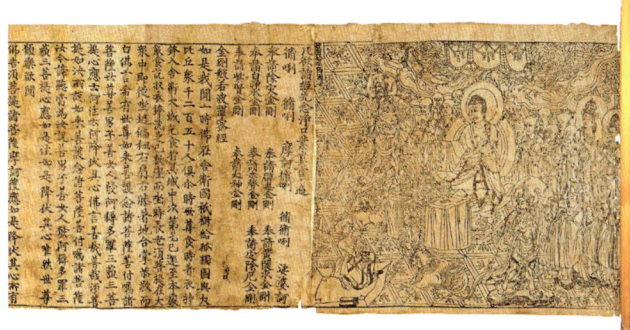

Figure 2.1.3 *The Scriptures of Mahayana Buddhism.* (大乘佛教现存最早的雕印本汉译《金刚经》,唐代咸通九年王玠刻本)

(http://img.bimg.126.net/photo/RmC6axwChGA9ue3nXB4l_w==/5749126399315762637.jpg)

Owing to his great achievement, Kumārajīva is regarded as one of the four master translators of Buddhist scriptures in ancient China together with Paramārtha, Xuanzang, and Yijing. In addition, Kumārajīva is also known as the "romantic monk", because he broke his vows as a Buddhist monk on two separate occasions: the first in 384 when he was forced to marry a princess of Kucha after the country's fall to Lv Guang; and the second in Chang'an when he took a courtesan in marriage in order to fulfill Yao Xing's request that he carry forward his "Holy Seed". In an attempt to explain why he had broken his vows, Kumārajīva compared himself to the lotus flower, which "grows out from the mud to emerge clean and unstained". He emphasized that the compliance of his translations with the teachings of Buddhism transcended the physical façade of breaking his vows. After his death, Kumārajīva was cremated in accordance with the ritual traditions of Tianzhu. But legend has it that Kumārajīva's tongue survived the cremation intact, even though his body had burned away and was no more. This was supposedly a sign that Kumārajīva's translations accorded strictly to the meaning of the Buddha, having been foreseen by Kumārajīva himself before his death.

Task 2 ▶ Discuss the historical note
(Students are required to do role play in groups by imitating the PRIMO's dialogue)

Owen: Wow, that historical note was quite long and detailed, wasn't it? That was the translator's whole life story, and what a life! But did you find any connection between his translations and Chinese publishing?

Irene: Well, Professor Phillips gave Miriam and me some background reading to do. I think we can probably answer your question between us, don't you think so, Miriam?

Miriam: I'm sure we can, Irene. You start off first.

Irene: Okay. I think Kumārajīva's story comes in three periods. The first part is his childhood and education. He was born in Kucha, which is in Xinjiang. His initial Sanskrit education came from his father, who was from India. Later, he studied Buddhism under the strict guidance of his mother and the scripture interpreters at the nunnery she had joined. This childhood education laid the foundation for his interpretation of Buddhist scripture.

Miriam: Yes indeed, but it was a very complicated life that he had. The second stage started when he was forced to leave his homeland, captured in war, imprisoned for many years, and even got married! Finally, he was brought east to the capital, Chang'an. This was when he started on his famous translations of the scriptures, first from Sanskrit to Tocharian, and then orally into Chinese.

Owen: Why didn't he translate straight into Chinese? And what is Tocharian?

Irene: Tocharian was the language spoken in Kucha, and therefore his mother tongue. He then translated the Tocharian orally into Chinese and his student scribes wrote it down. The Emperor Yao Xing asked him to translate many sutras, and had many temples and towers built. Under the influence of the Emperor's power and Kumarajiva's fame, reports say that 90% of the population became Buddhist.

Owen:	What a man, and what a life! And I think I can see the connection now between Kumārajīva's translations and Chinese publishing. With 90% of the population converting to Buddhism, the demand for copies of Buddhist scriptures would be enormous!
Irene:	You've got it, Owen! The last period of Kumārajīva's life was in fact his death and his reputation and fame after death. Even today we can still see how influential he was as a Buddhist translator and interpreter, one of the four great masters of ancient China. It was the pressure of demand for Buddhist scriptures that accelerated the invention of woodblock printing.
Miriam:	And this allowed the development of the whole publishing industry in the Southern and Northern Dynasty.
Owen:	There's so much behind this story, isn't there? Your proactive thinking has really set up a model for me. Next time, I want to lead the discussion, and I'll follow your example!
Irene:	And I'm sure you'll do it just as well!
Miriam:	Yes, I hope it's an even longer story and we can see Owen's analytical mind at work.
Owen:	Well, I'll do the best I can — but you girls were really terrific!

Task 3 ▶ Build up our vocabulary
(Drag and match exercises)

Match the English words or pinyin in column A with the Chinese equivalents in column B.

A		B	
1	the burning of Confucian classics	A	焚书坑儒
2	the reverence of Confucian classics	B	象形文字；表意文字
3	*Doctoral Chairs for the Five Classics*	C	《别录》
4	Confucianism	D	《汉书》
5	*Shuowen Jiezi*	E	《七略》
6	a bibliography	F	《齐民要术》

7　*Bie Lu*   G　《史记》
8　*Qi Lue*   H　《水经注》
9　*Yuandi Sibu Shumu*   I　《说文解字》
10　Confucian classics, history, masters   J　《四十二章》
　　and philosophers
11　Literary encyclopedias   K　《五经正义》
12　Rime dictionaries   L　《元帝四部书目》
13　Sutra of Forty-two Chapters   M　《韵书》
14　*Qi Min Yao Shu*   N　独尊儒术
15　Commentary on the Waterways Classic   O　肩胛骨占卜术
16　the Correct Meaning of the Five Classics   P　经史子集
17　the Records of the Grand Historian   Q　类书
18　the Book of Han   R　目录学
19　Scapulimancy   S　儒学
20　pictogram   T　五经博士
21　ideograph   U　象形图

Task 4 ▶ Reading activity

The following excerpt is recommended to PRIMO, some of which is from **Chinese History: A New Manual by Endymion Wilkinson**. *It is about* **"From the earliest signs and symbols to the construction of Chinese characters"**. *PRIMO believe their study of the history of Chinese history wouldn't have been possible without exploring the evolution of Chinese characters. So the following excerpt just fills in the gap in this regard.*

4.1 The earliest signs and symbols before characters

　　The appearance of oracle-bone script has long been regarded as the origin of Chinese characters. But actually, the origin of Chinese characters may have started much earlier with the practice of Pyromancy ['paırəmænsı] *n.* ((根据火或火的形状所作的) 火卜，火占卜) (Figure 2.4.1), which began to emerge in China during the late Yangshao (仰韶) period — the earliest traces discovered so far date from about 4000 BC. During the Longshan culture (from 2600-2000 BC) this method of divination with the generic name pyromancy and its specific term Scapulimancy (肩胛骨占卜术) (Figure 2.4.2) gradually spread over the rest of Northern China and into present day Korea. By the time of the Erlitou culture (二里头文化) (1900-1500 BC), just before the Shang, it was becoming even more widespread. Traces of prehistoric pyromancy have been found at numerous archeological sites. The materials were usually the shoulder blades of oxen, sheep, deer, pigs, and occasionally humans. They are less well prepared than those of the Shang. Several bear individual signs and symbols, but not characters.

Figure 2.4.1: One form of pyromancy involving divination (i.e. foretelling the future) by Kings of the Late Shang Dynasty, China (1200-1045 BCE), by using fire.（商代晚期用火占卜的一种形式）
(http://www.thegoddards.ca/alexgoddardblog/?p=652)

Turtles began being used as material in the lower Huai and Yangzi valleys from about 4000 BC. They were worshipped for their magical properties. Their plastrons are quite commonly found in tombs there, but they were not normally used for pyromancy. Instead, they appear to have been part of the paraphernalia [pærəfə'neɪlɪə] (*n.* 随身用具；设备) for a form of divination using small stones collected in the carapace. Then, at sites in Henan and Shangdong dating from the early second millennium BC, turtle plastrons used for hot-brand divination began to be found along with animal bones employed for scapulimancy. The application of northern scapulimancy to the divine turtle shell of the south and east reached its highest point several centuries later during the golden age of oracle-bone divination in Anyang, a period of roughly two centuries that starts in the reign of Wu Ding (ca. 1250-1192 BC) (Figure 2.4.3) and continues through the reigns of his eight successors until the fall of the Shang in 1046 BC.

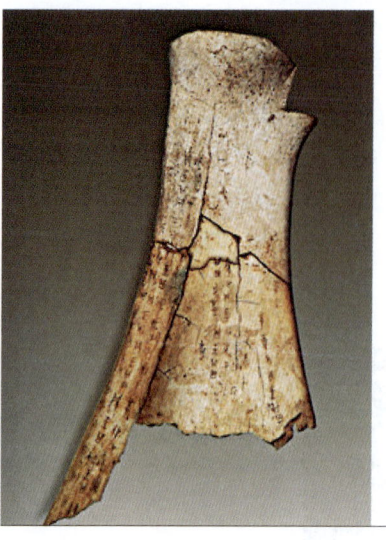

Figure 2.4.2: *Scapulomancy or Scapulamancy* — the practice of divination by use of scapulae (shoulder blades). (肩胛骨占卜术) (http://theweirdnewsdaily.blogspot.co.uk/2013/07/weird-wiki-21-scapulimancy.html)

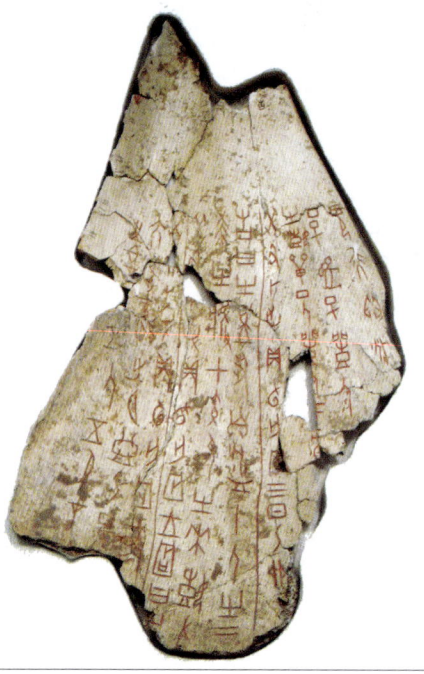

Figure 2.4.3: Ox scapula with a divination inscription from the Shang Dynasty, dating to the reign of King Wu Ding. (牛肩胛骨与商代占卜的铭文，可以追溯到武丁王的统治) (from http://www.thegoddards.ca)

The shells were first cleaned and polished, and then small oval-shaped hollows were prepared on the rough side, into which a red-hot bronze point or a heated brand of chaste wood (*jing* 荆) was inserted when the divination took place. Before the shell could be used for divination it had to be smeared with the blood of a sacrificed human or animal. Following each of the diviner's questions it was then scorched to produce a crack. This caused a fissure on the smooth side from which branched out horizontal cracks. As was mentioned in the previous lecture, "*bu* 卜 divine" and "⺈ *zhao* 兆" — divination cracks may have been originally graphic representations of these cracks. But these oracle-bone records were not documents intended for later consultation. As soon as an inscribed plastron or bone had served its purpose it was discarded, reused for something else or even destroyed on purpose. There was one exceptional case that an inscribed bone was kept for 179 days while waiting for the result of an omen to materialize.

Indeed, it appears that once the plastron had been used for one or more divination, especially once the King during whose reign the divinations had been made had died, the shells were buried in specially constructed garbage pits. They were buried because of the belief that they could otherwise bring harm to people. Diviners, too, in most cases changed as a new king came to the throne, making it possible to date bones on the basis of diviners.

The earliest traces of pyromancy and the long-lost inscriptions provided much more detailed insight into the formation of the Chinese language and characters than was previously possible.

4.2 The construction of Chinese characters

Chinese characters, unlike the writing system of any alphabetic language, are not formed with letters or combination of letters to represent the sounds of the Chinese language. Rather, they are symbols constructed and used to convey meanings as well as sounds that indicate meanings. From the previous discussion, we know that Chinese characters have had a history as a highly developed writing system for at least 3300 years. In the earliest known stages of written Chinese, there were six kinds of Chinese characters: 1) pictographic characters; 2) indicative characters; 3) associative characters; 4) picto-phonetic characters; 5) explanative characters and; 6) phonetic loan characters. The first five kinds are categorized according to the ways they were created, and the last one (6) complemented the other methods by borrowing existing characters to refer to new things that no characters had been created for.

These six kinds of Chinese characters, which were summarized and exemplified by Xu Shen in his *An Analysis and Explanation of Characters* (《说文解字》) at the beginning of the first century AD, reflect the earliest stages of the creation and use of Chinese characters (Figure 2.4.4).

The first major way of creating Chinese characters that came into use was the pictographic method. The human body or body parts as well as things that can be observed in nature were depicted in simple drawings based on their most conspicuous and differentiated traits. However, an abstract concept is not expressed easily by drawing a picture, so the indicative method, in which a

	Categories	Explanations	Examples*	
1	Pictographic Characters	Characters created by drawing a sketch to depict a material object	人 person	木 tree
2	Indicative Characters	Characters created by 1) drawing an abstract sign to indicate an abstract concept or 2) adding or changing a stroke to an existing pictographic character to indicate a new concept	上 upper	本 root
3	Associative Characters	Characters created by combining two or more pictographic components to infer a new meaning	木 + 木 = 林 tree + tree = woods	人 + 木 = 休 person + tree = rest
4	Picto-phonetic Characters	Characters created by combining a pictographic component that represents a meaning category and another component that indicates the sound of the whole character	氵+ 林 = 淋 water+(sound)=shower	氵+ 木 = 沐 water + (sound) = wash
5	Explative Characters	Characters created with a pictographic component to help explain the meaning added to another component that represents both the sound and meaning of the whole character	木 + 支 = 枝 tree + branch = branch (sound)	氵+ 益 = 溢 water + spill = spill (sound)
6	Phonetic Loan Characters	Characters originally created for one concept but borrowed to represent another concept with the same pronunciation	六 six (originally "hut")	北 north (originally "back")

Figure 2.4.4: Six categories of Chinese character construction.（汉字结构的六大类）

symbol was added to a drawing to indicate the concept, was adopted. When a meaning could be sensed or deduced by combining two existing pictographs, a combined form was produced to save the trouble of creating a new pictograph. This method of combining two existing pictographs is called the associative method. When a meaning could not be expressed by creating a character with the associative method, then the picto-phonetic method was deployed. The picto-phonetic method forms a character with a pictograph as one part to indicate the major category of meaning and the other part to indicate the pronunciation of the whole character. When a pictographic component representing both the sound and the meaning could not express the meaning clearly enough, another pictographic component was added to clarify or differentiate the meaning of the whole character from others. This method is the explanative method. The explanative method was also used when a character was borrowed (but never returned) to mean something else simply because this borrowed character had the same pronunciation as the new idea, which as yet had no character to express it. These borrowed characters are called phonetic loan characters. The picto-phonetic method has been the most productive in creating characters. Because the explanative method has not been clearly understood for many years and because a lot of work to distinguish explanative characters from picto-phonetic characters has still not been satisfactorily done, many explanative characters are confused with picto-phonetic characters. Nevertheless, it is widely accepted that over 90 percent of the characters used today are picto-phonetic in origin in a broad sense. Of course, because of developments and changes in the language over the past few thousand years, in modern Chinese no more than 30 percent of the picto-phonetic characters contain a phonetic component that can accurately represent the pronunciation of the whole character.

Regardless of how a character was created, when created it almost always had the trait of a pictograph one way or another. Over thousands of years, the pictographic essence slowly faded and is no longer visually obvious in modern Chinese characters. Now, formed with various kinds of lines, dots, and hooks, Chinese characters are highly symbolic. They mostly appear as logographs rather than pictographs. In other words, they look more like symbols than drawings.

Task 5 ▶ Reading comprehension

(Students are required to launch a discussion to pose new questions and answer all the questions raised in the dialogue, and do the role play based on the following)

Irene: So, characters are not only art, they're magic too! And they represent wisdom, don't they? I used to think I knew a lot about Chinese characters, but now I feel ashamed at my naivety. What I find incredible is that even though they have a history of more than three thousand years, we can still see

	their origins in the way they're constructed.
Miriam:	That's so true. But you can see why Chinese is regarded as one of the most difficult languages to learn by us second language students. The sheer complexity of those six construction methods is a real challenge for foreign learners!
Irene:	Yes, it's not surprising, especially when you consider that our writing system originated in the late Yangshao, developed through the Xia and Shang Dynasties, and then kept on developing all the way up to the present time. Both the history and the construction methods of Chinese characters are so complicated.
Miriam:	But not only long and complicated, it's also mysterious as well as ancient. Oracle bone script was the origin of Chinese characters, but it was also fundamental to the ancient Chinese system of worship — they actually believed in the magical power of the turtle shell! And all this was happening in the Yangshao period — that's about 4000 BCE!
Owen:	4000 BCE — wow! So the Yangshao takes you back into the Neolithic — that's the Stone Age!
Irene:	It is indeed. We call it the Yangshao culture after the small village in Henan province where the first Neolithic relics were excavated.
Owen:	You're amazing, Irene — a walking Chinese history book!
Miriam:	And you help me see the point of prehistoric pyromancy. It wasn't only superstition, it was also a representation of the ancient Chinese themselves. Those cracks on shoulder blades, just like the early woodblocks, helped to tell the life stories of your ancestors.
Irene:	Right! The Yangshao culture also saw the formation of settlement hierarchies on the ancient China Plain. Later, around 1900 to 1500 BC, the Erlitou culture developed and pyromancy increased in popularity. The shoulder blade then began to be used for oracle bone divination.
Owen:	Sorry to interrupt, but I'm a bit confused! When and where was the Erlitou culture? Is there a connection between it and the Yangshao culture.
Miriam:	Oh dear, Owen — confused again? But to be honest, it's all a

	bit mixed up for me as well!
Irene:	Don't worry about it you guys! That's the point of studying Chinese culture — to make us curious about the unknown, and then work it out between us. Yangshao was the oldest of the three cultures, dating back into the Neolithic and it was followed by the Longshan culture from about 2600 to 2000 BCE. Erlitou culture evolved from the Longshan culture, and was an early Bronze Age society from about 1900 to 1500 BCE. Its discovery was made in Yanshi, Henan Province, and it's normally called the Xia Dynasty by Chinese archaeologists.
Miriam:	Okay I get it now! So from Yangshao to Longshan to Erlitou, Chinese characters developed from pyromancy divination marks to oracle bone characters.
Owen:	Yes, the timeline in my head is getting clearer now. Turtle shells began to be used more and more and reached a peak in Anyang during the Shang Dynasty. That's why oracle bones were discovered in Anyang, as we were told in Unit 1.
Irene:	Right, and those symbols lay the foundations for the construction of Chinese characters.
Miriam:	But from the reading passage I gather that the structure of a Chinese character is not restricted to a symbol.
Irene:	That's correct. A character can be a combination of symbol, and meaning, and even of sound.
Owen:	After reading about the rules of character formation, I can see how visual some of the creation was. The Chinese character "人" looks like a person standing, and the character "上" actually demonstrates the meaning of "up".
Miriam:	Yes, and the characters with different components combine the original meaning of those components, so "溢" means water spill and "林" means woods.
Irene:	You two sound just like professional code-breakers!
Miriam:	(*Laughing*) Well, we are professionals — professional Chinese learners!
Owen:	Professional braggers more like it! (*They all laugh*)
Irene:	So, team, how about making a list of questions for the reading

	material and posting it on the online forum? That way we can have a discussion with more people online.
Owen:	Great idea! Let's work on it together.
Miriam:	The first question should ask about the origins and early evolution of Chinese characters.
Irene:	Next we should go on to the formation rules for the construction of characters.
Owen:	Okay, got it. Then how about a list of characters to exemplify each of the rules?
Miriam:	That'll be perfect! Examples are the best support for an explanation.
Irene:	Perfect indeed. Now we should finish the translation assignment so that we can talk about it either in English or in Chinese.
Owen:	And let's hope we do that perfectly too.

Task 6 ▶ Translation practice

(Students are required to translate the following Chinese paragraph into English individually, in pairs or in group)

Irene:	Hello again, team mates — are you ready for the translation task?
Owen:	Yes, I've done a lot of preparation on the topic, and I'm absolutely confident of getting a good translation of the paragraph.
Miriam:	Do you really mean that, Owen? Our learning's still a bit superficial. Are you really sure you can translate all the terminologies and sentences with no problems?
Owen:	I didn't mean I'm going to do the translation myself. I've got some basic knowledge of Chinese publishing, and with the help of you dear ladies, I'm sure we can arrive at a good translation.
Irene:	I'm sure we can, too, Owen. The paragraph is about

	publishing, or more accurately, Chinese publishing. We're acquainted with the different media and terms like "oracle bone script", "bronze inscriptions", "stone inscriptions" and so on from the first unit. In this unit we've developed an understanding of the origins and the formation rules of Chinese characters. So now, based on what we've learned so far, I think we're ready to deal with this translation exercise.
Miriam:	But some of the new terms will be a bit intimidating for me and Owen, won't they, Irene? There'll be characters we haven't learned before, and we'll have to practice them. We'll really need your help, Irene.
Owen:	Yes, but that's what I find so exciting — learning new words and new characters! Come on teammates, let's work this out!

　　出版的前提条件是文字、文字载体和印刷的产生。文字必须借载体才能得以表现，而文字与载体的结合，便是初期书籍的雏型。从现存的甲骨刻辞、青铜器铭文和早期石刻文字看，殷周时期是中国初期书籍发展的历史阶段。甲骨文，也称甲骨刻辞或卜辞，是记录性的档案材料，主要记载占卜的事项。此外还有石刻文字，世界上许多民族都有在石头上刻字的记载方法，中国古代也不例外，中国的石刻文字包括雕刻和书写在石鼓、玉、石片上的文字，战国及战国以前，在石头上刻字相当流行。我国初期雏形书籍还包括铸刻在青铜器上的文字，称为铭文，也称金文。殷人已有在青铜器上铸刻文字的习惯。到了周代初期，文字渐多，西周后半期到春秋中期，所刻文字出现多达几百字的长文。这些使旁人或后人从中获取一定的知识。从这个意义上来看，它们不失为初期书籍的形式，虽不是现代意义的正规书籍。中国的正规书籍大约产生在春秋末年以前。后世尊为"五经"的《诗》、《书》、《易》、《礼》、《春秋》相传就是经过大教育家孔子（公元前551—前479）整理编定的，这些可以证明在孔子生活的春秋末期，中国的正规书籍早已产生。进入战国时期，奴隶制社会急剧向封建社会转化，在思想界形成百家争鸣的局面。先秦诸子争相游说和著书立说，产生了大批私人著作，同时也不乏科学技术、天文、历法、农业、畜牧、历史、地理等方面的著作。在佛教自东汉明帝时传入中国以后，佛教经典也陆续地被翻译过来。后世的石刻儒家经典和释家经藏，则属于名副其实的正规书，或者称为"石头书"。竹木简书也随着正规书籍而产生并得以发展。而造纸和印刷术的发明，不但促进了写本书的繁荣与发展，也为书籍制作方法的改革提供了必备的条件。书籍的产生，实际上就意味着出版活动的产生。

Task 7 ▶ Attend Professor Richards's public lecture

Lecture 2

The Early Publishing in Ancient China
(The Evolution of Books During the Qin-Han, Wei-Jin and Sui-Tang Periods)
Professor Richards

Hello again. Today I'm going to present to you the second lecture in our lecture series on the history of publishing in ancient China. In my first lecture I reviewed with you the fundamental elements, i.e. the oracle bone scripts and development of Chinese characters. We elaborated on the various surfaces to which they were originally applied. Since people were able to transform what they knew mentally into visualized written forms so that their knowledge could be spread widely and passed down to their descendants. Therefore, given my introduction, today, it should come as no surprise that our lecture deals with the birth of books...

A major outward expansion in both book type and content took place from the Qin and Han up through the Sui and Tang periods in ancient China. A lot of the books I will talk about during this lecture are what you would refer to as reference books, from dictionaries to bibliographies, collected works to biographies and specialist works to histories.

The expansion of book form and content is interesting for a number of reasons, not the least of which is because it was this very consolidation of knowledge in book form which not only allowed for the transmission of knowledge, but also for the dispersal of ideas and culture on a scale not previously known. To a large degree this expansion of books represents the very essence of Chinese culture, you could say it is what made China become China and is responsible for instilling in you many of the values you possess today.

In this lecture I will list and then briefly address a number of different types of books, including, in order: dictionaries, bibliographies, literary encyclopedias, rime dictionaries, individual and general collections, family records, biographies, translations of Buddhist scripture, specialist works, interpretations of the Confucian Classics and books addressing history.

The Qin-Han period saw the emergence and solidification of centralized rule in China. From the burning of Confucian classics during the Qin Dynasty, to the reverence of Confucian classics during the Han Dynasty, and the establishment of the "Doctoral Chairs for the Five Classics" during the Western Han Dynasty, when Confucianism was declared the supreme school of thought for the country, this period of time in Chinese history provided a cultural stability which not only made possible the unification of Chinese characters, but also spurred the emergence of new types of books related to written language and academic study. One of the main types of books to proliferate during this time was dictionaries.

Dictionaries mainly came in two types, specialist reference books and literacy books that taught people how to write. Examples of the former include *Erya Fangyan* and *Shuowen Jiezi*. *Shuowen Jiezi*, written by Xu Shen during the Eastern Han Dynasty, is considered to be the first standardized dictionary in China (Figure 2.7.1).

Figure 2.7.1: Xu Shen（许慎）
(http://p3.so.qhimg.com/t01f0d82525ff8a1ed3)

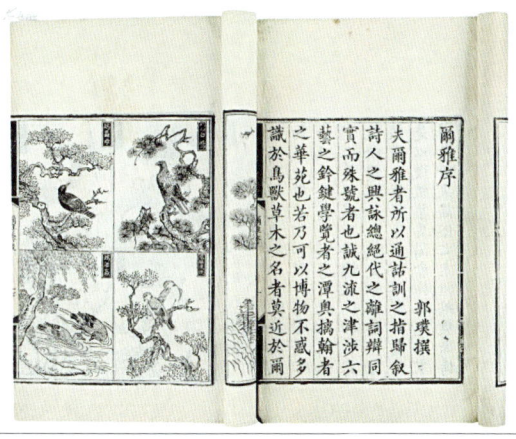

Figure 2.7.2: *ER Ya—The Elegant* written by Guo Pu in the Six Year of Jiaqing Period, Qing Dynasty.（《尔雅》，郭璞注，清嘉庆六年刻本）
(http://pmgs.kfzimg.com/data/pre_show_pic/2/42/4184)

It was the first book to classify Chinese characters into six categories according to differences in their composition, namely: pictograms, ideographs, compound ideographs, phono-semantic compounds, derivative cognates and loan characters. It also introduced the first method for the indexing of characters and the first method for ascertaining the meaning and origin of characters, by breaking them down into their component parts. *Shuowen Jiezi* was as original as it was profound and would eventually become an area of study in its own right (Figure 2.7.3).

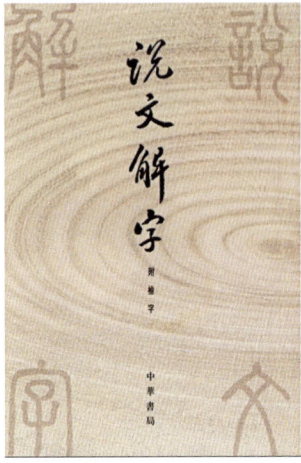

Figure 2.7.3: *Analytical Dictionary of Characters Language (Shuowen Jiezi)*, Modern Version, by Zhonghua Book Company in 1963.

The second type of dictionary, literacy books, were designed to teach children how to read and write. Examples of this type of book include *Cang Jie Pian, Xun Zuan Pian, Fan Jiang Pian,* and *Pang Xi Pian* (Figure 2.7.4). *Pang Xi Pian* was written in an easy to understand rhyme format and of the four books I just mentioned is the only one that has managed to survive.

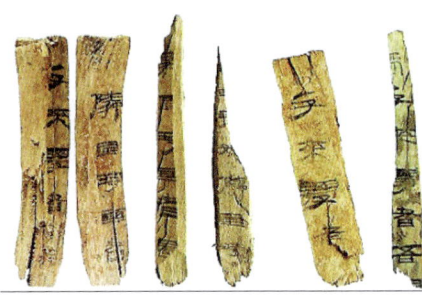

Figure 2.7.4: *Cang Jie — Unearthed Han Dynasty wooden tablets.* (《仓颉篇》，出土汉简)
(http://pic.gansudaily.com.cn/0/12/04/22/12042257_140696)

Aside from dictionaries, another way to reference materials, specifically other books, is to use a bibliography, which in case you don't know, is a book which contains a list and description of other books. In short, it is a reference tool which allows a user to quickly locate specific books addressing various subjects. One of the first bibliographies ever to be compiled was written in the Western Han Dynasty when the emperor commissioned an individual by the name of Liu Xiang to organize the royal book collection. Along with his son,

Liu Xiang wrote the *Bie Lu* (Figure 2.7.5), a catalog of the royal library that was itself 20 scrolls in length.

Figure 2.7.5: Liu Xiang and his *Separated Records* (*Bie Lu*), copied by Yu Jiaxi in 1930. (刘向《别录》，余嘉锡 1930 年手抄本，清代顾观光辑) (http://s14.sinaimg.cn/middle/64aa6ee9t73153407dd6d)

Based on the *Bie Lu*, Liu Xiang's son, Liu Xin, later wrote the *Qi Lue*, or *Seven Abstracts*, which was a comprehensive catalogue of the *Tian Lu Ge* collection of scrolls (Figure 2.7.6). Lu Xin's bibliography divided the collection of over 13,000 scrolls and 603 authors into 38 schools of seven different categories, including: the 6 arts, philosophy, poetry, military strategy, mathematics and astronomy, medicine, and arts and culture. Aside from the organizational benefits of the *Qi Lue*, Liu Xin also included summaries, general introductions and prefaces to his bibliography. His style was later emulated and other noteworthy bibliographies were compiled… notably the *Zhong Jing Xin Bu* (Figure 2.7.7) compiled during the Western Jin period used sequential characters Jia, Yi, Bing and Ding to classify works into four different categories, while the Jin *Yuandi Sibu Shumu* (Figure 2.7.8), also compiled during the Western Jin period, classified books into four separate categories entitled: Confucian classics, history, masters and philosophers, and anthologies and collected works.

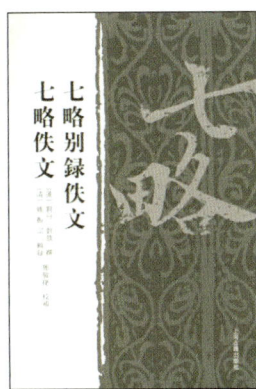

Figure 2.7.6: *Qi Lue,* or *Seven Abstract* by Yao Zhenzong, published by Shanghai Publishing House of the Ancient Books in 2008. (《别录佚文·七略佚文》，上海古籍出版社，2008 年)

Figure 2.7.7: *The Tian Lu Ge collection of scrolls divided into four categrories.*（建立在《中经新簿》《元帝四部书目》图书分类法基础上的清代四库全书分类法）

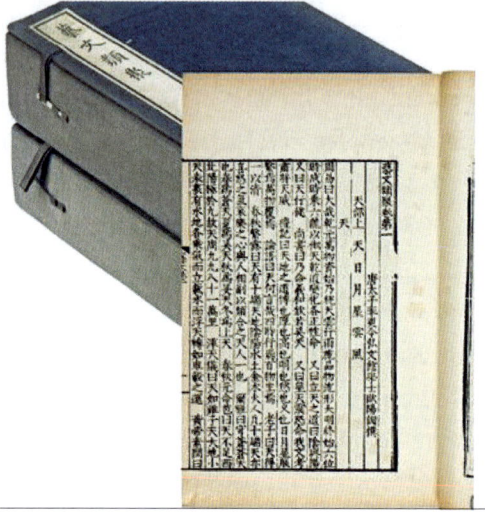

Figure 2.7.8: *The Carving Copy Anthologies and Collected Works* in Ming Dynasty.（明代刻本—《艺文类聚》）
(http://www.jguo.cn/uploads/allimg/140917/19_140917115032)

In addition to dictionaries and bibliographies, other book types emerged during the Qin-Han and Wei-Jin periods and then were subsequently improved upon during the Sui-Tang period. These book types include: literary encyclopedias, rime dictionaries, individual and general collections, family records, biographies, translations of Buddhist scripture, and specialist works. I will briefly address each of these book types in turn: Literary encyclopedias are large dictionaries arranged by theme. The earliest literary encyclopedia was the *Huang Lan* (Figure 2.7.9) which was written in the Cao-Wei period. Four other encyclopedias were commissioned during the Sui-Tang period and are named: *Beitang Shuchao, Bashi Liutie, Yiwen Leiju,* and *Chuxue Ji* (Figure 2.7.10), with the latter two being considered more advanced and better organized in their categorization and chapter arrangements.

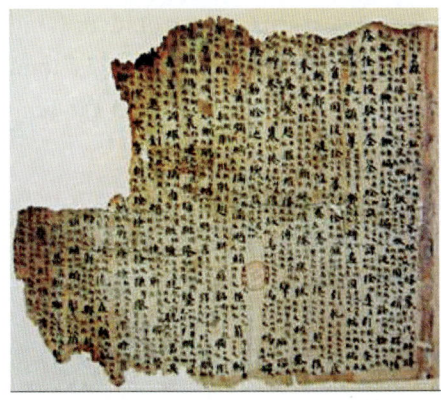

Figure 2.7.9: The remaining page of the copy version of the earliest literary encyclopedia in Tang Dynasty.（唐人抄本《切韵》残页）
(http://www.nlc.gov.cn/newgtkj/tssc/mzyj/201109/W020110919584018205329)

Figure 2.7.10: *The Zhaoming Anthology* by Xiao Tong.（萧统的《昭明文选》）
(http://www.guoxue.org/images/New/upfile/562dfb274af0e)

Rime dictionaries are reference books that organize Chinese characters according to their initial, vowels and tones. These books became popular after the emergence of rhythmic Yongming style poems during the Southern Dynasty period. *Sheg Lei*, written by Lei Ding in the Cao-Wei period is the first known rime dictionary. In the Sui Dynasty, Lu Fayen wrote *Qie Yun*, a dictionary which divided the four tones of Chinese pronunciation into 206 rimes. This work provided a standard format for subsequent rime dictionaries.

Individual collections consisted of collected works of individual authors while collected works consisted of collaborative works completed by multiple authors. Examples of renowned general collections include *Zhaoming Wen Xuan* and *Yutai Xinyong*, compiled during the Southern Dynasty period, by Xiao Tong and Xu Ling, respectively.

Originating during the Eastern Han Dynasty, family records were books used to trace lineage and help families distinguish between noble and common families. The name of a geographical region was often placed before a family name in order to help identify the various families; this practice was responsible for the emergence of clan politics. Family records were further used with the implementation of the nine-rank system for the selection of officials during the

Wei, Jin, Southern and Northern and Tang Dynasties. This system of identifying and ranking families was so popular that the Tang government compiled a total of three national family records, titled the *Shi Zu Zhi*, *Xing Shi Lu*, and *Da Tang Xingzu Xilu*.

Biographies were records concerning individuals; at least 40 of them were written between the Three Kingdoms period and the Sui Dynasty. The books were referred to as *Xianxian Zhuan*, which translates as biographies of former sages, or as *Qijiu Zhuan*, meaning biographies of elders.

Translations of Buddhist scripture broke the boundaries of the "six arts" system of categorization which had been maintained since the pre-Qin period. Buddhism spread rapidly throughout China during the Han Dynasty and the first known translation of a Buddhist work was the *Sutra of Forty-two Chapters*, said to have been translated by Tianzhu monks. More translations followed during the Southern and Northern Dynasties period; examples of officially compiled and translated scriptures include the *Catalogue of Buddhist Scriptures of the Wei* and the *Catalogue of Buddhist Scriptures of the Liang*. The most famous translations were produced by the Tianzhu monk Kumarajiva.

Another notable monk, Xuanzang, made a 17-year journey to India during the Tang Dynasty period in order to bring Buddhist scripture back to China. Successful in his quest he presided over the translation of 75 Buddhist scriptures and was credited with not only training a large number of translators, but also refining the translation process (Figure 2.7.11). Notably, it was during this same period, the Tang Dynasty, that China witnessed a peak in the translation of Buddhist scriptures into Chinese.

Figure 2.7.11: Xuan Zang — the famous Buddhist in Tang Dynasty.
(玄奘)
(http://blogcache.artron.net/201103/27/451944_13012231753ABB)

Specialist works include a number of different types of books which address varying subjects, including: mathematics, medicine, astronomy, agriculture, geography and poetry.

The traditions of writing on the subjects of mathematics, medicine and astronomy began in the Qin and Han periods with the writing of *The Nine Chapters on the Mathematical Art*, *Divine Farmer's Materia Medica* and the *Star Manual of the Masters Gan and Shi*, respectively (Figure 2.7.12). Medical knowledge was subsequently supplemented by Tao Hongjing's *Collective Notes to the Canon of Materia Medica*.

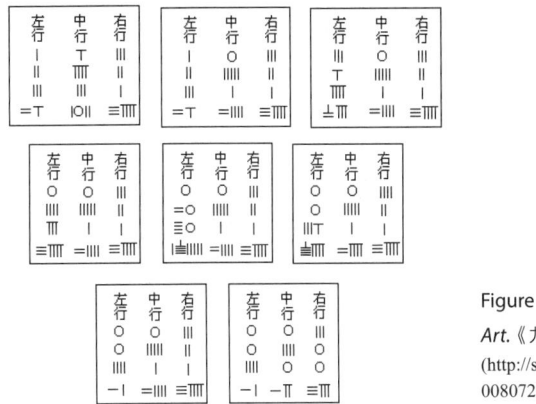

Figure 2.7.12: *Nine Chapters on the Mathematical Art*.《九章算术》
(http://se.risechina.org/kxwh/UploadFiles_8179/200807/20080723105618968)

The *Book of Fanshengzhi* and the *Qi Min Yao Shu* written during the Wei-Jin and Southern and Northern Dynasties periods set the standard for specialist works on agriculture.

Li Daoyuan's *Commentary on the Waterways Classic* greatly added to the ancient knowledge concerning geography with his use of the annotations to aid the reader. In the Tang Dynasty, the *Map of Long Mountain in the Guanzhong Plain and the Nine Prefectures of the South Mountains* drawn by Jia Dan, and the *Annals of Yuanhe County*, edited by Li Jifu, pushed the study of geography and map making to new heights (Figure 2.7.13).

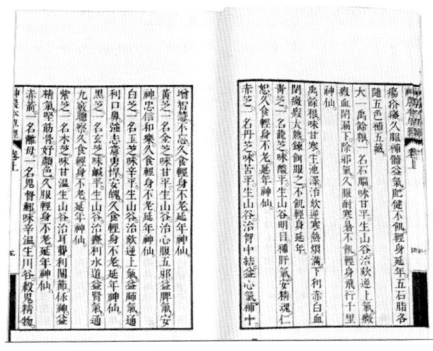

Figure 2.7.13: The carving version — *Sheng Nong's Herbal Classics*. (清代汲古山房刻本《神农本草经》)
(http://shopimg.kongfz.com.cn/20130102/1007721/1007721yaEEa0)

Lastly, the Tang Dynasty witnessed the emergence of great poets and outstanding poetry collections by the likes of Wang Wei, Li Bai, Du Fu, and Bai Juyi. The quality of their compositions and the number of poetry collections written during the Tang Dynasty surpassed those of previous dynasties, by a considerable margin.

In addition to the numerous book categories I have previously mentioned, interpretations and writings of Confucian classics were also very popular and first began to appear in the Han Dynasty and then to proliferate during the Tang Dynasty. The emperor of Tang not only ordered Yan Shigu to revise the *Five Classics*, but then ordered Kong Yingda and other experts to write the *Correct Meaning of the Five Classics* (Figure 2.7.14), which rearranged and then gave interpretations to the various annotations which had previously been made concerning the *Classics*.

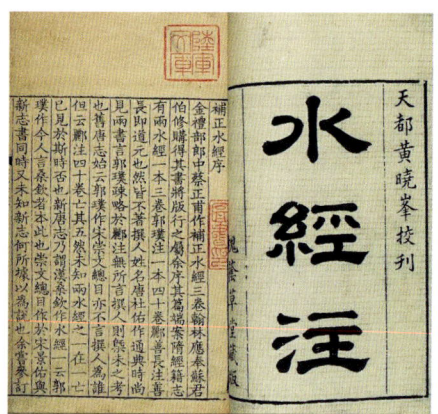

Figure 2.7.14: *Commentary on the Waterways Classic* carved during Qian Long period in Qing Dynasty.
（清代乾隆年间刻本《水经注》）
(http://www.hbswj.com/upload/news/201510/20151016153251777717)

History books were also popular and became one of the main forms of book produced during the Spring and Autumn periods and then witnessed significant development during the Qin-Han and Sui-Tang periods. Not only was the biographical format perfected, but this period also saw the compilation of books addressing history on a dynasty by dynasty basis. Noteworthy are four books: the *Records of the Grand Historian*, the *Book of Han*, the *Dong Guan Han Ji*, and the *Book of the Later Han*. All of the books were written using the biographical format and were mutually complementary with regard to Han history and the use of historical information. The books were used by future generations as models for the writing of histories and were subsequently followed by an additional eight books compiled during the Tang Dynasty, which altogether account for a third of China's official histories.

Conclusion

The writing and completion of such a wide variety of reference material not only allowed Chinese civilization and culture to develop more uniformly, but also provides us with an invaluable look into China's past. From the formation of a uniform system of categorizing Chinese characters, all the way to the compilation of histories addressing not only individuals, but dynasties… this time period and the books it produced offer us an enlightened and unmitigated view into the very development of Chinese civilization.

Task 8 ▶ Join the online forum and write a summary
(Students are required to have an instant and online post-talk discussion)

Miriam: Chinese cultural history is just so splendid, isn't it? Aren't you simply amazed by the sheer number and richness of the Chinese classics?

Irene: They are amazing indeed, but those classics are only a part of Chinese culture. There is a famous line of poetry "let a hundred flowers bloom, a hundred schools of thought contend". As Professor Richards mentioned in his lecture, a huge variety of books were produced, covering so many different categories.

Owen: Yes, but hold on! My brain is almost exploding with information overload. Do you guys really understand what all those books are actually about?

Miriam: I know what you mean. You can't get much just from the titles, but one of the things we can do is to note down some of them and then do some research on wiki.

Irene: That's ambitious. I think Professor Richards' objective in his lecture was to introduce us to Chinese history and culture in general by emphasizing the scope and variety of the classical publications rather than expecting us to have a detailed knowledge of their contents. Is that right, Professor?

Richards:	Partly, yes. You couldn't possibly read all those books! But it'd be a good idea to have an understanding of the contents of one or two representative books from the Qin-Han, Wei-Jin and Sui-Tang periods. There's actually quite a close connection between my lecture and Professor Phillips's. For example, we both mention the work of the Tianzhu monk Kumarajiva. My suggestion for you would be to make a list of a few representative works, and each of you researches one and then introduces it to the others on the forum, discussing their styles, cultural connotations, and symbolic meanings in Chinese history.
Owen:	That's a great idea — and that way we'll be uniting all the lectures we've had and the knowledge we've gained. Thank you so much, Professor Richards, Professor Phillips.
Richards:	My pleasure!
Philips:	You're welcome. If you get any more questions online, just let me know.
Irene & Miriam:	Thanks!
Richards:	Now I have two specific questions for you to discuss, as part of your forum. 1 Try to list at least five types of book during the Qin-Han, Wei-Jin and Sui-Tang periods. 2 Who was the Xu Shen mentioned in the lecture? And what was his work about?
Irene:	I'm sure we'll have a great time discussing those questions. See you on the forum, Professors.
Philips & Richards:	See you. Bye bye!
Owen & Miriam:	Bye!

Appendix: Vocabulary for Unit 2

Historical Note
devout /dɪˈvaʊt/ *adj.* 虔诚的；衷心的
longevity /lɒnˈdʒevɪtɪ/ *n.* 长寿，长命；寿命

nunnery /ˈnʌnərɪ/ *n.* 尼姑庵；女修道院
scripture /ˈskrɪptʃə/ *n.* (大写) 圣经；手稿；(大写) 圣经的一句
verse /vɜːs/ *n.* 诗，诗篇；韵文；诗节
sermon /ˈsɜːmən/ *n.* 布道；训诫；启示；冗长的讲话
      vt. 对……布道；对……说教
      vi. 布道
aptitude /ˈæptɪtjuːd/ *n.* 天资；自然倾向；适宜
tranquility /træŋˈkwɪlətɪ/ *n.* 宁静；平静
contemplate /ˈkɒntempleɪt/ *vt.* 沉思；注视；思忖；预期
        vi. 冥思苦想；深思熟虑
courtesan /ˌkɔːtɪˈzæn/ *n.* 宫女
compliance /kəmˈplaɪəns/ *n.* 顺从，服从；承诺
facade /fəˈsɑːd/ *n.* 外观；(法) 建筑物正面
cremate /krɪˈmeɪt/ *vt.* 火葬；烧成灰

Reading Activity
pyromancy /ˈpaɪrəmænsɪ/ *n.* (根据火或火的形状所作的) 火卜，火占卜
plastron /ˈplæstrən/ *n.* 胸饰，胸甲；胸铠
paraphernalia /ˌpærəfəˈneɪlɪə/ *n.* 随身用具；设备
scapulimancy /ˌskæpjʊˈlɪmænsɪ/ *n.* 肩胛骨占卜术
chaste /tʃeɪst/ *adj.* 纯洁的；贞洁的；有道德的；朴素的
smear /smɪə/ *vt.* 诽谤；弄脏；涂上；把……擦模糊
     vi. 被弄脏
fissure /ˈfɪʃə(r)/ *n.* 狭长裂缝或裂隙；裂伤；分歧；分裂
conspicuous /kənˈspɪkjʊəs/ *adj.* 显著的；显而易见的
differentiate /ˌdɪfəˈrenʃɪeɪt/ *vt. & vi.* 区分，区别
logograph /ˈlɒgəʊɡrɑːf/ *n.* 语标 (等于logotype，logogram)

Lecture
biography /baɪˈɒɡrəfɪ/ *n.* 列传；传记
bibliography /ˌbɪblɪˈɒɡrəfɪ/ *n.* 参考书目；文献目录
dispersal /dɪˈspɜːsl/ *n.* 分散；传播；散布；疏散；消失
instill /ɪnˈstɪl/ *vt.* 徐徐滴入；逐渐灌输
encyclopedia /enˌsaɪkləʊˈpiːdjə/ *n.* 百科全书
rime /raɪm/ *n.* (dictionary) 韵书
reverence /ˈrevərəns/ *n.* 崇敬；尊严；敬礼
proliferate /prəˈlɪfəreɪt/ *vi.* 增殖；扩散；激增
       vt. 使激增

pictogram /ˈpɪktəɡræm/ n. [数] 象形图
ideograph /ˈɪdɪəʊɡrɑːf/ n. 象形文字；表意文字 (等于ideogram)
semantic /sɪˈmæntɪk/ adj. 语义的；语义学的 (等于semantical)
compound /ˈkɔmpaund, kəmˈpaund/ n. [化学] 化合物；混合物；复合词
derivative /dɪˈrɪvətɪv/ adj. 派生的；引出的
index /ˈɪndeks/ n. 索引；标引
compile /kəmˈpaɪl/ vt. 编译；编制；编辑；汇编
emulate /ˈemjʊleɪt/ vt. 仿真；模仿；尽力赶上；同……竞争
entitled /ɪnˈtaɪtld/ v. 给……权利；给……定书名；授……以荣誉 (entitle的过去式和过去分词)
anthology /ænˈθɒlədʒɪ/ n. (诗、文、曲、画等的) 选集
collaborative /kəˈlæbərətɪv/ adj. 合作的，协作的
catalogue /ˈkætəlɒɡ/ n. 目录
annotation /ˌænəʊˈteɪʃ(ə)n/ n. 注释；注解；释文
prefecture /ˈpriːfektjʊə/ n. 管区，辖区；地方官的任期
unmitigated /ˌʌnˈmɪtɪɡeɪtɪd/ adj. 全然的；严厉的；未缓和的
cognate /ˈkɒɡneɪt/ n. 同族；同根词
ascertain /ˌæsəˈteɪn/ vt. 确定；查明；探知

3 Unit

Early Editing, Compilation and Publication in Ancient China

TABLE OF CONTENTS

Warm-up: Be proactive

Task 1 Listen to a historical note: The earliest bookshop in Ancient China — Chen Family Bookshop

Task 2 Discuss the historical note

Task 3 Build up our vocabulary

Task 4 Reading activity: Early Publishing and Media Prior to Paper Book

Task 5 Reading comprehension

Task 6 Translation practice

Task 7 Attend a public lecture: The Compilation and Publication of Diverse Books in the Song and Yuan Dynasties

Task 8 Join the online forum and write a summary

Appendix: Vocabulary for Unit 3

Unit 3
Early Editing, Compilation and Publication in Ancient China

WARM-UP: Be proactive

Irene: Nice to see you again, PRIMO partners! You got here so early today.

Owen: You bet — I just can't wait to get on with the course. Those lectures last week by Professor Phillips and Professor Richards really opened a door for me into the wonderful world of Chinese publishing. Now, every Chinese character I read, I'm thinking about its origin and the best way to translate it into English. Even my shirt, made of best Chinese silk, reminds me of ancient Chinese icons.

Miriam: Hey Owen, you're really becoming a genuine Chinese expert! But I know what you mean. That discussion we had last time about Kumārajīva and his translation methods really shed light on my own translation study.

Irene: Yes, a good translator has to be immersed in both the target language and the culture of that language. That's why the great translators like Kumārajīva, Paramārtha, Xuan Zang, and Yijing were so accurate and convincing in their translations of the Buddhist Scriptures — they had all explored the different countries and cultures along the great Silk Road.

Miriam: Right. And it was those translator monks, with their writings and teaching, who made Buddhism so popular in China. This popularity increased the demand for books and scriptures, which in turn contributed to the growth and prosperity of the

	publishing industry. I remember in a Chinese TV series, seeing people read from bamboo scrolls and even from inscriptions on stone.
Owen:	Bamboo, stone! That TV series must be as old as Adam!
Irene:	Yes, it certainly sounds like some remote period. But don't forget, people in ancient times wrote on bronze and even bones.
Miriam:	It makes sense, though, doesn't it? The Erlitou excavations proved that the people of that culture wrote on bones for oracle divination, and in the Xia and Shang Dynasties they inscribed words on bronze because of course they didn't have paper. That's a relatively modern thing, from the Tang and Song Dynasties.
Irene:	Exactly, Miriam, and that's what we're going to be discussing today — books and their early compilation. Professor Philips will introduce us to the earliest bookstore in China and the family story of its owners. He told me he also has a video clip from a TV series that features early literature on different media before paper books. I'm sure the video will help us understand that better.
Owen:	Video! That'll be great! I really can't quite understand how those ancient Chinese managed to write on bamboo strips or wooden slats. It's like when you see an actress wearing an ancient costume and you can't imagine how it was made.
Irene:	After we've discussed the video, Professor Richards will give us a lecture on the compilation and publishing of books in the Song and Yuan Dynasties. I think you have already read something about some of the famous books and their editors and authors in Chinese history?
Owen:	Yeah, I know a bit about it, but I'm sure I'll get a lot more from Professor Richards' lecture — he's always so interesting.
Miriam:	The first lecture today is by Professor Philips. I'm sure his introduction to the Chen family legend will be fascinating.

Owen:	Oh he's definitely my guide to the study of Chinese publishing. But the legend of the Chen family…that sounds rather mysterious.
Irene:	It is a fantastic family story, and after we've heard about the Chens we'll continue with a reading and discussion on early writing media before the invention of paper, and then finally end with the publication of books in the Song and Yuan Dynasties by Professor Richards.
Owen:	That's going to be brilliant. So, let's go and meet Professor Philips and begin our class.

Task 1 ▶ Listen to a historical note: The earliest bookshop in Ancient China — Chen Family Bookshop

Irene: Owen, have you been to any book stores recently?

Owen: Yeah, sure. The bookstore is the place I usually go with my friends. Yesterday I went to the Xinhua Bookstore and read *Chinese History* there.

Miriam: Yes. I always buy books from the Xinhua. It's the most well-known franchised bookstore in China, right?

Irene: Yes, it is now. But in ancient times, when bookstore first started, some of them even became household names. One example, the most famous bookstore in the Song Dynasty, will be introduced by Professor Philips.

Miriam: I know about it — the Chen Family bookstore from Song Dynasty. Actually I've been to Hangzhou many times, and the legend of the Chen family is mentioned over and over again by the tour guides.

Owen: I have a question, though. Why did the most well-known bookstore ever appear in the Song Dynasty? Why aren't there any examples from the Tang Dynasty? After all, that was the summit of national strength and influence in ancient China?

Irene: I can tell you why. The Tang Dynasty was indeed the peak of national military and political power in ancient times; however it was the Song Dynasty that represented the best instances of official, private, and workshop printing in ancient China. As a symbol of excellence, the woodblock-printed books of the Song Dynasty made the book popularization become possible. Even workshop-made books, which prior to the Song period had never been held in high regard, became things of beauty in the hands of the Song people.

Owen: Oh. I see now. Thank you, Irene, you are so well-informed.

Miriam: So really it was the perfection of woodblock printing in the Song Dynasty that made books more readily available, therefore leading bookstores to spring up all over the place.

Irene:	Yes, and the most famous of them being the Chen family! "Da Chen daren", Chen the senior and "Xiao Chen daren", Chen the junior were the successive owners of that store. Both of them contributed a lot to the compilation and publication of books. Moreover they were spoken highly of by men of letters in the Song Dynasty for their generosity and courtesy.
Owen:	The family story sounds intriguing, but I'm particularly interested in learning more about woodblock printing in the Song Dynasty. And here's Professor Philips to tell us all about it.
Philips:	Hello there. So pleased to meet you all again. The last time I talked to you, it was about the great interpreter — Kumārajīva — his story and his contribution to the spread of Chinese characters. His translations, just like other social and scientific knowledge, caused a huge demand for wider range of transmission. People heard of his translations and wanted them for themselves. Hence, new ways of providing copies of his translations gradually developed into a distinctive entity. It was the bookshop. Today I am going to give you a second historical note, and it concerns the earliest bookshop in ancient China — the Chen Family Bookshop. (You are required to fill in the blanks with the words and phrases you hear while listening)

The Chen Family Bookshop was founded by Chen Qi and his son, Chen Jieyuan. The books they printed were marked with the name of either the father or the son, depending on who had made the book. Chen Qi, known more commonly as Chen Daoren, had the courtesy name Zongzhi and the style name Yunju. Chen Jieyuan, known more commonly as Xiao Chen Daoren, had the style name Xu Yun. Chen Qi's bookshop was located in Muqin Alley on Pengbei Road in the city of Lin'an (today's Hang Zhou) (Figure 3.1.1). The bookshop faced a river and was flanked on one side by a group of Chinese parasol trees. The river provided plenty of 1) _____ and the parasol trees provided cover from the sunlight, 2) _____ that were both cool and pleasant. Despite being a bookseller by trade, Chen Qi had the 3) _____ a famous scholar and 4) _____ to match. A generous man, he would happily lend or sell books on credit to 5) _____ scholars visiting his bookshop. In some cases, he would even give books away for free. Chen Qi was an accomplished poet (Figure 3.1.2) and singer who enjoyed 6) _____ wandering poets from around the land. Many of these poets wrote poems especially for him. More than just 7) _____, these poems expressed sincere admiration for Chen Qi's generous and 8) _____, as well as envy for the casual lifestyle he managed to lead in such 9) _____, which was described as "sitting amidst ten thousand 10) _____; living a life of ease" (See *To Chen Zongzhi*, by Huang Youfu). Chen Qi's bookshop mainly printed small collections of lyrical and uplifting poetry from the Tang and Song Dynasties. Thanks to its popularity and the fine reputation it built for itself, the bookshop attracted an almost constant stream of 11) _____. Chen Qi was once 12) _____ in a crime during a 13) _____ on poetry led by the censor Li Zhixiao. The reason for the charge was his inclusion of banned poetry by Zeng Ji in the *Jianghu Collection*. However, owing to his 14) _____ in the imperial court, Chen Qi was helped in secret by the PRIMO minister. As a result, he was only 15) _____. Not long after, he was pardoned and allowed to return to the capital.

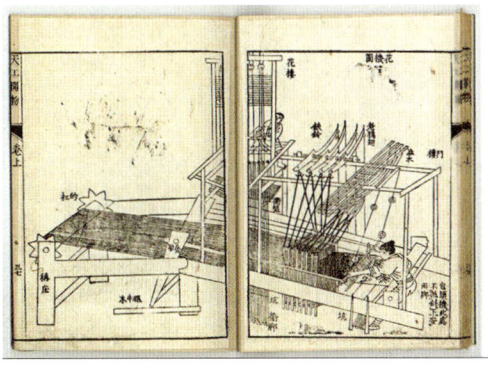

Figure 3.1.1: The Lin'an palace engraving industry situation in the Sounthern Song Dynasty. (南宋临安府刻书业的状况)
www.yhsz.gov.cn

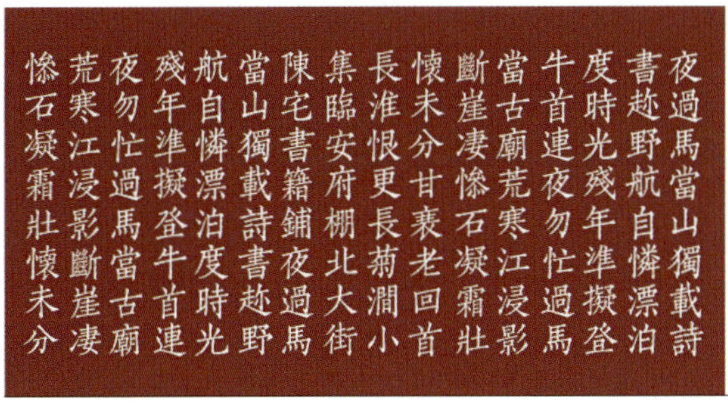

Figure 3.1.2: The anthology of Lin'an book shed version stored in Chen's Bookstore. (陈起宋朝体, 临安书棚本 《南宋群贤小集》, 1208-1264 年, 陈宅书籍铺)

As I said at the beginning, the books produced by Chen Qi and his son did not carry the same names at the end of each scroll, even though they were produced in the same bookshop. Books marked with the words "Chen Daoren" or "Chen Family Bookshop" were produced by Chen Qi; while books marked with the words "Chen Jieyuan Bookshop" were produced by Chen Jieyuan. There were also differences in the types of book that the two produced, with

Chen Qi mainly producing collections of Tang poetry, while Chen Jieyuan tended to print literary sketchbooks and collections of Song poetry. Together, Chen Qi and his son compiled and published almost 100 different titles. The most notable were *Poems of the Tang Female Poet Yu Xuanji*, *Collection of Poems by Zhu Qingyu*, and *Collection of Poems by Zhou He*, which were carved and printed by Chen Qi; and *Collection of Poems by Chang Jian*, *Collection of Poems by Wang Jian*, *Wencui*, and *Shuji*, which were carved and printed by Chen Jieyuan. These books were mostly printed using high quality ink and paper. The carvings and the prints were also expertly made. In terms of quality, the finest books of the Chen Family Bookshop were roughly equivalent to the books produced by the imperial academy in the Song era. However, Chen family books boasted a squarer and more widely spaced script, which was developed on the basis of Ouyang Xun script.

So that's all for this short note on a very famous bookstore of the Song Dynasty. On this DVD there's a little episode that shows people of the era before woodblock printing reading scrolls made from bamboo strips. Have a look at it later, and discuss what it must have been like in those days.

Task 2 ▶ Discuss the historical note
(Students are required to do role play in groups by imitating the PRIMO's dialogue)

Irene:	It seems to me that the Chen Family Bookstore wasn't just a bookstore in the modern sense, it was much more than that, don't you agree?
Miriam:	Oh, absolutely right. In our terms they were printers and publishers. They didn't just sell books, they actually made them! They collected and edited texts. They carved the woodblocks, printed the books — and then sold them.
Owen:	And I guess once Bi Sheng had invented movable type, that meant that books could be mass-produced, bringing down the price enormously. Local printers could afford to print and publish their own copies of literature.
Irene:	I can see you've been researching on the Internet, Owen. Well done. Woodblock printing probably reached its peak of

	excellence in the Song Dynasty, and even workshop-made books became things of beauty. After that, movable-type printing made book production even more efficient and so altered society in many ways.
Owen:	One thing I didn't quite understand from Professor Philips' talk, though, was why books produced by the father and son didn't share the same name — was there any disagreement between them?
Miriam:	Owen, you're always looking for mysteries below the surface, but I don't think there's anything sinister here, is there Irene?
Irene:	No, not at all. It's simply that father and son produced different kinds of books. Chen Qi mainly compiled collections of Tang poetry but his son tended to print literary sketchbooks and collections of Song poetry.
Owen:	Okay, I've got it now — different books, different names.
Miriam:	The important thing about the advent of widespread printing was that it helped to educate more and more citizens. As literacy spread, so did the ability to take the national exams in order to enter the imperial civil service.
Irene:	Yes, I think it's fair to say that social mobility reached a summit during the Song Dynasty as a result of the improvements in publishing. But we'll discuss this point at greater length later on, I think.
Owen :	Wow, we've really traveled a long way from the family bookstore we started with, haven't we? But on that journey we've seen the landscape of the whole of Chinese history. That's amazing!

(*Miriam and Irene smile and nod in agreement*)

Task 3 ▶ Build up our vocabulary
(Drag and match exercises)

Match the English words in column A with the Chinese equivalents in column B.

	A		B
1	editing of books	A	百科全书
2	sketchbook	B	编辑
3	the imperial examination system	C	编年史，年代记；记录
4	*Dream Pool of Essays*	D	参考书目；文献目录
5	compilation	E	《梦溪笔谈》
6	inscription	F	地图制作，制图；制图学，绘图法
7	verify	G	二等分
8	halve	H	纲要；概略
9	pictograph	I	核实；查证
10	neologism	J	《文苑英华》
11	bibliography	K	考古学
12	*Finest Blossoms in the Garden of Literature*	L	矿物学；矿物学书籍
13	encyclopedia	M	气象状态，气象学
14	meteorology	N	题词；铭文；刻印
15	mineralogy	O	小品集；写生簿；随笔集
16	cartography	P	新词；新义；新词的使用
17	archeology	Q	科举制度
18	pharmaceutics	R	制药学；配药学
19	chronicle	S	图书编校
20	compendium	T	象形文字

Task 4 ▶ Reading activity

*The following excerpt is recommended to PRIMO. It is about **Early Publishing and Media Prior to Paper Books.** PRIMO members hope to be clear about what were the media before paper and about how early Chinese publishing came into being. The following excerpt will help to meet their needs.*

With the emergence of Chinese characters and the maturing of the writing system, people experimented in order to discover and create media to preserve and transmit their experience and idea. Those who were righteous were praised in their own times, and their deeds were recorded with inscription, sometimes written on bamboo and silk (Figure 3.4.1), inscribed on bronze and stone (Figure 3.4.2), or incised onto vessels (Figure 3.4.3) in order to pass them down to later generations. Such experimentation in the transmission of text went on a considerably long period before the so called books came into being. These inscriptions showed some elements of publishing since procedures were developed during the process of researching, writing, collecting and verifying, which can be regarded as the original editing process before the emergence of formal books. Perhaps when mentioning ancient books, most people would think of bamboo or silk scrolls, which were involved in the early publications.

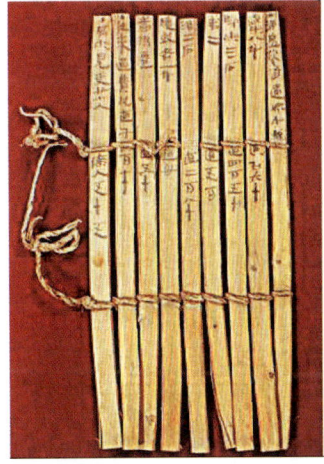

Figure 3.4.1: The shape of bamboo slips. (简牍的外形)
(http://p4.so.qhimg.com/t01a6b9d23b908ee554)

Figure 3.4.2: The Western Zhou Dynasty bronze inscription in Duke Mao Tripot. (西周青铜器毛公鼎内的铭文)
(http://www.mjrd.gov.cn/UpFiles/Article/200911/2009111623254472868)

Figure 3.4.3: The Warring States period pottery. (战国陶文)
(http://file.gucn.com/file//CurioPicfile/200903/Gucn_20095_200939212310CheckCurioPic7)

It is recorded that writing on bamboo had already begun at least during the later Shang. The writer would hold the top end of the strip in the left hand with the other end resting against the body to steady it (this explains why the longest strip was never more than an arm's length). He would then write vertically down the length of the strip using his right hand to hold either a brush or whatever other inscribing carving tool. This way of holding the strip had the advantage of minimizing the risk of smudging the wet ink because the characters written first were full length of the strip away from the writer's hand and sleeve (had the strip been laid horizontally in front of the writer the distance between his sleeve and the wet ink at the beginning of the row would have been halved). Using the same method to avoid smudging and to keep a clear line of sight, the strokes furthest away from the writer, that is the strokes at the top of each successive character, were written first. For similar reasons, almost all writing that does not run from top to bottom runs from left to right.

The strips were then laid out next to each other, the second one to the left of the first and so on to the end. They were bound together — *bian* (编) (Figure 3.4.4), usually with two or four longer strips, three hemp threads to form a bundle — *ce* (册) (Figure 3.4.5). Silk or leather was also used for threads. Sometimes short wooden tablets and bamboo strips were bound together with a single thread at the top.

Figure 3.4.4 和 Figure 3.4.5: The "code", "bamboo books". (竹简， "编"、"册")
(http://imgx.xiawu.com/xzimg/i4/i1/18121021687432995/T1zu5bXAVaXXXXXXXX_!!0-item_pic)

Later, for long texts, it became more practical to bind the strips before writing on them, although even as late as the Han the binding was still sometimes done after the writing, for example, for lists of funerary objects. The writer would lay the bundle out horizontally before him to write on, starting from the second strips on the right (the first was reserved for the cover and title). The characters were then written with a brush and ink vertically down the strips following the grain, usually on the inside surface. After they were tied together, the strips were bundled up, from the last one to the first one on the left functioned as the spindle of the bundle and the beginning of the text on the first strips to the right was the first to appear when the scroll was unrolled. The title was often written on the reverse of the first strips. This way of writing on columns and rolling up the strips into bundles helps explain why old Chinese records started at what for us today is the end. It was an arrangement that was retained when books began to be printed in the seventh century and it lasted until the 1950s. Then ironically, just at the time that Chinese writing shifted from vertical columns to horizontal lines, Chinese books moved in the opposite direction: cloth-bound books with horizontal lines of text were designed to stand vertically on the shelf where before thread-bound volumes with their columns of text had been piled flat. Before the introduction of modern printing and binding practices, the only exception to writing in vertical columns were counting-rod numeral (*suanchou shuzi* 算籌数字), which were written horizontally from left to right. Writing in vertical columns is still often used for newspaper headlines and sometimes for book titles. The old way of rolling up a bundle of bamboo strips or a paper book roll is retained for pictures scrolls to this day; So the beginning of the scroll is on the right and the end is on the left.

This has been taken to suggest that bamboo was the original medium for writing, because of the arrangement of the characters from top to bottom in vertical columns on some of the pottery inscriptions, on late-period oracle-bone inscriptions and on bronze inscriptions. The fact that non-bamboo cultures (such as Greece) also sometimes wrote from top to bottom and from right to left need not necessarily invalidate this argument. It is also an arrangement that helps explain the stretched forms of the characters for long-bodied animals, birds and fishes in the oracle-bone script. Many other creatures are all shown looking sideways with their tails or fins at the bottom of the character and the head at the top. Had the script first been written on a medium other than thin strips of bamboo there would perhaps have been no need to write such long characters vertically.

Apart from writing on bamboo and wooden strips, shorter documents, or those such as maps, which required a larger surface, were written on tablets, usually of wood (Figure 3.4.6). They came into general use in the Han. The tablets were usually broader and shorter than the strips and could accommodate a short document with several rows of characters. For letters, two were often notched into each other face-to-face and then tied together. The top tablet was used to record the addressee and the sender. Wooden tablets were also sometimes used as the table of contents of a bamboo record.

Figure 3.4.6: The wood tablet in the Han Dynasty. (汉代书写文字的木牌)

The normal scribal practice appears to have been to make drafts on bamboo strips, which were easily corrected with the scraping knife. Final copies would be made on bamboo or in some cases on silk, the advantage of which was that it was less bulky than the strips, and hence, more easily consulted, read, stored, or transported. Its disadvantages were that it was expensive, copyist's mistakes could not easily be corrected, and once written on, it could not be reused.

Both the strips and the tablets varied in length according to the type of writing. By the Han there were regulations that government laws should be written on strips of 3 *Chi* (尺) — 1 *Chi* was by that time about 23 *cm*; the classics on 2.4 *chi* strips; and correspondence on tablets 1 *Chi* long. This was why the old name for a letter — *chidu* 尺牍. In practice, we know from excavated strips that there was considerable variation in length.

There were many words and compounds for different types of compilation. *Jiance* (简册), along with *jiandu* (简牍) — strips and tablets, was one of the most common early ones. Others were *dianji* (典籍), *jiance boshu* (简册帛书), or *zhubo* (竹帛), — documents on bamboo and silk. *Dianji* (典籍) came to mean writing in general (perhaps even books) only after the Han. The principal meaning of the modern word for books, *tushu* (图书), was maps and documents from its first appearance in the Zhou Dynasty until after the Han Dynasty. *Ce* (册) is still used to mean book in one of the Minnan dialects. The word for book or volume (册), for example, is often explained as a pictograph of two vertical bamboo or wooden strips held together with threads. A swatch of bamboo or wooden strips forms a complete work or section, which in the modern usage is now *yipian wenzhang* — meaning an article.

Much of the vocabulary for books and publishing in use today still reflects the bamboo and wooden origins of Chinese writing and early compilation. All the classics of very ancient dynasties, such as the Spring and Autumn and Warring States periods were originally written in the form of what are conventionally called "bamboo records" or in ink. How long and which ones were handed down by word or mouth before being written down is unfortunately not known.

Task 5 Reading comprehension

(Students are required to launch a discussion to pose new questions and answer all the questions raised in the dialogue, and do the role play based on the following)

Irene:	Hey you guys, if there was a time machine, which dynasty would you like to travel to? And why?
Owen:	Nice question. Impossible, I know, but I'd like to go back to ancient China and see how people created the four great inventions, especially paper making.
Miriam:	Hmm… If I could, I would choose the Tang Dynasty. I'm absolutely fascinated by the dress style of that age. How about you then, Irene?
Irene:	I would like to go back to the Shang Dynasty to see how people left their words on bronze or go back even further to explore how Chinese characters were first created and recorded.
Miriam:	That would be a fantastic journey of exploration and discovery! We've already seen that the most ancient characters were carved on stones or bones. After bones, or shells, they used bronze, and then they used bamboo strips and rich people used silk until paper was invented. The trouble is, I can't imagine how they were able to write on those materials, or how they could read them easily.
Irene:	In the Shang Dynasty they used brush and ink to write on the bamboo, and they used small knives to scrape off the ink if they needed to make a correction. I looked at the

	video episode from *The Great Qin Empire*, and you can see people reading bamboo scrolls vertically from right to left, the opposite of how we read today. In the video, when the emperor wants to read a bamboo scroll, one servant holds the beginning of the scroll, while another one unrolls it to the left.
Miriam:	You've really researched ancient characters and early Chinese writing, but did anybody research when they first started using paper?
Owen:	Yeah, I looked that up because I'm really interested in the subject. It was in 105 CE that Cai Lun, who was an official attached to the court during the Han Dynasty, first produced sheets of paper. And that invention put an end to the laborious work of writing and reading bamboo bundles. One of the great inventions!
Miriam:	You've put your finger on it, Owen. The invention of a new material for writing and printing on brought the publishing industry into an entirely new era.
Irene:	You've both obviously gained a lot from the reading passage and your own research. One thing that fascinated me was how you can trace the origins of some Chinese characters to writing on bamboo. For example, "编" (*bian*) means to bind strips together with thread. The Chinese silk radical denotes the silk threads, so from the actual structure of the word itself you can see its meaning. It's the same with the other characters like "册" or "版" or "本" etc.
Miriam:	Yes, I just loved that explanation of the word for "volume". You can actually see the two bamboo strips tied together with a thread, can't you? It's a real pictograph.
Owen:	There's one thing I still don't quite get, though. Before the Han Dynasty, people wrote on bronze or bamboo. But how did they do that? Bronze and bamboo aren't as smooth and soft as paper — it must have been very difficult.
Irene:	Oh, I think I can help you sort that out, Owen. They didn't use a brush on bronze — the ink wouldn't really stay on bronze, it's too hard. Instead, they used short, sharp knives to inscribe or incise on to the bronze vessel. Bamboo was different. They used brush and ink, and wrote on the inside

	surface of the bamboo strip, which was slightly rough and would hold the ink well. Of course, neither method would be as easy as writing on nice smooth paper.
Owen:	Okay, I get it now. And that's why only the rich could afford to study in ancient China. Bronze inscriptions and bamboo books couldn't be easily duplicated, and so wouldn't be available to ordinary people.
Miriam:	Now that's a good example of how discussion can make the content of a reading passage clearer, isn't it? Let's do some more reading on the subject and continue our discussion online.
Irene:	Good idea, Miriam.
Owen:	Let's take a break, and then we can continue our translation task in the next section.
Irene & Miriam:	Okay!

Task 6 ▶ Translation practice

(Students are required to translate the following Chinese paragraph into English individually, in pairs or in group)

Irene:	Okay, PRIMO group, we are going to finish a new translation task about the geopolitical background of the Song Dynasty and publishing at that time. Do you know much about the Song Dynasty?
Owen:	Of course, it's a very famous part of Chinese history, and I've read a lot about it. The Song Dynasty, began in 960 and continued until 1279. It came after the Five Dynasties and Ten Kingdoms period, and was followed by the Yuan Dynasty. It's normally divided into two historical eras, the Northern Song Dynasty and Southern Song Dynasty. Have I got that right?
Irene:	Completely right! Owen, well done!
Miriam:	I read in my history book that the Song Dynasty was the first

	government in world history to issue national banknotes or true paper money, which was called *jiaozi*. Since the paper currency was issued nationally, you can only imagine the prosperity that brought to the printing and publishing industry.
Irene:	Yes. It was a major factor in the blossoming of the publishing industry. But other elements mentioned in the translation text also facilitated the development of publishing. Why don't we work together to translate the passage into English right now?
Owen & Miriam:	Okay! Let's get down to business.

公元11和12世纪前后，与宋朝并立的王朝有辽、西夏和金。辽王朝笃信佛教，辽代以官刻佛经为主要特点，并设有印经院。金王朝的重要官刻机构则是国子监，其首要任务是养士育才，同时兼有刻书任务。辽代和金代统治时期是早期北京地区出版业快速发展的时期，其主要推动力量有出版技术，即雕版印刷的发展和普及；此外就是政府对出版活动的积极参与，当时也存在私刻，包括以牟利为目的的坊刻和不以牟利为目的的家刻，辽金时期没有家刻，只有坊刻。辽、金时期的出版活动总体上存在如下特点：第一，出版主体是政府，家刻比较缺失，一些大型丛书，如儒家经典、佛教典籍的翻译和出版，基本上是由政府组织完成的；第二，由于宗教、儒道和史学等正统文化的一统性，世俗文化以及大众文化读物稀缺，出版内容主要是佛道典籍、儒家经典和史学著作；第三，这个时期的译撰工作初见成效，大量佛道典籍和儒家经典被翻译并刊刻，为文化的交流融合做出了不可磨灭的贡献；最后，这个时期的出版活动扮演着文化交流和融合的重要角色，其代表性的区域就是北京，这主要是由于其重要的社会地位和地理位置所决定，北京长期充当辽、金两朝的陪都或首府，又处在农耕文明与游牧文明的交汇点，这些都促进了出版的发展。

Task 7 ▶ Attend Professor Richards's public lecture

Lecture 3

The Compilation and Publication of Diverse Books in the Song and Yuan Dynasties
Professor Richards

Hello again. This is the third lecture in this series of lectures concerning the history of publishing in China. In my last lecture I outlined for you the tremendous advances in the production of reference books and historical texts compiled during the Qin-Han, Wei-Jin and Sui-Tang periods. I also elaborated on what you would refer to as reference books, from dictionaries to bibliographies, collected works to biographies and specialist works to histories. In this lecture I will also address the compilation of books from three aspects. First I'd like to talk about how book compilation grew to blossom and who assumed the role of the editorial staff; Next, I hope to introduce some of the most influential Chinese bibliographies; and finally, I will spend a little time on three Chinese ancient historiographies. My talk will unfold chronologically during the subsequent time periods of the Song and Yuan Dynasties and with more of an emphasis on how they were organized.

7.1 Editorial staff in the Song and Yuan Dynasties

The innovation of the imperial examination system in the Song Dynasty contributed greatly to the prosperity of book publication. It was during the Song Dynasty that the imperial examination system was expanded to become approximately four to five times larger than the previous scheme implemented during the Tang Dynasty. As a result, and in conjunction with an expansion of the education system, China experienced a proliferation of scholar-officials as never before seen. Interestingly, these officials were not necessarily born to royal families; based on improvements in the imperial testing system it became possible for individuals of lower social status to rise to political prominence by doing well in the examination. In part, it was this innovative approach to education, examinations and governance that allowed the Song Dynasty to be as successful as it was.

With a focus on promoting and advancing talented individuals, the Song

Dynasty soon developed a system for the administration of the imperial book collection. The Chongwen Library was the focal point of what was to become an extensive system charged with the upkeep of the royal book collection and the organization and editing of books. Scholars from around the country were chosen to correct, organize and revise books from the imperial collection and were treated with great respect. They became the early professional editorial staff, who doubled as scholars and editors. They comprised individuals selected from the pool of successful candidates from the imperial examinations, were required to have a wide knowledge of culture and a love of learning. Additionally, the compilation, editing and revision work was managed by a stringent set of rules. For instance, editors were required to proofread a total of 21-pages per day, while manuscript writers were required to complete between 2,000 and 2,500 characters every day. Work output was dutifully recorded, reported to a secretary every ten days and to the Department of State Affairs once a month. The imposition of this work ethic made it possible for these scholars, or senior civil officials, to compile four very noteworthy national bibliographies and four encyclopedias.

Due to the large numbers of talents fostered by the examination system, the liberal cultural policies of the time and the widespread application of printing techniques, the production and compilation of books during the Song Dynasty increased dramatically. The books of the time are noted for their better organization and superior editing and revision, an increase in the number of larger books and innovative book formats. These same qualities continued into the Yuan Dynasty.

7.2 The Compilation of bibliographies

The first national bibliography of the Song Dynasty, the *Chongwen Catalogue*, was completed in the year 1034. Divided into 66 volumes, the catalogue consisted of more than 30,600 scrolls. Two noteworthy bibliographies were completed thereafter, the *Zhongxing Library Catalogue* (Figure 3.7.1) in 1177, and the *Zhongxing Catalogue Continued* in 1220. The former included 44,000 books while the latter contained 59,000. The Song government also commissioned a fourth bibliography, which was considered a specialist bibliography and was entitled the *Record of National History, Art and Literature*.

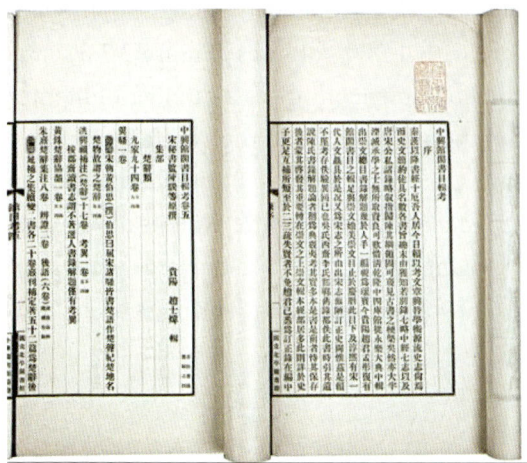

Figure 3.7.1: The Library Catalogue stored in Zhong-xing-ge by Zhao Shiwei, printed in Minguo period. (赵士炜撰《中兴馆阁书目辑考》民国印本)
(http://pmgs.kongfz.com/data/pre_show_pic/15/75/082)

Aside from nationally sponsored bibliographies, private individuals also engaged in the pursuit of compiling information. You Mao produced the *Library Catalogue of the Suichi Hall* (Figure 3.7.2), a massive undertaking which took him years to complete and which deviated from the normal bibliography format by introducing separate book versions. His four encyclopedias were all published in separate years:

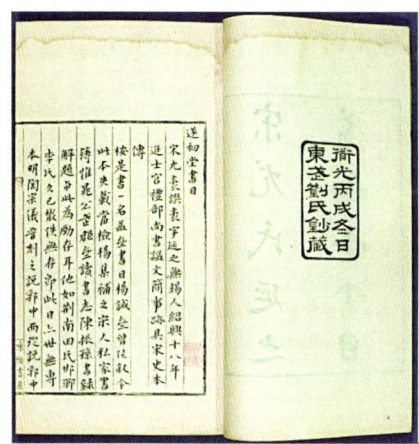

Figure 3.7.2: *The Library Catalogue of the Suichi Hall* — carving version in the Qing Dynasty. (宋代尤袤编《遂初堂书目》清刻本)
(http://www.cssn.cn/ts/ts_slcs/201402/W020140225399998148498)

Extensive Records of the Taiping Era (Figure 3.7.3), is a collection of unofficial novels and miraculous events recorded in Buddhist and Taoist scriptures dating from the Han to the Song Dynasties. The compilation was completed in 978 and contains 500 volumes. By contrast, the *Imperially Inspected Anthology of the Taiping Era* (Figure 3.7.4), is a comprehensive encyclopedia which contains more categories and entries than any bibliography preceding it. The sections which address the histories of the Tang Dynasty and Five Dynasties periods are especially prized by historians. This compilation was completed in 983 and contains 1,000 volumes. After that another book *Finest Blossoms in the Garden of Literature* with 1,000 volumes (Figure 3.7.5), was successfully compiled in 986. This bibliography comprises a number of literary works by authors dating from the Southern Dynasties to the late Tang and Five Dynasties periods. Last, but not least, the *Prime Tortoise of the Record Bureau* (Figure 3.7.6), is a historical encyclopedia documenting the exploits of previous emperors and ministers. It finally came into being in 1031. The large amount of historical documents arranged in 1,000 volumes made it the largest of the four encyclopedias.

Figure 3.7.3: *Extensive Records of the Taiping Era* — the photocopy version in the Republic of China period. （民国影印本《太平广记》五百卷）
(http://pmgs.kongfz.com/data/pre_show_pic/3/69/431)

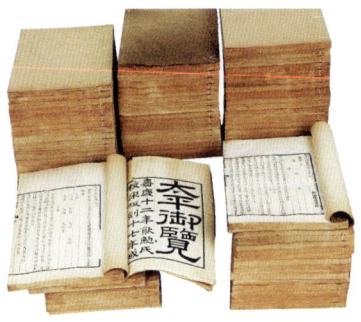

Figure 3.7.4: The *Imperially Inspected Anthology of the Taiping Era* — carving version in the Qing Dynasty. （清代刻本《太平御览》一千卷）
(http://pmgs.kongfz.com/data/pre_show_pic/2/117/3602)

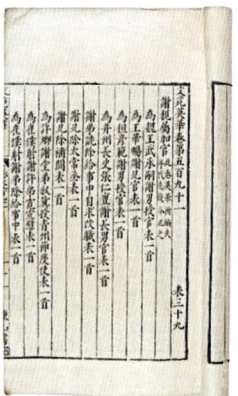

Figure 3.7.5: The *Finest Blossoms in the Garden of Literature* — the copy version in the Ming Dynasty. （明代抄本《文苑英华》书影）
(http://p0.so.qhimg.com/t014ffdb103e4c66daf)

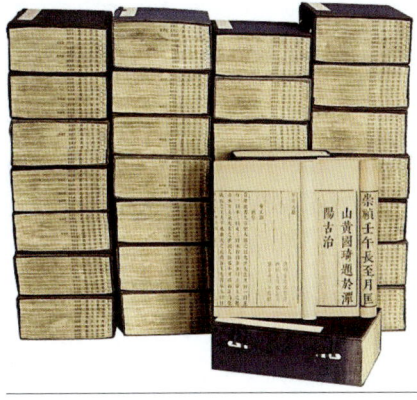

Figure 3.7.6: The *Prime Tortoise of the Record Bureau* — carving version of the Ming Dynasty. (明代刻本《册府元龟》一千卷)
(http://pmgs.kfzimg.com/data/pre_show_pic/3/278/107560VkjniF)

Other compilations addressing a variety of subjects were also compiled during the Song Dynasty. During the Northern Song Dynasty, She Kuo, compiled the *Dream Pool of Essays* (Figure 3.7.7), which includes a large collection of writings on the subject of the scientific and technological achievements of the time. The book is organized into 26 volumes and addresses a variety of subjects, including law, mathematics, physics, chemistry, astronomy, calendars, meteorology, biology, geology, mineralogy, geography, cartography, engineering, archeology, architecture, agriculture, medicine, pharmaceutics and the military.

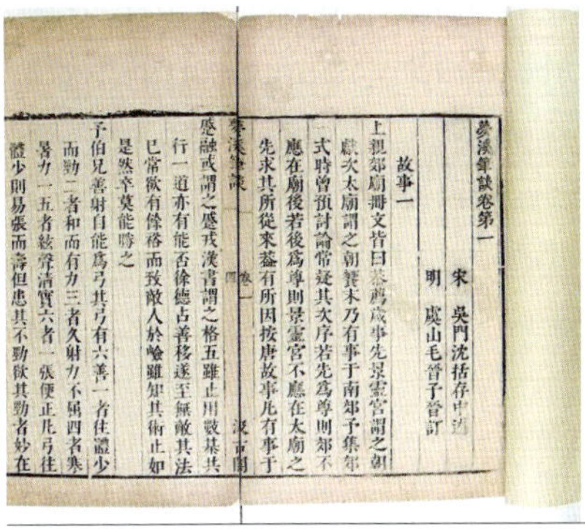

Figure 3.7.7: The *Dream Pool of Essays* — carving version in the Ming Dynasty. (明代毛晋刻本《梦溪笔谈》)
(http://pmgs.kongfz.com/data/pre_show_pic/1/506/276)

Dream Pool of Essays, is truly a noteworthy collection and has been described by the modern English scholar Joseph Needham as, "a milestone in the history of Chinese science and technology". Not only does the encyclopedia cover a number of different subjects, but it is also very precise, objective and insightful, and bridges the gap between the social and natural sciences. The collection is considered unique for its ability to demonstrate the overall cultural and scientific achievements of Song society in a way no other book from the time was able to.

85

7.3 The Compilation of historical books

Aside from bibliographies, compiling histories was also a very popular pursuit during the Song and Yuan Dynasties periods. Of particular note are three books compiled by three different authors, which together are referred to as the "Three Tongs". The "Three Tongs" are the *Zizhi Tongjian* compiled during the Northern Song Dynasty, the *Tong Zhi* written by Zheng Qiao, and Du You's *Tong Dian*.

The *Zizhi Tongjian*, compiled during the Northern Song Dynasty, provided a template for the subsequent compilation of histories and its format was emulated by historians for many generations. The accompanying books include *Tongjian Kaoyi* (corrections and amendments), *Tongjian Shili* (annotations), *Tongjian Juyao Li* (a record of major events), *Jigu Lu* (a concise historical reference) and *Linian Tu* (a timeline). Altogether the main book, in conjunction with the complementary books, is known as the *Zizhi Tongjian* collection. The book can best be described as a monumental historical chronicle which took 19-years to complete and was compiled from records in the national library.

The *Zizhi Tongjian* (Figure 3.7.8), was edited by Fan Zuyu together with Liu Shu and Liu Ban under the direction of historian Sima Guang and is more than 3 million characters in length. The book covers Chinese history from 403 BCE to 959 CE and the work was divided between the previously mentioned authors on a section by section basis. The bibliography is noteworthy for its editing which involved application of a more rigorous compilation process, with the editors compiling the individual entries and then merging the entries into longer sections before finalizing the entire book. Part of the compilation plan also involved the completion of a number of subsidiary books which were based on the book's main content.

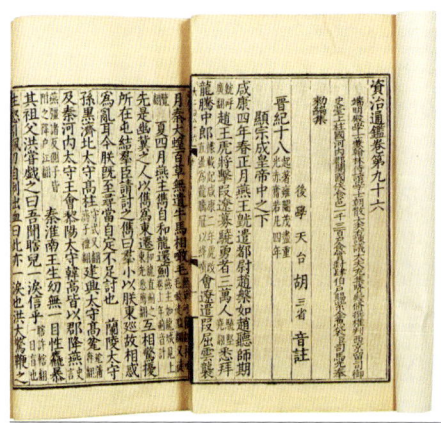

Figure 3.7.8: The *Zizhi Tongjian* — The Qing Dynasty carved Yuan edition. (清代影刻元刊本《资治通鉴》)
(http://pmgs.kongfz.com/data/pre_show_pic/78/236/2026)

The second book of the "Three Tongs", the *Tong Zhi* (Figure 3.7.9), written by Zheng Qiao, recorded the history of law and regulations dating from the Three Dynasties to the Sui and Tang periods. The book resembles a modern encyclopedia in form and was groundbreaking for the reason that it used a number of different formats, including the biographical format similar to the *Records of the Grand Historian* and the accepted legal format, or "Dian Zhi". The 20 abstracts included in the *Tong Zhi* eventually became a book of their own and are referred to as the *Tong Zhi Lue*.

Figure 3.7.9: The *Tong Zhi* — the Precious Collection Series of Wu Ying Dian Palace in Qing Dynasty. (清代武英殿聚珍版《通志》二百卷)
(http://pmgs.kongfz.com/data/pre_show_pic/10/120/044)

The third book, Du You's *Tong Dian* (Figure 3.7.10), was a compendium of philosophies, rites, music, law and principles of governance that spanned over 200 volumes and covered 1000-years of history. The emperor it was presented to, Emperor Dezong, issued an edict praising the work and it went on to become a valuable resource for the people. In fact, the *Tong Dian* influenced the Yuan Dynasty scholar Ma Duanlin, who used the book as a blueprint for his compilation *Wenxian Tongkao* (Figure 3.7.11). This increased the number of subject categories in the *Tong Dian* from 8 to 24, and covered a period of history from ancient times to the reign of Emperor Ningzong of the Song Dynasty. The book comprised three parts: "Wen" basic documents and their examination and correction, "Xian" the opinions of elders, and "Kao" comments by the author. The compilation is noteworthy for refining the "Zheng Shu" format of recording laws and regulations.

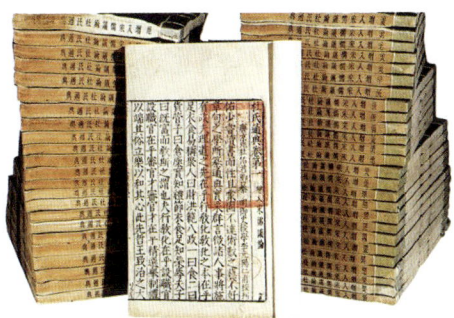

Figure 3.7.10: The *Tong Dian* — carving version in Ming Dynasty. (明代刻本《通典》二百卷)
(http://pmgs.kongfz.com/data/pre_show_pic/10/32/64)

Figure 3.7.11: The *Wenxian Tongkao* — the carving version in the Ming Dynasty. (明代刻本《文献通考》) (http://pmgs.kfzimg.com/data/pre_show_pic/16/501/634)

Altogether, the "Three Tongs" and the *Wenxian Tongkao*, contain invaluable historical records dating from the Northern and Southern Song and Yuan Dynasties and exemplify the groundbreaking work scholars endeavored to achieve during the time.

7.4 Conclusion

The innovative approach to governing and promoting smart and talented individuals allowed the governments of the Song and Yuan Dynasties to prosper. This fact is reflected in the large number of books which were written, compiled and published during this period of China's history. The books of the time are noted for their better organization, superior formats and the wide range of topics that they covered.

That's all I want to say for today, but I'll leave you with two homework questions that we can discuss on the online forum. First, how were the different tasks of publishing — editing, compilation, book production — carried out before paper was created? And secondly, what were the influential publications of books in the Song and Yuan Dynasties, and why were they so influential? When answering these questions, I'd like you to introduce as many of the major works as possible, and to share your comments with your team. I will be with you on the forum to answer any questions you may have. Until then, goodbye!

Task 8 ▶ Join the online forum and write a summary
(Students are required to have an instant and online post-talk discussion)

Irene:	I really appreciated the way Professor Richards organized his lecture in terms of the time sequence through the Song and Yuan Dynasties, and I was particularly struck by what he said about the role of editorial staff. What do you think about the way they were selected?
Miriam:	It was one of the reasons why the Song was such a dynamic era, wasn't it? Editors were selected through the imperial civil service exam. Those who passed would be chosen to serve the Dynasty, and the most eminent among them would work in the Chongwen Library, the royal institution in charge of book collection and editing. Imagine the prestige of a job like that!
Irene:	You make a very good point, Miriam. The competitive system of the Imperial Civil Service Exam guaranteed that the Emperor got the top scholars of the day. They were outstanding individuals and they took up their editing duties under the management of the royal family.
Owen:	Yes, it was a top job, but a really tough one as well. Did you catch how many pages they had to edit every day? 21-pages a day! And writers had to write 2,500 characters a day. No wonder they managed to compile the four great national bibliographies during the Song. What were they called again, Irene?
Irene:	They were the most authoritative works of their time — the *Chongwen Catalogue*, the *Zhongxing Library Catalogue*, the *Zhongxing Catalogue* and the *Record of National History, Art and Literature*.
Owen:	You really are a learning prodigy, Irene. But see if you can explain this problem I have. To me a bibliography is just a list of books or sources you've used in a term paper. What's so great about a list of book titles?

Miriam:	Can I butt in here, Irene? I had the same question as Owen, so I researched it. The great bibliographies were not just titles and authors — that's just a library catalogue. But the great classical bibliographies had commentaries and evaluations and publication history — isn't that right Irene?
Irene:	That's some excellent research, Miriam, and you've hit the nail on the head. A bibliography in the classical Chinese sense gives you a description of content as well as obvious things like dates and author's name. The fourth of the great bibliographies, *The Record of National History, Art and Literature* is, as you can imagine, more like an encyclopedia of the arts than a simple bibliography in the modern sense. And it's the same thing with the historiographies like the first of the three Tongs, *Zizhi Tongjian*. It records the history of 16 dynasties and spans almost 1,400 years with more than 200 volumes and 3 million Chinese characters. Now that's a real history book, is it not?
Owen:	Wow, Irene! You amaze me. The amount of extra preparation you put in ahead of just one lecture!
Irene:	We all did research, and now we're all sharing the results. That's what our team is for.
Miriam:	I agree — that's the benefit of teamwork. The four great bibliographies present an overall picture of the Song Dynasty. But another point I picked up was that the publications of that era were not only those of official scholars working for the government. There were also compilations and anthologies produced by private editors and printers that perhaps more properly reflected folk culture and customs. I think we should take a look at the *Extensive Records of the Taiping Era* for example.
Owen:	Sorry, I don't quite get the point. How can private collections reflect people's lives better than the work of elite officials of the Song Dynasty? Who could outperform them in editing and compilation?
Irene:	Well, no one could, but you said it yourself — they were elite officials doing incredibly comprehensive work but regulated by the royal family. They dealt with great historical and

	political events — but not the lives of ordinary people. What the unofficial compilation did was to complement the official work by adding stories about common folk.
Miriam:	That's exactly what I meant, Irene, only you said it better. *The Extensive Records* contains hundreds of folk tales and magical stories from Buddhist and Taoist literature, whereas *The Finest Blossoms in the Garden of Literature* is a collection of very literary works for very educated people.
Owen:	Okay, I take your point. Private collections catered to the demands of common people, and that's why they were preserved and passed down from generation to generation.
Irene:	That's right, Owen. And another unofficial publication was Shen Kuo's *Dream Pool Essays* which he wrote privately in retirement. He revealed many scientific facts including the concept of true north in terms of the direction in which a compass needle points. This is regarded as a milestone in Chinese scientific history, but it wasn't an officially compiled book.
Miriam:	So really we should be grateful for all the hard work of both the official and unofficial editors and compilers and what they contributed to our store of knowledge.
Irene:	We should indeed. But we must also remember that it was due to woodblock and movable type printing that the work of those scholars could be dispersed and shared with the whole community, to form the basis of our education and culture.
Owen:	I couldn't agree more. This discussion has really given me a lot to think about. I'm looking forward to continuing these themes when we look at Professor Richards' homework questions on the online forum.
Miriam:	Yes, I think we'll have a lot more new members to join us, and Professor Richards said he'd be there to join in, too.
Irene:	Okay team, see you online!
Miriam & Owen:	See you!

Appendix: Vocabulary for Unit 3

Historical Note

flank /flæŋk/ *vt.* 守侧面；位于……的侧面
                vi. 侧面与……相接
parasol /ˈpærəsɒl/ *n.* (~tree) 梧桐树
demeanor /dɪˈmiːnə/ *n.* 风度；举止；行为
chivalry /ˈʃɪvəlrɪ/ *n.* (复数 chivalries) 骑士精神；骑士制度
mingle /ˈmɪŋg(ə)l/ *vi.* 混合；交往
                vt. 使混合；使相混
patron /ˈpeɪtr(ə)n/ *n.* 赞助人；保护人；主顾
equivalent /ɪˈkwɪvələnt/ *adj.* 等价的，相等的；同意义的
sketchbook /ˈsketʃbʊk/ *n.* 小品集；写生簿；随笔集

Reading Activity

incise /ɪnˈsaɪz/ *vt.* 切；切割；雕刻
vessel /ˈves(ə)l/ *n.* 船，舰；脉管，血管；容器，器皿
inscription /ɪnˈskrɪpʃ(ə)n/ *n.* 题词；铭文；刻印
verify /ˈverɪfaɪ/ *vt.* 核实；查证
halve /hɑːv/ *vt.* 二等分；把……减半
hemp /hemp/ *n.* 大麻；麻类植物；大麻烟卷
spindle /ˈspɪndl/ *n.* 轴；纺锤，锭子
neologism /nɪˈɒlədʒɪz(ə)m/ *n.* 新词；新义；新词的使用
scribal /ˈskraɪbl/ *adj.* 抄写的；抄写员的

Lecture

conjunction /kənˈdʒʌŋ(k)ʃ(ə)n/ *n.* 结合；[语] 连接词；同时发生
proliferation /prəʊˌlɪfəˈreɪʃən/ *n.* 增殖，扩散；分芽繁殖
prominence /ˈprɒmɪnəns/ *n.* 突出；显著；突出物；卓越
focal /ˈfəʊk(ə)l/ *adj.* 焦点的，在焦点上的；病灶的
stringent /ˈstrɪn(d)ʒ(ə)nt/ *adj.* 严格的；严厉的；紧缩的；短缺的
proofread /ˈpruːfriːd/ *vt.* 校对；校正；校勘
imposition /ɪmpəˈzɪʃ(ə)n/ *n.* 征收；强加；欺骗；不公平的负担
miraculous /mɪˈrækjʊləs/ *adj.* 不可思议的，奇迹的
meteorology /ˌmiːtɪəˈrɒlədʒɪ/ *n.* 气象状态，气象学
mineralogy /mɪnəˈrælədʒɪ/ *n.* 矿物学；矿物学书籍
cartography /kɑːˈtɒgrəfɪ/ *n.* 地图制作，制图；制图学，绘图法

archeology /ˌɑːkɪˈɒlədʒɪ/ *n.* 考古学
pharmaceutics /ˌfɑːməˈsjuːtɪks/ *n.* 制药学；配药学
chronicle /ˈkrɒnɪk(ə)l/ *n.* 编年史，年代记；记录
compendium /kəmˈpendɪəm/ *n.* 纲要；概略

Unit

The Requirements of Publishing — Book-Sellers, Authors, Editors and Printers

TABLE OF CONTENTS

Warm-up:	Be proactive
Task 1	Listen to a historical note: Hua family bookshop in Ming Dynasty
Task 2	Discuss the historical note
Task 3	Build up our vocabulary
Task 4	Reading activity: Authors, Editors and Editing
Task 5	Reading comprehension
Task 6	Translation practice
Task 7	Attend a public lecture: The Technology-based Expansion of publishing in the Dynastic Period
Task 8	Join the online forum and write a summary
Appendix:	Vocabulary for Unit 4

The Requirements of publishing — Book-Sellers, Authors, Editors and Printers

Unit 4 The Requirements of publishing — Book-Sellers, Authors, Editors and Printers

WARM-UP: Be proactive

Irene: Welcome back, PRIMO group! Today we will set out on another journey into Chinese publishing. Can you remember what we learned in the last unit?

Miriam: Oh, very clearly. We discussed the Chen Family Bookstore — how the Chen family became the most esteemed book sellers and publishers of their time. Then we discussed the elements of books publication and the Chongwen Library, the royal institution for book collection and editing.

Owen: That's right, and on the online forum we discussed the Three Tongs that Professor Richards introduced. Three great publications covered all aspects of history, the arts, the sciences of a thousand years of Chinese civilization. Amazing stuff!

Miriam: I agree, Owen, the Tongs are fantastic, but what fascinates me about them is that technological innovations in publishing allowed them to circulate more widely, which helped to raise general literacy. This then led to more social mobility through the Imperial examination system, because ordinary people could succeed through passing public exams — just like today!

Irene: Yes, that's one of our great themes, isn't it? Throughout our history, technological enhancement in publishing has always contributed to great social change. Today we'll be looking at another stage in Chinese publishing — copper movable type printing. Copper was an advance on ceramic or tin

	movable type because it was easier to make, took ink better and so produced a better page. Copper printing plates were also more endurable for mass production. Based on this innovation, another legendary name — the Hua family book business — began to prosper.
Owen:	Yes! That's what I'm waiting for — the Hua Family story!
Miriam:	Me too! And after that we have a reading passage on the authors and editors of books before their publication. The whole unit will end with Professor Richards' introduction to the publishing institutions in the Ming and Qing Dynasties and the different types of publications they produced.
Irene:	So our task in this unit is to continue our journey through the Ming and Qing Dynasties by learning about another legendary printing family and also the great printing establishments of the time with all their technological innovations.
Owen:	That'll be fantastic — why don't we post those topics online to get more online learners involved? I bet a lot of people will be interested in Professor Philips's opening lecture.
Irene:	Good idea, Owen. Our class will be more inclusive with online as well as offline learners.
Miriam:	Ah, here comes the Professor now.

The Requirements of publishing — Book-Sellers, Authors, Editors and Printers

Task 1 ▶ Listen to a historical note: Hua Family Bookshop in Ming Dynasty

Philips: Hello again everybody, nice to see you all.

In today's lecture, I want to illustrate the multiple connections between the different crafts and technologies involved in book publication, from authoring and editing, to advanced copper-type printing and overall book quality as influenced by the Hua family research and development in this regard. Now, do you remember what I talked about last time?

Miriam: Of course we do, Professor. Your historical notes are very memorable. You told us about the Chen Family Bookshop in ancient China. It was one of the earliest and most famous bookshops in Chinese history. We're eager to know how it compares to the Hua Family Bookshop.

Philips: This is exactly what I hope to address. The Chen Family Bookshop was the forerunner, perfecting the printing of books with their hand-carved woodblocks. The Hua family contribution to Chinese publishing and printing lay in its technological improvements in plate-making, and the creation of copper type printing techniques, as well as to a more disciplined approach to the collection and correction of manuscripts. I will describe the Hua family development from the following three aspects: First, an introduction to the Hua family and their development of copper type printing technology; Second, the contribution of outstanding members of the Hua family; Third, the achievements of the Hua family as a whole. (You are required to fill in the blanks with the words and phrases you hear while listening)

  The Hua family of Wuxi contained some of the most renowned book sellers and contributors to the craft of book printing in the middle of the Ming Dynasty at a time when the technique of copper and bronze movable type printing was reaching maturity. Because of the family's success in fashioning and casting movable metal type, many members of the family committed themselves to the innovation of printing technology for the pursuit of maximum profit. The Hua family's rise to 1) _____ in the printing industry came as a result of intellectual prowess combined with an 2) _____ and the family, thus, became very celebrated among movable type printers of that time. This may also explain why, at that time, the most advanced metal movable type printing was found in the Zhejiang region, wherein the most active city was Wuxi, where family-based printing was the norm and the Hua family the exemplar.

The Hua family traced its 3) _____ back to Hua Bao, the 5th century "Filial Son of the Southern Qi." Influenced by a long-standing family tradition of 4) _____ respect, which had begun with Hua Bao, the members of this ancient and 5) _____ local family were all highly cultivated. Hua Bao was the progenitor of Hua Sui who lived 1,000 years later in the Ming Dynasty. Hua Sui (Figure 4.1.1), who led the Hua family's 6) _____ in copper movable type printing, was already known as an 7) _____ learner before he took up printing. Hua Sui began reading the classics from an early age. In addition to demonstrating 8) _____ interests, he was also highly attentive and focused in everything he did. Sometimes he would stand in the street and read at the top of his voice, seemingly 9) _____ to the people around him. Later in his life, he 10) _____ researching books and correcting texts. After copying out and correcting a text, he would bind it together and take it with him wherever he went, often asking others for their advice. As his collection of manuscripts grew increasingly large, Hua Sui naturally began to ponder the question of printing duplicates. This led to him developing an entirely new printing technique that involved the use of copper movable type. Compared to clay and tin movable type, printing plates that used copper movable type produced more attractive prints, were easier to use, and boasted superior physical properties. In addition, the printing process was more efficient, allowing more than 1,000 booklets to be printed in a single day. Hua Sui's invention brought him great fame.

Figure 4.1.1: Hua Sui (华燧)

One of the most representative achievements of the Hua family was the "Huitong Gallery". At the beginning of the Hongzhi Emperor's reign, Hua Sui expanded the scale of his printing activities and began printing the name "Huitong Gallery" (Figure 4.1.2) on his books. The Huitong Gallery was originally the name of Hua Sui's personal study. In choosing this name, he wanted to emphasize that a scholar should seek to gain mastery of a subject through comprehensive study. From the third to the eleventh year of the Hongzhi Emperor's reign (1490-1498), the Huitong Gallery produced a total of around 15 titles, including *Memorials of Ministers of the Song Dynasty*, *The Valley of Brocade Flowers*, and *Miscellaneous Notes from the Tolerant Studio* (Figure 4.1.3). In each of the books, the name "Huitong Gallery Movable Type Copper Plate Print" (Figure 4.1.4) was printed at the bottom of the pages below the center. The book *Memorials of Ministers of the Song Dynasty* consists of 150 manuscript scrolls divided into 50 booklets. Recording 1,630 precious memorials from 241 ministers of the Northern Song Dynasty, it is currently the oldest surviving copper movable type publication in the world.

Figure 4.1.2: The Ruins of Hua Sui's Museum Site in Wuxi Dangkou Town. (无锡荡口古镇的华燧会通馆遗址)
(http://a1.att.hudong.com/21/83/20300543494169144569831946921_140.)

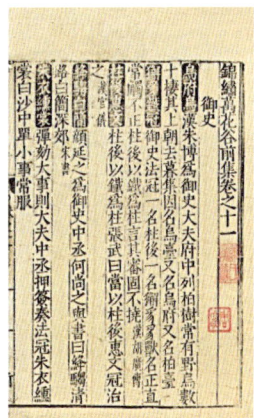

Figure 4.1.3: *Splendid Blossoms Valley* — Huitong Gallery Movable Type Copper Plate Print. (明代华燧会通馆铜活字印本《锦绣万花谷》)
(http://bbs.thmz.com/data/attachment/forum/201204/27/18274186ds6djtbbd688kg)

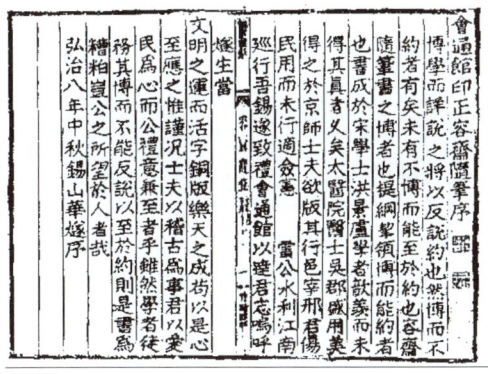

Figure 4.1.4: *Miscellaneous Notes from the Tolerant Studio* — Huitong Gallery Movable Type Copper Plate Print. (明代华燧会通馆铜活字印本《容斋随笔》)
(http://big5.ce.cn/gate/big5/i1.ce.cn/cathay/pieces/200904/01/W020090401340301441260)

The second most accomplished printer in the Hua family was undoubtedly Hua Sui's nephew, Hua Jian. Hua Jian's studio, the Orchid Snow Hall (Figure 4.1.5), did not print books in large quantities, but mainly recreated Song Dynasty prints of renowned literary collections from the Tang Dynasty, such as the *Anthology of Bai Juyi* and *Yiwen Leiju* (Figure 4.1.6). Books produced by the Orchid Snow Hall were marked with the words "Xishan Orchid Snow Hall Hua Jian Yun Gang Movable Type Copper Plate Print and Issue". Hua Jian's books also employed a unique line structure whereby each line housed two rows of characters, leading to the name "Orchid Snow Hall Double Line Books". Hua Sui's uncle Hua Cheng and younger brother Hua Yu were also engaged in the printing of books using copper movable type. Hua Cheng was an avid collector of old books and paintings, which meant that printing was more of a hobby to him. Using a set of copper movable type he had made personally, he printed rare versions of the *Weinan Wenji* (Lu You's Collected Articles) and *Jiannan Shigao* (Lu You's Collected Articles), which boasted more refined script and better print quality than their originals.

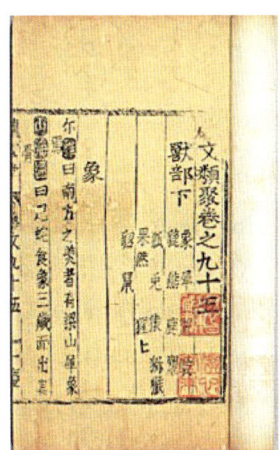

Figure 4.1.5: *Yiwen Leiju* — the version of Copper Movable Type by the Orchid Snow Hall of Hua Jian's studio. (华坚兰雪堂铜活字印本《艺文类聚》)
(http://www.ccnt.com.cn/htm/yssc/y0305/text/images/03_0014.002)

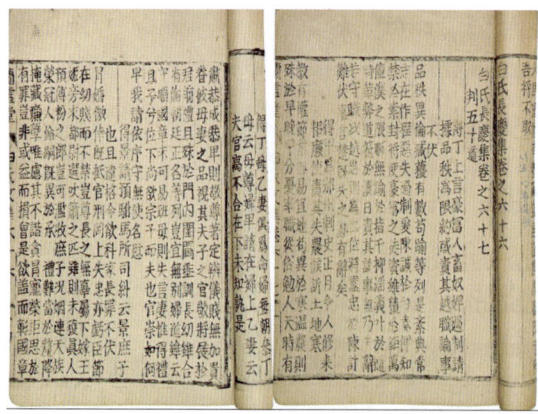

Figure 4.1.6: The *Bai Changqing Anthology* — the version of Copper Movable Type by the Orchid Snow Hall of Hua Jian's studio. (华坚兰雪堂铜活字印本《白氏长庆集》)
(http://www.ccnt.com.cn/htm/yssc/y0305/text/images/03_0014.002)

As the first books to be printed in Chinese using copper movable type, Hua family print editions were sold around the country in large numbers, being recognized for their unique cultural value. However, in the opinion of later generations, their corrections were generally inferior in quality to those of the An Family Guipo Gallery of Wuxi. Even the famous *Memorials of Ministers of the Song Dynasty* has been found to contain numerous mistakes and omissions. This is directly related to the inherent character of Hua Sui and the other members of the Hua family, who conducted themselves more like scholars than business owners, and whose primary interests were learning and trying new things. However, the new things they tried were revolutionary in their way, and movable copper or bronze type printing processes became the norm for the next few centuries.

Task 2 ▶ Discuss the historical note

(Students are required to do role play in groups by imitating the PRIMO's dialogue)

Irene: The Hua family story is such a legend! They went several steps further than the Chen family, didn't they? They didn't only collect and edit and print like the Chens did, they also led the way with technological inventions in movable type that allowed them to print more efficiently and effectively.

Miriam: I agree! It was a business empire based on updated technology and consistent research and development from Hua family

	members. I think their business prosperity also benefited from its favorable location in Wuxi, which was where the most advanced work in movable type printing was being done. And of course it didn't hurt to have the ancient Hua family tradition of fidelity and virtue behind them — that's always going to be big in China. No wonder they were so esteemed.
Owen:	Make perfect sense when you put it like that, Miriam. But I'm still a bit unclear about the differences between Bisheng's clay or tin movable type and copper type printing. What was it about copper that made it possible to open a new era in Chinese printing and publishing industry?
Irene:	That's a good question, Owen, and I think I can answer that with some hints from the historical note. Clay or porcelain movable type and a metal like tin had problems to do with holding the ink for clear printing. Porcelain was also a little fragile for multiple printing, and a soft metal like tin would also easily deform. It was the same with movable wood type. But copper — and in particular its alloy, bronze — took ink much better, gave cleaner edges for attractive print, and was very much more durable — it could be used over and over again for hundreds and thousands of copies. In the note, Professor Philips mentioned more than 1,000 booklets in one day. Imagine that, in the 15th century!
Owen:	Okay, I get it now, thank you, Irene.
Miriam:	And that mass production of printed works led the publishing industry into a new age in which the Hua family were important players. But the family legend really rests upon three key figures in the Hua family genealogy. You know which ones I mean?
Irene:	That must be Hua Bao, Hua Sui, and Hua Jian?
Miriam:	Right — the three family members who carved their names in publishing and printing history.
Owen:	Let's see if I've got them right — I made notes of course. Hua Bao was "the filial son of the Southern Qi" — isn't that great description? He was the ancestor who started the family tradition of fidelity and virtue. Then there was Hua Sui, the founder of the Hua family business a thousand years later, an

	avid learner with wide interests. His nephew, Hua Jian, went in for more refined printing. Higher quality reprints of classic poems, but in smaller quantities.
Miriam:	Full marks, Owen — better than my notes!
Irene:	Great stuff, Owen. But what about the actual products — what did they all do?
Owen:	I take your point. Hua Bao of course wasn't a printer, so he didn't produce any books. But he set the moral guidelines for future generations of the Hua family.
Miriam:	Right. Then Hua Sui was the key founding figure who took his family business to its summit. The Huitong Gallery, the most comprehensive family institution, collected and published more than 1,600 memorials of ministers.
Irene:	The third key figure — though there were other Hua family members in the business, of course — was Hua Jian, Hua Sui's nephew. He reprinted the *Anthology of Baijuyi* and *Yiwen Leiju*. Altogether, as the first family printing house to adopt copper or bronze movable type, the Hua family should be respected and remembered. Now let's do the vocabulary exercise to consolidate the text we have discussed.
Miriam & Owen:	Good idea!

Task 3 ▶ Build up our vocabulary
(Drag and match exercises)

Match the English words in column A with the Chinese equivalents in column B.

A		B	
1	Inner Palace books	A	赵孟頫体
2	Director of Ceremonies	B	绣像本小说
3	the Scripture Workshop	C	修书处
4	Zhao Mengfu script	D	线装书
5	a Book Production Office	E	铜版活字印刷
6	private printing	F	宋版翻刻
7	copying the style of Song	G	私刻

	Dynasty books		
8	*Eight Collections of Tang Poems Selected by the Tang People*	H	司礼监
9	*One Sky Pavilion Collection*	I	内府刻书
10	*Jing Ke Ben*	J	经厂
11	calligraphic engraving	K	包背装
12	*Shili Studio Collection*	L	《通志堂经解》
13	*Commentaries to the Classics from Tongzhi Hall*	M	《天一阁集》
14	Illustrated novels	N	《唐人选唐诗八种》
15	thread-bound books	O	《士礼居丛书》
16	back-binding	P	写刻
17	copper-type movable broze print	Q	精刻本

Task 4 ▶ Reading activity

The following excerpt is recommended to PRIMO. It is partially from **Chinese History: A New Manual by Endymion Wilkinson.** *It is about* **Authors, Editors and Editing.** *PRIMO may distinguish the concepts of authors, editors and editing as well as their relationship through reading this excerpt.*

4.1 Authors and Editors

Creative writing was clearly distinguished from editing, compiling, and translating. But the meaning of these concepts changed over time.

In early China when writing was on heavy and difficult media and most works circulated in short paragraphs or by word of mouth, it became conventional to say, as Confucius did in the *Lunyu* (《论语》), "I edit and do not create". Such an attitude regarding the authorship also fitted perfectly with a culture that valued the wisdom of the past and actually frowned on innovation. After the introduction of paper during the Later Han, as the number of authors began to increase, the length of literature also began to expand as frequently they were now written by the single individual. And Zuo ceased to mean "create" and was used then to mean simply "write". Based on Confucius, *Shu* is often translated as "transmit" (述而不作). Whereas *Zhu* (著), *Zuo* (作), and *Zhuzuo*

(著作) were all used for creative writing or innovative works. Sima Qian, the great historian and thinker in the western Han Dynasty, says in his post-face to the *Shi Ji* (Figure 4.4.1) that he wrote "the basic annals of the Five Emperors " (作五帝本纪). He expressed ancient matters and arranged past traditions, but did not create a single word in the same way that Confucius produced the *Spring and Autumn Annals* (Figure 4.4.2). Thus the difference between the original authors and compilation editors can be clear.

Figure 4.4.1: *Shi Ji* (Historical Records) — the revised version by Zhong Hua Book Company, 2013. (《史记》修订本，中华书局 2013 年版)
(http://image.chinawriter.com.cn/cr/2011/1031/1559673982.)

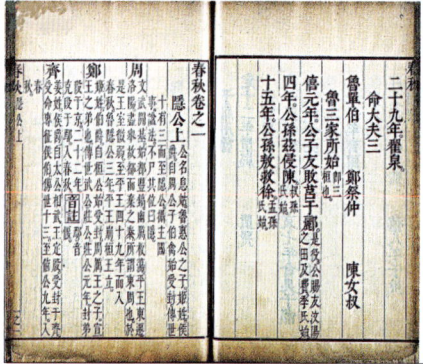

Figure 4.4.2: The *Spring and Autumn Annals* — the carving version in Qing Dynasty. (清代刻本《春秋》)
(http://image.chinawriter.com.cn/cr/2011/1031/1559673982.)

Then an interesting side point is that the authors often preferred their pen names or pseudonym to their real names. Beginning in the Tang and Song Dynasties, authors chose to use a variety of alternative names (笔名) instead of using their own names or their courtesy names. In addition to their regular names (*xing* 姓，*ming* 名，*zi* 字), members of the elite in imperial China used many different kinds of names called *Hao* (号), which were often qualified, as in *Guohao* (国号)，*Hanghao* (行号)，*Huihao* (徽号) and so on. In its narrower sense, *Hao* is short for alternative name. Sometimes the terms *Hao* and *Zi* were used interchangeably and sometimes it is not easy to distinguish a peroson's *Hao* from his *Zi*.

Apart from the authors' names, the works published in a dynastic age were also labeled differently, especially for imperial works. In the Ming and

Qing Dynasties, imperially authored works including prefaces, paintings or calligraphy were often published with the prefix (*Yuzhi* 御制), which normally means "by imperial command" or "imperially commissioned" . Works with less imperial involvement in the writing, compilation, editing, or annotating were indicated with prefix like *Qinding* (钦定), meaning imperially commanded or commissioned or authorized; *Yuding* (御定), imperially edited, reviewed, commissioned or a combination of these; *Yuzhu* (御注), imperially annotated and the like. The titles of imperially commissioned works that were published during the ruling dynasty usually had *Da* (大) added before the dynastic name, as in *Da Tang Liudian* (大唐六典) (Figure 4.4.3)，*Da Minglu* (大明律). (Figure 4.4.4) In many cases such dynastic indicators were dropped from titles after the dynasty ended.

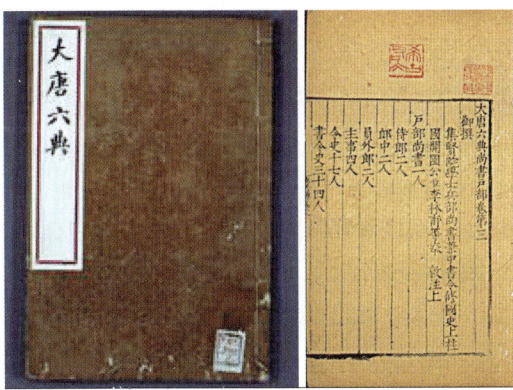

Figure 4.4.3: *Da Tang Liudian* — the Six Canon of Tang Dynasty. (《大唐六典》) (http://image.digitalarchives.tw/ImageCache/00/07/97/5d)

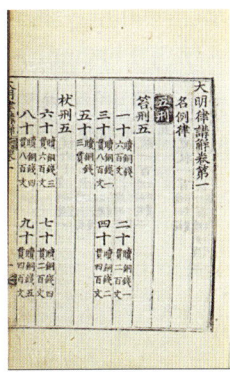

Figure 4.4.4: *Da Minglu* — the criminal law of the Ming Dynasty. (《大明律》) (http://image.digitalarchives.tw/ImageCache/00/07/96/ce)

4.2 Editing

The work of editors of pre-Qin texts in Han China was more arduous than that of an editor today. Often they had to begin by transcribing the characters from one of the ancient scripts. Next, they had to collate the bamboo or wooden strips in a coherent order into bundles. An early definition of the *bian* (编) in *bianji* (编辑) was to put the bamboo strips in order and bind them together. If, as often happened, the threads had perished, the editors had to put the strips back into the correct order before rethreading could take place. If there were missing or broken strips, missing characters would have to be replaced. This is a common cause of confusion and variant readings. Sometimes a previous editor had put the strips in the wrong order or had been tempted to add material at the end of a bundle if there were blank strips left, thus creating a puzzle for future editors.

Next, the editors had to assign to each bundle a heading or as we would say, a chapter title. This was often chosen as it was in ancient Greece from the key words in the first sentence of the first strip in each bundle.

Finally, the bundle had to be arranged into a coherent order. In the course of his work, the editor often had to compare various editions, usually with the aim of producing a single reliable text, but in some cases recognizing the validity of several versions of a single work. Another task was to choose the title from one of several available alternatives or to invent one and, in some cases to attribute an author. In later Chinese history, many works continued to have alternative titles, but for different reasons. The results of an editors labors were often recorded in a colophon (*xu* 序). One thing that editors did not have to do was to correct the punctuation, since there was none.

Textual criticism often fell into editors' missionary domain. The object of textual criticism is to establish an uncorrupt master version of a text by comparing all known editions and by removing copyists' errors and other faults of transmission. Textual criticism was called *Choujiao* (雠校) or Jiaochou (校雠), which refers to probing the enemy, from the Han and *Jiaokan* (校勘) beginning in the Six Dynasties. This is among the chief jobs of editors, and is usually done by two people working together, with one reading the original, and the other correcting the proof.

The main assumption of textual criticism as it had been practiced in China is that there was at one point in time an original text established by a master. However, the excavation of hitherto unknown early texts of several classical works called into question the *stemma codicum* model (真本树模型). The *Laozi* for example, was committed to memory and then written down at different times in different parts of the country. Which is the most authentic among the newly discovered earlier version of the *Laozi*? If a passage in them is the same as the transmitted version, are we to conclude that it is correct? When a passage diverges from the transmitted versions, do they automatically indicate a more authentic reading? There is no easy answer to these questions, because a transmitted version may have been based on an earlier version. Clearly, the stemma codicum model with its tree diagram of textual transmission does not work for the Confucian and other Classics because in most cases they were memorized and written down often centuries after the master was dead. Nor was there a simple progression from oral to written. Consequently, the discovery of new copies of ancient texts profoundly affects textual criticism on the one hand, and it throws out a challenge to all editors as well.

Task 5 ▶ Reading comprehension

(Students are required to launch a discussion to pose new questions and answer all the questions raised in the dialogue, and do the role play based on the following)

Irene:	I think that passage describes clearly the differences between editing and compiling, and the act of creative writing, don't you think so PRIMO team?
Miriam:	I think the concept of editing and compiling is expressed by the ancient Chinese "*shu*" or "*bian*", which indicate that the editor is not the writer of the book.
Owen:	I'm still not very clear about the ancient Chinese ideas on editing and writing — can you give me some more examples?
Irene:	Okay, let's take the *Analects (Lunyu)* as an example. It's a collection of sayings and ideas attributed to Confucius, the great philosopher. When we quote him, we usually say "As Confucius once said" but in fact the Analects were actually written down and edited by Confucius's students and followers after his death in the Warring States period. The sayings originated from Confucius, but they were recorded and edited by others. And that's the difference between the Chinese "*shu*", "*zuo*", and "*zhuzhuo*".
Miriam:	An even better example is perhaps the *Shiji*, the *Records of the Grand Historian*, written by Sima Qian. It's a monumental history of ancient China, covering 2500 years from the Yellow

Emperor to the Emperor Wu of the Han Dynasty. We say it was written by Sima Qian, but he himself says that he used official archives and Imperial records for all his sources, and he even collected eye-witness accounts. For examples, the material on Jing Ke's attempt to assassinate the Emperor of Qin was supposed to be taken from an eye-witness account passed on by the great-grandfather of his father's friend. So we can see from all this that the great Sima Qian didn't regard himself as the writer of the *Basic Annals* or *Hereditary Houses,* but rather as the compiler of historical records that had existed for centuries.

Owen: I see. So the ancient Chinese "*bianzhu*" is quite different from the contemporary "*bianji*", right?

Irene: Exactly right. The editor in ancient times had to do things no modern editor has to do. For example, since most texts before the Han Dynasty were on wooden or bamboo strips whose binding may have decayed, the editor might have to put all the strips back into the right order and then re-thread them. No modern editor has to do things like that!

Owen: And you'd really have to know your original materials, wouldn't you, to be able to put them all back in the right order.

Miriam: That's true. But I've got another problem — do they give themselves all those different names? I understand having a pseudonym or a nom de plume, but half a dozen names in one lifetime? What was that all about?

Irene: I suppose it does look strange to a Westerner, but it's easily understood in Asian countries. In Chinese culture, the *Hao* — as opposed to the birth name — was used to denote some great changes in the person's life time. So for example, Su Shi was dismissed from his official position and retired to Dongpo to write poetry, and so he took the new *Hao* of "the man who went to Dongpo". Similarly Tao Yuanming, when he retired from his official position, went to his country home that had willow trees in its garden, so he called himself "Mr Five-Willows" — *Wuliu Xiansheng*. Do you see now how it works?

Miriam: Yeah, I really get it now — it's rather lovely, don't you think so,

	Owen?
Owen:	Yeah, that's a great explanation, Irene, thank you.

Task 6 ▶ Translation practice
(Students are required to translate the following Chinese paragraph into English individually, in pairs or in group)

Irene:	Okay, PRIMO team, are we ready for the translation task? This passage is about the different book publishing institutions in the Yuan, Ming, and Qing Dynasties.
Miriam:	I've researched this a bit online. The Yuan, Ming, and Qing are the last three dynasties in Chinese history, of course. Each one of them created policies to restrain the publishing industry but the Qing Dynasty enforced the strictest guidelines.
Owen:	That's interesting! And in this text I'm going to find out the names of the different publishing institutions — that'll be good. I want to start with the first line about publishing in the Yuan Dynasty.
Miriam:	Good for you, Owen. If there are any words we don't know, we can ask Irene for help.
Irene:	Of course you can — we're a team, and team work is the way to overcome all obstacles. Let's get going!

　　从元朝开始，出版就已基本形成了编纂、审查、雕刻、印刷分工的出版雏形，而翰林国史院、国子监、御史台、集贤院等在编书这一点上与现在的出版社类同。到明朝，图书出版政策变得比较宽松，免除了出版税。明政府对民间的学术和创作活动一般不予干涉，但对其统治地位有危害的除外。所以，一些视野开阔、远见卓识的知识分子和外国学者可以切磋学问，编纂和刻印活动十分活跃，涌现出大量的科技类图书和天主教图书。随着明朝的私刻技术的空前发达，通俗文化读物包括小说、戏曲剧本等成为坊刻的重要出版物，而且为了满足人们审美的需求，在通俗读物中广泛采用插图版画。到清朝年间，尤其是康熙、雍正、乾隆三世编修出版了大型丛书和类书，规模达到万卷，内容涉及经学、史学、诗词、天文、历法、农艺等方面。清代的出版由考据学发展出校勘学和辑佚学，校勘人才层次较高，基本上都是全国有影响力的学者，而且

皇帝亲自把关，曾制定"有一误字，罚俸一年"的措施。这个时期的私刻也形成鲜明的特点：坊刻的市场定位是面向普通市民大众，具有浓厚的商业经营意识，出版了注重轻小灵活的袖珍本和巾箱本。清朝坊本还有一个特点，即注重广告效应，在书前加封面、题书坊名称，注明刻行及藏版。

Task 7 ▶ Attend Professor Richards's public lecture

Lecture 4

The Technology-based Expansion of Publishing in the Dynastic Period
Professor Richards

  Hello PRIMO members, you're all looking fine. I hope that's because you've all been looking forward to my lecture. But before I begin, I have a question for you: Have you ever wondered where books come from? It seems a stupid question, doesn't it? Books come from publishing houses. But can you tell me where books came from before the development of modern publishing houses? Don't bother to answer me now. In any event, the answer to that question is the subject of our next lecture on the history of publishing in China. In my previous lecture I addressed the production of books during the Song and Yuan Dynasties. Today, I'm going to talk to you about the technology-based publishing expansion during the Ming and Qing Dynasties, in another word, the maturing process of the publishing industry in China during the Ming and Qing Dynasties.

  To begin, you have to understand that the Ming and Qing Dynasties constituted a time of highly developed systems of central government in Chinese history. The time period saw not only vast fluctuations in policies concerning Chinese culture, but also an increase in the exchange of trade and culture with foreign countries. The diversity of ways in which books were produced, i.e. printing technology, and the books published through these different ways played the role of bridging China and other countries. Here, I will address the three major printing institutions which greatly promoted publishing during the Ming and Qing Dynasties: First, official publications made in the Wuying Palace (Figure 4.7.1); Secondly, private publications produced by scholars; and Thirdly, workshop prints completed in shops and sold for profit, and other kinds of books. Finally I will say a few words about the physical construction of these books and the different types of book that were published during this time. I will briefly address each of these separate and distinct sections in turn.

Figure 4.7.1: The Wuying Palace. (故宫武英殿)
(http://p4.so.qhimg.com/t01cbdc5125957e6d6e)

7.1 Officially produced books

1) Inner Palace books

During the Ming Dynasty the highest quality prints produced by the government were no longer made in the Imperial Academy, but rather at the Inner Palace. Superior prints produced by the government were referred to as Inner Palace books and they were completed under the supervision of the Director of Ceremonies at the Scripture Workshop (Figure 4.7.2).

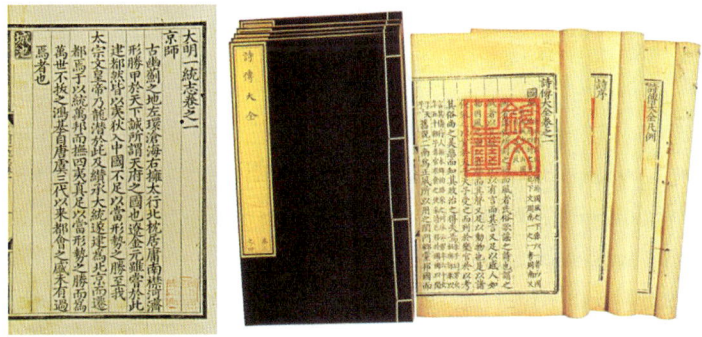

Figure 4.7.2: *Poetry biography* — the carving version by Inner Palace in Yongle Period, Ming Dynasty. (明代永乐年间内府经厂刻本《诗传大全》)
(http://p4.so.qhimg.com/t01cbdc5125957e6d6e)

Interestingly, the editing of books in the Scripture Workshop was performed entirely by eunuchs. The eunuchs were supervised by a special secretary who would oversee the completion of imperial orders. In the beginning the printing workshop produced mostly classics and histories, Confucian and Taoist teachings and collections ordered by officials, although the range of book content gradually increased over time. Ironically, the majority of the books were often re-supplied to the special secretary and the eunuchs for study.

Inner Palace books were printed on quality paper using the best ink and are noteworthy for their thick borders, widely spaced lines, very clear characters and punctuation marks. The choice of Zhao Mengfu script (Figure 4.7.3) for the text additionally made the resulting editions appear more like works of art than pages for a book. The carvings of the woodblocks and the resulting prints used to make the books were in a word: exquisite.

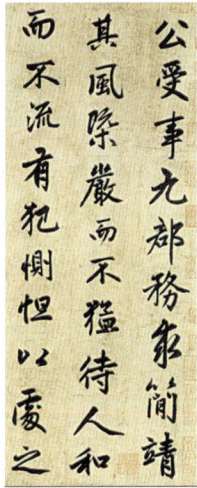

Figure 4.7.3: The Collection of Calligraphy Works by Zhao Mengfu — *Check Zhai Paste.* (赵孟頫书法作品《止斋贴》)
(http://s10.sinaimg.cn/bmiddle/82aa88a5gba02e548d629&690)

2) Wuying Palace books

The finest official prints of the Qing Dynasty were printed in the Wuying Palace which possessed a Book Production Office divided into both a production supervision section and a text revision section (Figure 4.7.4). The production office was supervised by an academician selected from the Hanlin Academy who would oversee the scholars chosen to complete the editing, checking and printing processes. To give you an idea of the scope of this operation, the production supervision section itself was led by a council of princes and high officials and contained a records office, writing workshop, printing workshop, copper type storehouse, a medicine storehouse and a gallery of prized works.

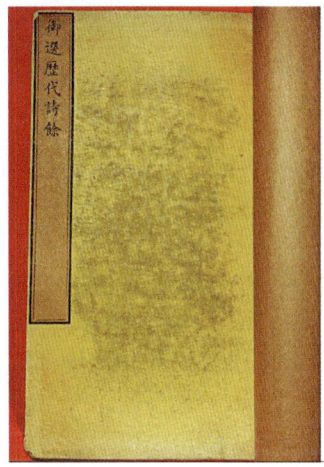

Figure 4.7.4: *The Main Book Cover* by Wuying Palace in Qing Dynasty.（武英殿刻书的书衣）

The Wuying Palace is credited with advances in woodblock printing and both wooden and copper movable type print. The texts were corrected using quality manuscripts dating from the Song and Yuan Dynasties and although the style of block carving sometimes varied, it always remained masterful. (Figure 4.7.5). The prints completed in the Wuying Palace during the Qing Dynasty represented a high point in the history of printing, which reached its peak in the Qianlong and Yongzheng periods, until it later fell into decline during the reign of the Jiaqing Emperor.

Figure 4.7.5: *The Sample Illustration in the Carving Copy* by Wuying Palace in Qing Dynasty.（清代武英殿刻本《御製武英殿聚珍版程式》插图）
(http://s9.sinaimg.cn/mw690/0025mOp5zy6NeV0znQIe8&690)

7.2 Privately printed books

Aside from official or government sponsored printing, private printing also took place during the Ming and Qing Dynasties. In fact, private printing during this time surpassed that of all previous dynasties in terms of both scale and quality. The majority of privately printed books was done by scholars, who themselves were often book collectors. As a result, their finished prints were well regarded for both their academic and artistic qualities. The private printers of the time especially appreciated books which had been printed in the Song Dynasty and so it became fashionable to emulate them. This trend of copying the style of Song Dynasty books was eventually adopted by both government and workshop printers.

Ming and Qing period scholars who engaged in producing their own editions mainly produced secret versions of books, family documents, selected poems with comments and articles and passages grouped by category. Some of the best known works completed by private printers during the Ming and Qing periods are: *Eight Collections of Tang Poems Selected by the Tang People*, the *Selected Works of Ming Monk Hongxiu*, and *Thirteen Classics Explanatory Notes and Commentaries*, by Mao Jin, who alone printed more than 600 books (Figure 4.7.6).

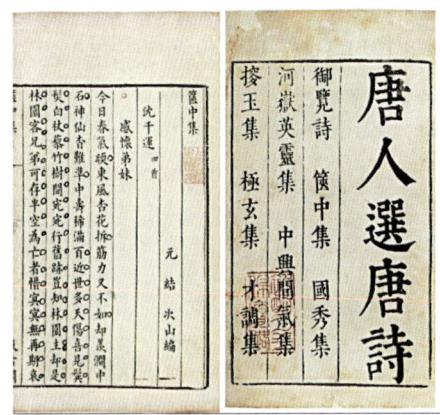

Figure 4.7.6: *The Carving Copy—the Anthology of the Poetry in Tang Dynasty.* (毛晋汲古阁刻本 —— 唐人选唐诗八种)
(http://pmgs.kfzimg.com/data/pre_show_pic/6/343/1125)

During the Qing Dynasty, private printers were producing very high quality books, to the extent that their woodblock prints were considered the most valuable of the time. The quality of compilation and carving were unprecedented. Strict standards were also employed in the selection of paper and ink and along with improvements in the quality of revisions, the renowned private printers were able to produce many artistically superior titles which were referred to as "Jing Ke Ben" or finely engraved books.

The majority of these books were independent writings and collections of poems from great poets of the past. Interestingly, a number of printing trends also took place during the time, including the practice of 包背装 where an engraver would copy the look of brush written characters, the practice of collecting, carving and printing previous collections which had become scattered, and the practice of making exact replicas of older versions of books.

With regard to this latter trend, the book *Shili Studio Collection* by Huang Pilie was reprinted with such precision that it was almost indistinguishable from the Song Dynasty original (Figure 4.7.7).

Figure 4.7.7: *The Anthology of Scholar series* by Huang Pilie. （黄丕烈辑《士礼居丛书》）
(http://pmgs.kfzimg.com/data/pre_show_pic/3/56/446)

7.3 Books printed by workshops

In addition to government sponsored printers and private printers, the number of printing workshops also grew in scope and scale during the Ming and Qing Dynasties.

Although workshops existed prior to this time, Ming and Qing Dynasties workshops, known as *Shu Si* or *Shu Pu* (Figure 4.7.8) are noteworthy for the reason that they consolidated the functions of editing, publishing and distribution and made publishing a thoroughly commercial operation. These shops established themselves in commercial and cultural centers with the aim of selling as many books as possible and realizing a profit, many of them became so renowned that they were able to survive the transition from one ruling dynasty to the next. During the Ming Dynasty workshops concentrated in Fujian, Zhejiang, Nanjing and Beijing. During the Qing Dynasty printing workshops were mostly seen in Beijing, Nanjing, Suzhou and Hangzhou.

Figure 4.7.8: The recent picture of Studio of Glorious Treasures in Azure Stone Factory of Qing Dynasty. （清代北京琉璃厂书肆荣宝斋近影）
(http://images.visitbeijing.com.cn/20121119/Img214777275)

7.4 Other kinds of books

You now probably know more about how printing boosted publishing during the Ming and Qing Dynasties than you thought possible… but lucky for you, I still have some material to cover. I have reviewed who were printing books during the period: the government, private individuals and workshops… but exactly what types of books were they printing? I am going to answer this question in two ways, first by describing the physical aspects of the books being made, and second, by reviewing the content of these books.

By the Ming and Qing Dynasties thread-bound books had become the standard book format in China. Although thread-bound books existed as early as the Tang Dynasty, they did not become commonplace until the middle of the Ming Dynasty.

The technique of thread-binding books (Figure 4.7.9) derived from the practice of back-binding. Instead of using a one-piece cover for back-binding, thread-bound books utilized two covers, one for the top and one for the bottom of the book, with holes punched through both covers and the pages containing the text and then bound together with string. I call it the bottom cover because books in those days would be stacked on their sides, not end-up as in our day. Thread-bound books were easier to read and more easily distinguishable than their predecessors. The emergence of thread binding also made it easier to compile and organize large collections and encyclopedias.

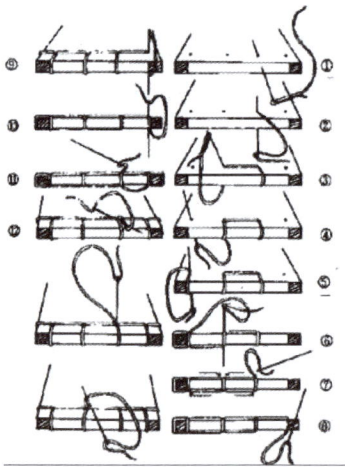

Figure 4.7.9: The Sketch of book binding process. (线装书装订流程示意图)
(http://p2.so.qhimg.com/t015faca917ce66b5ec)

Regarding content, a number of different types of books were published. I have already mentioned some well known titles, and of course there were the standards, including the Confucian Classics, histories, philosophy, anthologies, collected works and Buddhist and Taoist classics. Additionally, there were the popular books made for the masses which I have previously mentioned.

However, there is yet another category of book which I have not mentioned... those being written in the West and then translated into Chinese by Jesuits priests of the Roman Catholic Church.

From 1552 to 1773, a number of Jesuits arrived in China and were responsible for the translation of over 400 titles. Many of the prized translations concerned the natural sciences... books covering topics such as astronomy, geography, physics, mathematics, engineering and medicine being highly coveted. Interestingly, the Jesuits often worked in conjunction with a Chinese counterpart on their translations and to a large degree these men are responsible for the initial transmission of the Western sciences to China.

7.5 Conclusion

So now you know a little more about the history of publishing in China, more specifically, you know the various ways books were produced during the Ming and Qing Dynasties and by whom. You also know not only who were producing books at the time, but what types of books were being made and the content of those same books. The Ming and Qing Dynasties represent a flourishing publishing era in China, which is reflected in the various ways books were produced and which directly pre-dates the advent of modern day printing practice, which I will cover in a subsequent lecture.

I will leave you with three questions for you to discuss after this lecture or in you online forum as you wish. First the simple question that I started my lecture with: Where do books come from? It's a simple answer in today's world, but what is the more complicated answer that you now appreciate as students of the history of publishing in China? My second question is: How were books constructed, how were they put together in the Ming and Qing dynasties? And the final question: What different sorts of books were produced in that period? And with that question I will say goodbye for this time, and I'll see you next time.

Task 8 ▶ Join the online forum and write a summary

(Students are required to have an instant and online post-talk discussion)

Irene: So, PRIMO team, what's the answer to Professor Richards'

The Requirements of publishing — Book-Sellers, Authors, Editors and Printers

	first question at the beginning of his lecture? Where does a book come from?
Owen:	Well, I think we all understand why the Professor started with that question. To most people, the answer is simple: books come from a bookstore. But we know that it's more complicated than that, don't we?
Miriam:	Yes, books have been produced in different ways ever since woodblock printing reached its summit in the Song Dynasty. We've learned about the great family bookshops of Chen and Hua, but of course they were essentially private printers, scholars for whom book production was almost a work of art. There were also the official printing institutions of the Imperial Palace, as we learned from Professor Richards' lecture.
Irene:	Yes indeed. The Ming and Qing Dynasties saw the peak in the development of central government monopoly. The authorities gradually controlled publication with more and more regulations, especially in the Qing Dynasty.
Owen:	So to understand the history of publishing in China, we really have to know about the books published by the imperial authorities. But who exactly was in charge of compiling and editing at that time?
Miriam:	Ah, that was the Inner Palace, wasn't it? Professor Richards said that the editing and writing was all done by eunuchs. The books were all produced with the best quality ink and paper so that they were more like art works than reading material. I imagine they were so expensive that they would only be owned the royal groups themselves.
Owen:	I guess so. And that imperial system continued under the Qing Dynasty, didn't it?
Irene:	Yes. The best official printing branch in the Qing Dynasty was the Wuying Palace. Scholars were chosen to edit, check and print the books under the supervisions of professionals from the Hanlin Academy. The Wuying Palace survived and prospered for several decades but then declined during the late Qing period.
Owen:	So the Ming and Qing Dynasties saw the rise of official publications. But there were still lots of private bookstores

	and printing houses, weren't there? Professor Richards mentioned *Shu Si* or *Shu Pu*, bookstores that had opened up in the major cities and some of the ports along the Yangzi River.
Miriam:	Yes, books were spreading everywhere because of the new printing technologies. But what I found really interesting was the way that books were actually put together.
Irene:	Oh, you mean the way the pages were bound together with thread and with a front and back cover, which Professor Richards called a top and bottom cover, because the books would be stacked on their sides, and not upright as we keep them in shelves today.
Owen:	And of course there was a wide variety of titles and topics covered by all the books being produced in all these private workshops, weren't there?
Miriam:	Oh yes. All the official standards, of course — the Four Books, the Five Classics and so on — but also popular books like novels to educate and entertain the masses.
Irene:	And one very important type of book that looked very much towards the future: there were Jesuit priests in China who, along with Chinese counterparts, translated important Western books on mathematics, physics, engineering and medicine into Chinese.
Owen:	You know, Irene, this discussion is so interesting I think we should continue it in our online forum, don't you?
Irene:	I agree — let's do that. See you both online later!
Miriam & Owen:	Okay, See you, Bye!

Appendix: Vocabulary for Unit 4

Historical Note
prowess /ˈpraʊɪs/ *n.* 英勇；超凡技术；勇猛
aptitude /ˈæptɪtjuːd/ *n.* 才能；天赋

lineage /ˈlɪniɪdʒ/ n. 血统；家系，[遗] 世系
filial /ˈfɪlɪəl/ adj. 孝顺的；子女的，当作子女的
oblivious /əˈblɪvɪəs/ adj. 遗忘的；健忘的；不注意的；不知道的
ponder /ˈpɒndə/ vi. 考虑；沉思
　　　　　　 vt. 仔细考虑；衡量
duplicate /ˈdjuːplɪkeɪt/ n. 副本；复制品
avid /ˈævɪd/ adj. 渴望的，贪婪的；热心的
inherent /ɪnˈhɪərənt/ adj. 固有的；内在的；与生俱来的，遗传的
orchid /ˈɔːkɪd/ n. 兰花；[植] 兰科植物；淡紫色
miscellaneous /ˌmɪsəˈleɪnɪəs/ adj. 混杂的，各种各样的；多方面的，多才多艺的

Reading Activity

pseudonym /ˈsjuːdənɪm/ n. 笔名；假名
annotate /ˈænəteɪt/ vt. 注释；作注解
　　　　　　 vi. 注释；给……作注释或评注
arduous /ˈɑːdjʊəs/ adj. 努力的；费力的；险峻的
transcribe /trænˈskraɪb/ vt. 转录；抄写
coherent /kə(ʊ)ˈhɪər(ə)nt/ adj. 连贯的，一致的；清晰的；凝聚性的；互相耦合的
colophon /ˈkɒləf(ə)n/ n. 书籍的末页；版本记录，版权页标记
hitherto /hɪðəˈtuː/ adv. 迄今；至今
stemma /ˈstemə/ n. 家谱
diverge /daɪˈvɜːdʒ/ vt. 使偏离；使分叉
　　　　　　 vi. 分歧；偏离；分叉；离题

Lecture

eunuch /ˈjuːnək/ n. 太监；阉人
academician /əˌkædəˈmɪʃ(ə)n/ n. 院士；大学生；大学教师
unprecedented /ʌnˈpresɪdentɪd/ adj. 空前的；无前例的，前所未有的
consolidate /kənˈsɒlɪdeɪt/ vt. 巩固，使固定；联合
　　　　　　 vi. 巩固，加强
predecessor /ˈpriːdɪsesə/ n. 前任；前辈
covet /ˈkʌvɪt/ vt. & vi. 垂涎；觊觎
advent /ˈædvənt/ n. 到来；出现；基督降临；基督降临节
exquisite /ˈekskwɪzɪt/ adj. 精致的；细腻的；优美的，高雅的；异常的；剧烈的
Buddhist /ˈbʊdɪst/ n. 佛教徒
Confucian /kənˈfjuːʃən/ adj. 孔子的，儒家的；儒家学说的
Taoist /ˈtɑːəʊɪst/ adj. 道教的；道教信徒的

punch /pʌntʃ/ *vt.* 开洞；以拳重击
　　　　　　vi. 用拳猛击
oversee /ˌəʊvəˈsiː/ *vt.* 监督；审查；俯瞰；无意中看到

5 Unit

Artistic Design and Book Collection of Ancient Chinese Publications

TABLE OF CONTENTS

Warm-up:	Be proactive
Task 1	Listen to a historical note: Beijing Liulichang
Task 2	Discuss the historical note
Task 3	Build up our vocabulary
Task 4	Reading activity: The Artistic Design of Bookbinding and Page Layout
Task 5	Reading comprehension
Task 6	Translation practice
Task 7	Attend a public lecture: Official Book Collecting from the Xia Dynasty to the Five Dynasties
Task 8	Join the online forum and write a summary
Appendix:	Vocabulary for Unit 5

Unit 5: Artistic Design and Book Collection of Ancient Chinese Publications

WARM-UP: Be proactive

Irene: Hello again PRIMO team, it's time for the next unit on Chinese publishing. What's the most important thing you remember from the last Unit?

Miriam: Oh, there were lots of things, but I suppose the most important single thing was Professor Phillips' story of the Hua Family Bookstore and how they prospered in Wuxi, in the south of China.

Owen: That's right, and it was a real family effort, wasn't it? There were several outstanding family members, and their prosperity came from their use of advanced printing technology, in particular movable bronze type printing.

Irene: The reading passage showed us the difference between authors and editors, and explained how complicated it must have been in the days when editors had to re-arrange bamboo strips. Then Professor Richards gave us a lecture on the difference between official publications from the Imperial Government compared with the books published for the general public by the increasing numbers of private bookstores and printing houses. We had a really interesting discussion on our online forum about it.

Miriam: Yes, it was good, wasn't it? So what's the program for today?

Irene: Well, Professor Phillips is going to give us a historical note about a very beautiful part of Beijing with a rather strange name. It became a cultural centre in ancient China, and today is a well-known tourist attraction.

Owen: You say it has a strange name — you mean like Dashilan? That was a famous historical site, and the name meant "big fence". There aren't any fences there now, but they still use the same name.

Miriam: It's not a cultural center, though, is it? I've been there. It's a commercial area.

Irene: You're right, Miriam, Dashilan's a very well-known business area. The place I'm thinking of has a name that actually means Glass Factory, though there hasn't been a glass factory there for hundreds of years.

Owen: Oh, I've been there! You mean Liulichang? It's a fabulous place, full of antique shops and old bookstores and wonderful art galleries!

Miriam: Well, I get the Chang bit — that means factory — but what are *Liuli*?

Irene: *Liuli* are those coloured glaze tiles that they decorated palaces and temples with in ancient times. So Liulichang started as a factory, but then in the Ming Dynasty the factory was relocated and the area became an important cultural and intellectual center, especially for books, and continues to be so today.

Miriam: Well, I haven't been there yet, so I'm really looking forward to the Professor's lecture — and here he is!

Task 1 ▶ Listen to a historical note: Beijing Liulichang

Philips: Hello there, nice to see you again. You are all such keen students. This time I am going to talk about the famous cultural center — Liulichang in Beijing. I will cover the origin of Liulichang, its prosperity and its peak, its function as the distribution center of antiques, calligraphy, books and paintings, and why scholars and book sellers swarmed to this place and made it the heart of intellectuality and culture. I hope you will find my talk interesting. (You are required to fill in the blanks with the words and phrases you hear while listening)

Liulichang (Figure 5.1.1-2), which 1) _____ means "glass factory," takes its name from a famous glass kiln that was located in this part of the city during the Yuan, Ming, and Qing Dynasties. Boasting 2) _____ and pleasant surroundings, Liulichang was only a short distance from Xuannan, an area of Beijing where many scholars and 3) _____ . When Emperor Qian Long was in power (1736-1795), Liulichang flourished, reached its peak, and then became the collecting and distributing center of a diverse range of antique products, paintings, ancient books, and the Four Chinese Treasures Studio.

Figure 5.1.1: Antiques stall in Azure Stone Factory during the Republic of China era. (民国时期琉璃厂古玩摊)

Figure 5.1.2: Azure Stone Factory during the early period of the Republic of China era. (民国初年的琉璃厂)
(http://www.artintern.net/update/english/201309/484a7323906195767d77b3d07a9729d3)

Bookshops took over most of Liulichang. In the early years of the Qing Dynasty, most of Beijing's bookshops had been located in the area around 4) _____ , within the Guang'an Gate. However, after the Temple was destroyed in an earthquake in 1679, the number of bookshops in this part of Beijing gradually decreased as the book industry 5) _____ By 1769, there were more than 31 bookshops in Liulichang, among which Rongbaozhai (Studio of Glorious Treasures) (Figure 5.1.3) enjoyed great popularity. Moreover, Qianlong himself particularly favoured this place.

Figure 5.1.3: Studio of Glorious Treasures (Rongbaozhai) during the Republic of China era. (民国时期的荣宝斋)

In 1773, the Qianlong Emperor established a library to house the *Imperial Collection of Four*, and initiated 6) _____ to seek out privately collected books for 7) _____ the collection. Scholars from the library began appearing in Liulichang in large numbers, looking to locate and purchase books for the collection. At the same time, book sellers and books from the south of China began to flow northwards in increasingly large numbers as the center of China's woodblock printing industry gradually 8) _____ Suzhou, Hangzhou, and Nanjing in the south to Beijing in the north. The number of renowned bookshops in Liulichang soon neared 40, making it the center of Beijing's book industry. During the 9) _____ of the Xianfeng and Tongzhi emperors, many southern scholars who were unsuccessful in the imperial exams but reluctant to leave the rich cultural atmosphere of the capital decided to stay in Beijing as booksellers. The majority of these scholars were from Jiangxi. Towards the middle of the Guangxu Emperor's reign, large numbers of people from Hebei Province, most of whom were from Ji County, began to take up residence in Liulichang. A renowned scholar from the kingdom of Josean Yi Tongmu, who had traveled to Beijing as 10) _____ in 1778, described several of his visits to the bookstores of Liulichang in his travel memoir *Ru Yan*

Ji. In addition to recounting his experiences, Yi also recorded the names of 12 bookshops and more than 100 titles on sale. These records offer us some insight into the huge diversity of books available in bookstores at that time. The most renowned bookshops in Liulichang at that time were the Jiangu Hall, Wencui Hall, and the Wuliu Residence. The owners of all three bookshops were held in high regard for their familiarity with different book editions, and for their deep knowledge of books from both the north and the south of China. The owners of the Wuliu Residence and Wencui Hall, whose surnames were Tao and Jin respectively, were both booksellers from Suzhou. Every year they would purchase large numbers of books from Suzhou, which they transported to Beijing by boat. With the most extensive book collections in Liulichang, their bookshops were often visited by private buyers and officials from the imperial court. Yi Tongmu and his entourage were able to purchase several rare books from the Wuliu Residence, including *Commentaries to the Classics* (140 scrolls) by Zhu Yizun, *History Unraveled* by Ma Su, and the *Tinglin Collection*, all of which were forbidden books.

By the early years of the Guangxu Emperor, the number of bookshops in Liulichang had risen to more than 220. And yet in 1885, following a century of change, coupled with the confused fighting between the warlords, Liulichang met its waterloo. Consequently, only one bookshop from the Qianlong era was still present in Liulichang — the Erjiu Tang.

Task 2 ▶ Discuss the historical note
(Students are required to do role play in groups by imitating the PRIMO's dialogue)

Irene:	So, that's Liulichang — much more than just a book-selling center, eh Miriam? Did you say you'd never been there?
Miriam:	Not yet, but I'd love to go there with you guys. I've seen pictures, of course, all those traditional Chinese stone buildings covered in colored tiles and the shops selling all sorts of craft work and antiques.
Owen:	Yeah, let's all go together, you'll love it! You get this real feeling of history walking along the street — as Professor Phillips pointed out, it's been a flourishing cultural center for

	nearly 500 years, and it's still a favorite hangout for all sorts of scholars and artists and calligraphers, a real mixture of history and today's Beijing.
Irene:	Well put, Owen — a mixture of history and today.
Miriam:	I still have a question, though. How does a glass factory at the beginning of the Ming Dynasty become a famous cultural centre by the Qing Dynasty? I thought the cultural center of China was in the south, along the Yangzi River. That's where all the famous bookstores like the Chen and Hua Family Bookstores came from.
Owen:	Yeah, I have that problem too — why did they all move from the sunny south to the cold north, all those scholars and writers and publishers from Suzhou, Hangzhou, Nanjing?
Irene:	It's a good question, and I can answer it from general Chinese history. The glass factory was well-used by the Ming rulers who began to build their palaces in Beijing. But as Beijing expanded, the factory was relocated to the suburbs, leaving behind only its name. With the foundation of the Qing Dynasty, the ruling class established Beijing as the capital of the new dynasty. Nanjing, the old capital, gradually lost its influence. Naturally, the leading institutions of the south began to follow the government to the north. By this time, the glass factory road, which is pretty close to the center of the city, had become a center for intellectuals and artists and therefore of bookshops. Publishing moved north with the Emperor.
Miriam:	Right, so then when Emperors like Kangxi and Qianlong began to patronize the Liulichang bookshops, that would naturally attract other booksellers.
Irene:	Absolutely right! And don't forget that when Qianlong set up his Imperial Collection, he started a nationwide movement to collect and preserve ancient books. Huge numbers of scholars were attracted to Beijing and booksellers transported hundreds of thousands of books from all over China to the capital.
Owen:	So Liulichang flourished because of the political decisions and cultural policies of the Qing Dynasty! Thank you, Irene, that has really clarified things for me.

Miriam:	Me too, Irene. It really does help to be part of a team!	
Irene:	I agree — I get a lot from it, too. So, how about a trip to Liulichang this weekend, the three of us? With what we know about it now, it should be a really fruitful trip. All that history, and the wonderful artwork and craft on display — we should have a great time.	
Miriam:	Wonderful, Irene, I'm really looking forward to it.	
Owen:	Me too!	

Task 3 Build up our vocabulary
(Drag and match exercises)

Match the English words in column A with the Chinese equivalents in column B.

	A		B
1	bamboo strips	A	装盒
2	*Records of the Grand Historian*	B	《史记》
3	box-packaging	C	《太初历》
4	*Taichu Calendar*	D	编目
5	scroll rolling	E	单抬
6	*Buddhist Scriptures*	F	分色装潢制度
7	whirlwind binding	G	佛经
8	library for housing books	H	古抄本
9	compile bibliographies of titles	I	蝴蝶装
10	butterfly binding	J	集贤院
11	single elevation	K	简册文献
12	equal elevation	L	卷装
13	manuscript	M	秘书监
14	codex	N	平抬
15	the Virtuous	O	手抄善本
16	hand-copied versions	P	手稿；原稿
17	color coding system	Q	旋风装

Task 4 ▶ Reading activity

The following excerpt is about **The Artistic Design of Bookbinding and Page Layout,** *which is extracted from On the History of the book in China by Brokaw, Cynthia J., and Chow, Kai-Wing, eds. Studies on China. PRIMO members can expand and probe more complete aspects concerning publishing through reading.*

4.1 The Art of early Chinese bookbinding

Binding refers to the generic term for the artistic design and craft process of constructing books. It ultimately aims at protecting the interior part, facilitating reading and embellishing the exterior. The earliest book form in China was *Jian Ce* (简策), (Figure 5.4.1) i.e. bamboo strips strung together, which began in the Zhou Dynasty and became prevalent in the Qin-Han Dynasties. This was the earliest method of binding. At the same time, the *Ban Du* (版牍) (Figure 5.4.2) method was also in use. Ban referred to a blank wood tablet, while Du meant a wood tablet with characters engraved in it. After this, *Bo Shu* (帛书) (Figure 5.4.3), silk manuscripts in English, came into being. The three early types of binding were folding (折叠), which was often applied to large silk manuscripts or paintings, box-packaging (函装) (Figure 5.4.4), used for rectangular silk pages of similar sizes placed in the box in sequence, and scroll rolling (卷装) (Figure 5.4.5), joining all the silk pages together in the form of one long strip convenient for both rolling and hanging. All these fall into the category of early Chinese Bookbinding.

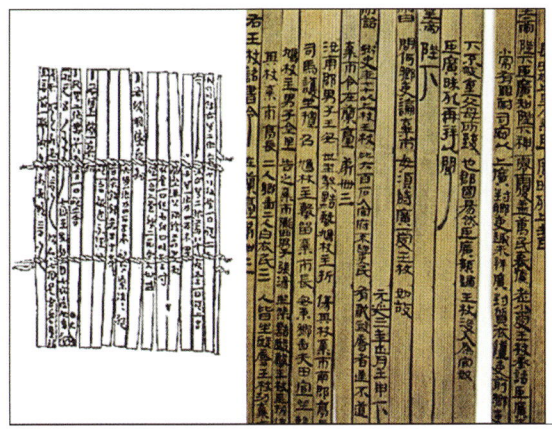

Figure 5.4.1: Bamboo strips for writing — *Jian Ce.*（简策）
(http://image53.360doc.com/DownloadImg/2012/07/2013/25632734_1)

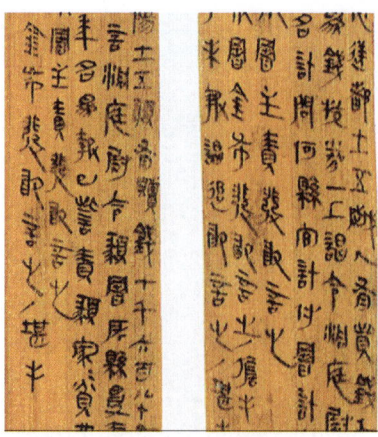

Figure 5.4.2: Wooden slips for writing — *Ban Du*. （版牍）
(http://img.blog.163.com/photo/exSYe67v8ezNlRBTqsesyw==/5759540973453515918)

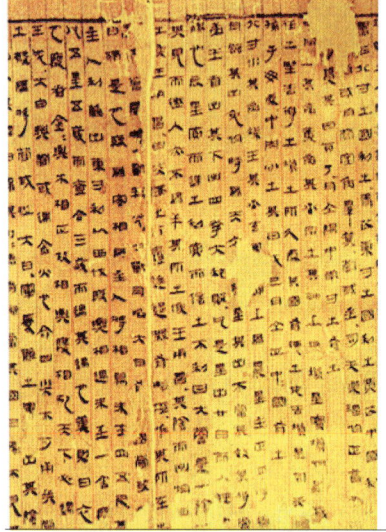

Figure 5.4.3: Silk Scroll unearthed in Mawangdui — *Bo Shu*. （马王堆出土的帛书）
(http://image83.360doc.com/DownloadImg/2015/03/2108/51415004)

Figure 5.4.4: *Box-packaging*. （函装）
(http://auction.ig365.cn/sdb/oldimg/1b52/1b52dc0c0358d22fe225d817a0456f0f)

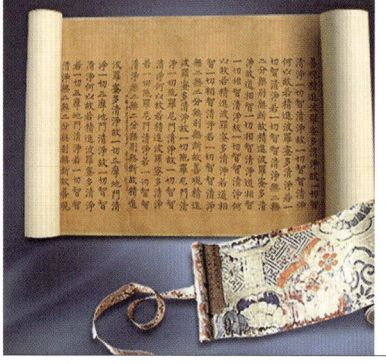

Figure 5.4.5: *Scroll rolling*. （卷装）
(http://tech2.npm.edu.tw/sutra/web/reason/images/b1_2)

Later on, the invention of paper and printing technology led to the increasing number of paper books, which in turn gave rise to the diverse methods of binding, for example, Sutra Binding and Thread-binding. In the Tang Dynasty, paper scroll rolls were gradually replaced by concertina (Sutra) binding (*jingzhe zhuang* 经折装) (Figure 5.4.6) in which the pages were folded flat rather than rolled up. This may have begun in imitation of the palm-leaf books of Buddhist scriptures imported from India (*fanjia zhuang* 梵夹装) (Figure 5.4.7).

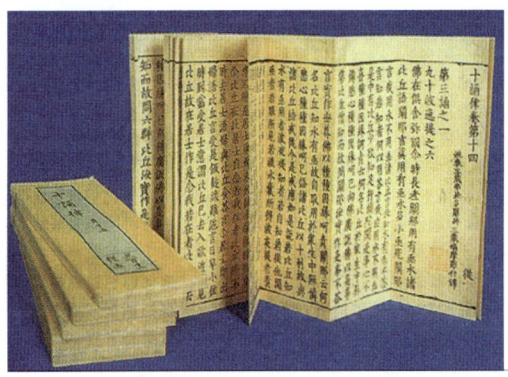

Figure 5.4.6: Accordion binding — *Jingzhe zhuang.* (经折装)
(http://image83.360doc.com/DownloadImg/2015/03/2108/51415004_41)

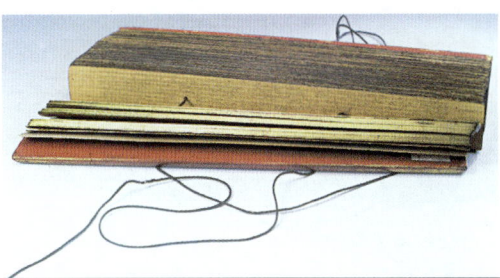

Figure 5.4.7: A kind of ancient Indian Sutra binding way — *Fanjia zhuang.* (梵夹装)
(http://s4.sinaimg.cn/middle/682341f84941eaa698de3&690)

The shift in ancient Rome from rolls to codex (a book made from leaves of folded paper; originally a wood tablet notebook not unlike the Chinese *pian* (篇) had begun at the end of the first century AD. By 300 AD, half of the extant books were written on rolls and half on codices. By 500 AD, 90 percent of all books were in codex form.

In China, a change to a new style of binding began in the seventh century and was well advanced by the ninth century. It was an adaptation of the scroll format, but had the advantage that both sides of the pages could be printed on. A series of pages, the first inscribed on one side, the rest inscribed on both sides, was pasted onto a long paper scroll, in overlapping sequence. When pasted, the leaves were read from left to right. When unrolled, the separately pasted pages swirl out and open as if blown by the wind. This method is known as whirlwind binding (*xuanfeng zhuang* 旋风装) (Figure 5.4.8). With the spread of printing, it became convenient to fold printed pages into two forms of facing pages that were bound together by pasting the backs of the folds, a method known as butterfly binding (*hudie zhuang* 蝴蝶装) (Figure 5.4.9). The disadvantage of this method was that after every two pages the reader encountered two blank pages. By the thirteenth century this had been overcome by folding the folio page backwards, that is, with the print on the outside of the pages, and then by pasting together the edges of the pages so that the reader encountered no blank pages (*baobei zhuang* 包背装) (Figure 5.4.10)A strong paper cover was wrapped around the pages, and the format was called wrapped-back binding. In the late Ming and early Qing Dynasties, thread stitching replaced pasting or paper for the binding to produce the familiar thread-bound book (*xianzhuang shu* 线装书) (Figure 5.4.11) with soft covers. Here and there these techniques of binding may have been used much earlier than this neat evolutionary picture suggests. Many photographs of these binding types can be found among the Dunhuang manuscripts.

Figure 5.4.8: Accordion-based bookbinding method with one piece of paper pasted on both book face cover and back cover — *Xuanfeng zhuang.* (旋风装)
(http://image48.360doc.com/DownloadImg/2012/01/1916/20852410_2)

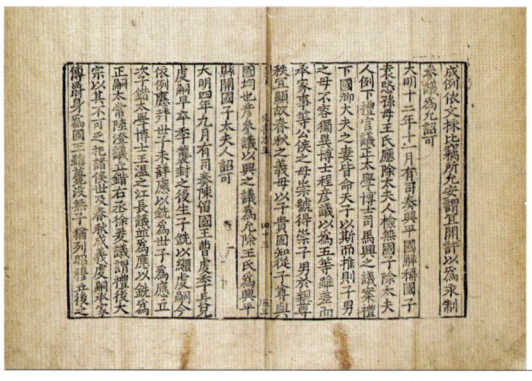

Figure 5.4.9: Butterfly binging—*Hudie zhuang.* (蝴蝶装)
(http://a3.att.hudong.com/18/86/01300535533055139213861646636)

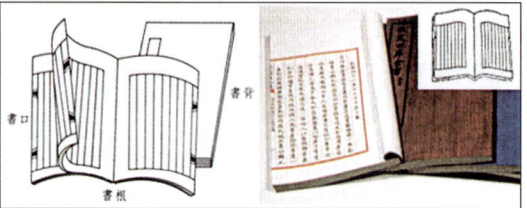

Figure 5.4.10: Wrapped-ridge binding — *Baobei zhuang.* (包背装)
(http://image53.360doc.com/DownloadImg/2012/07/2013/25632734_7)

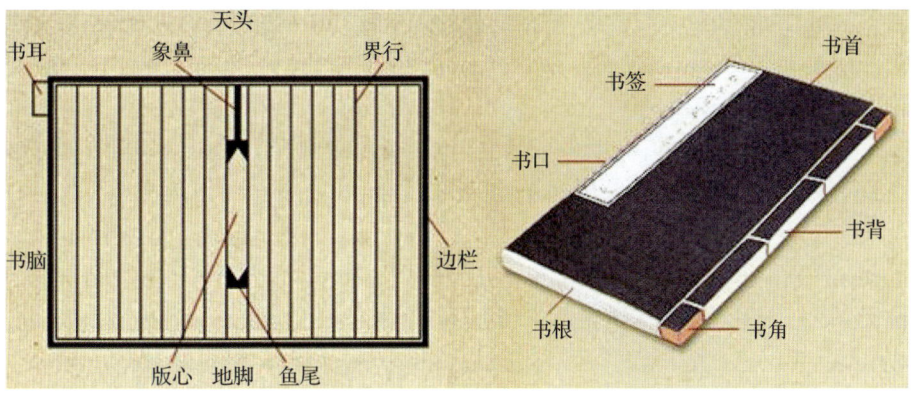

Figure 5.4.11: The sketch of the thread binding — *xianzhuang shu*. (线装书结构示意图)
(http://a.cvimg.cn/UploadFile/UserFiles/2012/5-16/d8ad5429-1dd9-4f1a-b787-7c1fc1941d8a.)

4.2 The design of page layout

Book binding embodies the exterior design of books. From ancient times, Chinese people also attached importance to the interior design of books, in other words, the design of page layout. The following three kinds of page layout are representative, of the most notable ones.

Taitou (抬头) in which the head of the column is elevated, *Taixie* (抬写) (Figure 5.4.12) being the general term. As a mark of respect, references to an emperor of the reigning dynasty either directly or indirectly, or to the titles of his close relatives or senior officials, or to the imperial buildings were usually elevated between one and three characters above the height of the regular columns of characters (the previous text simply stops elevated references to start a fresh column). The functional equivalent of *Taitou* in European and American orthography is the use of capitals, for example, " the President and First Lady returned to the White House." The first glimpses of *Taitou* can be seen on the bamboo strips of the Han Dynasty. Later, it was continued on paper and other stationery as well as in books. By the end of the Qing Dynasty the rules laid down in the *Huidian* were as follows:

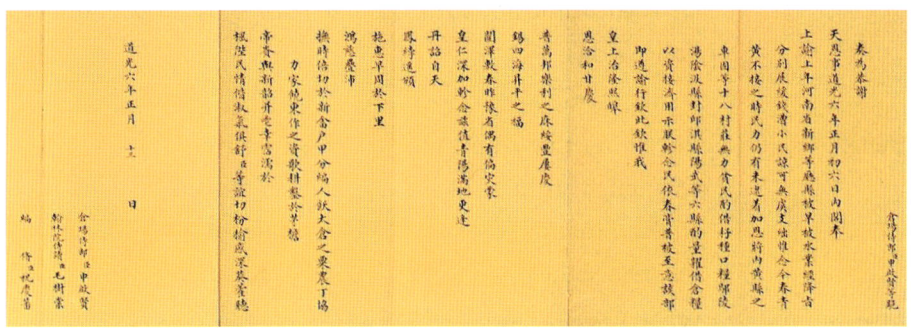

Figure 5.4.12: The way of addressing the title in Qing Dynasty. (清代奏折的"抬头"格式)
(http://pmgs.kongfz.com/data/pre_show_pic/1/10/003)

Single elevation (*Dantai* 单抬) for references to the abodes of majesty, the attributes of government, proceedings addressed to the sovereign, and reference to supernatural powers.

Double elevation (*Shuangtai* 双抬) was allocated to characters referring to the person, attributes, or actions of the reigning sovereign or his consorts.

Triple elevation (*Santai* 三抬) for references by the sovereign to his ancestors, to their places of interment, and to the powers of nature and places of worship. If the words that received double elevation for a reigning sovereign were used in connection with a deceased sovereign of the dynasty in power they received triple elevation. References to an emperor of a previous dynasty were not normally elevated.

The Ming system of *Taitou* was somewhat more elaborate in that several hundred words were specified for elevation on the page. Another relevant design worth mentioning is *Taihang* — raising the line. It was customary in letters to elevate the name or attributes of the recipient by two characters above the regular column, compared to the widespread practice in English letter writing of placing the greeting and name of the recipient on the line above the body of the text.

At the end of the Qing Dynasty, in diplomatic correspondence between foreign powers and the foreign ministry, both sides in referring to the other elevated the reference to the head of the next column. This treatment was appropriately called "equal elevation" (*Pingtai* 平抬).

Task 5 ▶ Reading comprehension

(Students are required to launch a discussion to pose new questions and answer all the questions raised in the dialogue, and do the role play based on the following)

Irene: The thing that impresses me from reading that excerpt is how much art there has always been in the craft of producing books. From the external binding to the internal page layout, we can see the beauty as well as the function of a book.

Miriam: What I found fascinating was the relationship between the binding techniques and the writing materials available —

	threading bamboo strips into rolled bundles is the only way to do it, isn't it?
Owen:	True. The thing I liked was the way Chinese culture interacted with other cultures to produce things like the sutra translations and also the sutra binding method.
Irene:	Should we try to draw a timeline and then put each binding method on it in a time sequence? We might be able to understand it better that way.
Miriam:	I think we will — but we also have to remember, as Owen pointed out, that this timeline describes other eastern cultures as well — the Koreans, the Japanese, and the Vietnamese. The first stage was from the Zhou to the Qin-Han Dynasties — their earliest book form was *Jian Ce* — bamboo strips bound together with twine or thread.
Owen:	You could also have *Ban Du*, which were tablets of wood linked together with twine, and that was the same sort of time, wasn't it?
Irene:	Yes, and after that came *Bo Shu*, which was printing or writing on silk — can you remember the three ways of storing *Bo Shu*.
Miriam:	Yes, it wasn't exactly binding, was it? You had folding, box-packaging individual squares or pages of silk, and then scroll rolling.
Owen:	The really big change came with paper, though, didn't it? Didn't you have different forms of binding starting in the Tang Dynasty.
Irene:	Yes, you mentioned it before, Owen. In the Tang Dynasty you had sutra folding, which originated in India with folded palm leaves that opened out like a concertina. It made it easier to read the middle section of a book, as you didn't have to open a whole scroll to get there.
Miriam:	Another scroll-like arrangement was whirlwind binding — I love that name! Pages that were printed on both sides were pasted by their edges onto a long scroll, but overlapping, so one page at a time came up as you unrolled.
Owen:	I prefer the name of the next technique — butterfly binding.

	It's the first binding that begins to look like a modern book. A big folio leaf that had two pages printed on it was folded in half, with the words on the inside. Lots of these folded leaves were stacked together and then pasted together at the folds to form a book. The leaves opened up and closed like a butterfly's wings.
Irene:	That's a good description, Owen. But butterfly binding had a disadvantage — pages 1 and 2 had words on them, but pages 3 and 4 were blank, all the way through the book.
Miriam:	The solution was simple, though, wasn't it? With wrapped-back binding, they simply folded the folio pages the other way round, so that the words were on the outsides of the pages. Then they pasted and stacked the edges together so that the blank pages were on the inside and therefore not seen. Then you had a book that looked just like a modern book.
Irene:	Absolutely right, Miriam, you understood that perfectly. All of those binding methods affected the outside of the book, but even more importantly, there were design considerations that affected the internal layout of the pages. Did you get a good idea of the three different levels of character elevation?
Owen:	I think I got that — weren't they used to refer to different levels of the people or things being addressed? Single elevation was for abodes of majesty, attributes of government and so on, while double elevation was for the person or actions of the reigning sovereign and his consorts.
Miriam:	That's right. And triple elevation was used by the emperor for reference to his ancestors, the power of nature, and places of worship. In other words, elevation was used to denote the relative status of the two sides. Is it still used in modern China, Irene?
Irene:	Not really. Nowadays you may see *Taitou* printed at the head of an invoice or some formal business letter to show respect to the addressee, but otherwise, in normal daily life, there's no special requirement to use elevation.

Task 6 ▶ Translation practice

(Students are required to translate the following Chinese paragraph into English individually, in pairs or in group)

Owen: So, we've established the timeline for different binding methods. We've discussed the design and page layout. Shall we get on with the translation task now?

Miriam: Good idea, Owen. But I've had a quick look at it, and it's all about publishing in the Five Dynasties and the Ten Kingdoms. Ancient Chinese history is not my strong point — we're going to need a lot of help from you, Irene.

Irene: Don't worry. I can give you any historical background you need — just let me know when there's anything you don't understand.

Owen: Great! Let's get going.

唐末时期刻印书籍很多，人文荟萃，由于纸张和印刷术的日趋成熟，为印造书籍提供了良好的客观条件。接下来的五代十国是历史上紊乱的时期，国内四分五裂，出现各地军阀割据的局面，短短五十三年换了五个朝代。但是在印造书籍史上却呈现出前所未有的繁荣时期，印刷术在五代十国时期大为流行，成为蒸蒸日上的新兴事业。五代十国时期刻书除民间私刻外，政府复出版大批课本，比如，当时的四川已有很多书坊，成为全国出版业的中心。五代十国时期刻书对后世影响最大的是冯道，当冯道发现吴蜀之人贩卖的各色各类的印板文字，唯独缺少儒家经典时，就发起雕版群刻，刻板印卖。他先召集能书人才，依照唐代的石经文字，端楷写出，然后再召雇雕字匠人进行雕刻，历经数十年，完成了《九经》经典著作。五代十国时期的刻本除佛、道及儒家经典外，还有文学、史书、法律、类书、历本等，遗憾的是多数没能传承下来，现存的五代十国时期印刷品有一些珍藏在敦煌，也有许多早已流落到国外。由于五代十国时期的统治阶级对印刷事业的大加提倡，刻书不只是民间书坊或和尚、道士的事，而成为政府的出版事业，对印刷出版起到了很大的推动作用。

Task 7 ▶ Attend Professor Richards's public lecture

Lecture 5

Official Book Collecting from the Xia Dynasty to the Five Dynasties
professor Richards

Hello again. You may remember that in my last lecture concerning the history of publishing in China, I addressed the various methods of Chinese publishing during the Dynastic periods, especially in the Ming and Qing Dynasties. Today I am going to talk about the history of book collecting in ancient China.

Book collecting has a long tradition in China. Generally speaking, there are two types of book collectors: official collectors, and private collectors. Of course, official collectors are government sponsored, while private collectors are, well, just about everybody else… and perhaps falling somewhere in between would be the collection of books by educational academies and either Buddhist or Taoist temples.

Today's lecture will focus on the history of book collecting by official collectors, basically emperors, and span a time period beginning with the Xia Dynasty and ending with the Five Dynasties period. The lecture is in three parts: the beginning, the evolution and prosperity, and the decline of book collecting. The history is interesting, not only from the standpoint of how the various governments organized their collections, but also from the perspective of how the success or failure of the practice of book collecting fluctuated depending on the political and social agendas of a given time period.

7.1 The Beginning of Ancient Chinese books collection (Xia, Shang and Zhou)

Historically, official book collectors included royal families and various government designated organizations. The collections these organizations amassed served an important role in the compilation, editing and storing of national archives. The archives included histories, bibliographies and encyclopedias, all of which contained the information necessary for the continuation and proliferation of cultural traditions in ancient China.

Official book collecting began as early as the Xia Dynasty. At that time historians were appointed to make records of what was said in the royal court.

These records were then arranged and stored in the ancestral temple of the ruling dynasty. It was also during this period that the practice of attaching ten pieces of writing together to make one *Juan* or scroll developed a tradition that carried through to the Shang and Zhou Dynasties.

During the Shang Dynasty the royal family collected both oracle bone inscriptions and bamboo scrolls, although they were careful to store the two separately. The bones and scrolls were each catalogued and then arranged in sequence for storage pursuant to a system based on heavenly stems and earthly branches. The system was highly organized and only designated historians were allowed access to documents, with each addition or withdrawal being recorded.

The system for storing Zhou Dynasty records was even more elaborate; books and various documents were stored in a number of different locations by specified organizations, including the Ancestral Temple, the Historical Commission and the Hall of Treaties. The primary function of these groups was to provide reading material and political advice for the royal family. Records kept by the Zhou kings consisted mainly of bamboo strips, although oracle bones and copper carvings were also stored. Additionally, written materials from previous generations and writings presented to the kings as gifts were also stored. Consequently, the content of the collection of the Zhou kings was varied, and covered the six domains of the arts, law, astronomy, geography, literature and engineering. Other texts included the writing of the Zhou kings, official documents, national histories and writings collected from vassal states.

7.2 Evolution of book collecting through the Qin, Han, Wei, and Jin Dynasties

The Qin Dynasty was very severe in its treatment of books from previous eras and books containing content which did not fit into its philosophy. Qin Shihuang, the first emperor of a unified China, ordered many books to be burned and that strict controls be placed on private collectors (Figure 5.7.1). Of the few books that have survived from that time, the majority are Qin histories, books collected by scholar officials, and books on medicine, fortune telling and agriculture.

Figure 5.7.1: Ruins of burning books and burying the literati in pits in Qin Dynasty. (陕西渭南地区传说中的秦朝"焚书堆"遗址)
(http://www.dictall.com/picture/bkimg/da_6/F0683_0)

The Han Dynasty took a different approach to collecting books and it began with an individual by the name of Xiao He, the first PRIMO Minister of the Han Dynasty, who under orders from the emperor, began to amass a large book collection. The collection comprised official books from the former residence of the Qin PRIMO Minister, public donations, and through efforts to locate and acquire surviving texts. As a result of his endeavors, Xiao He was able to fill three halls with the imperial book collections (Figure 5.7.2). Over time the collection of books grew until nine halls were required for their storage. The halls were given different names, and the more important or rare books housed separately. During his reign, Emperor Wu of Han ordered a major overhaul of his imperial library. The overhaul resulted in the first known Chinese bibliography called the *Qi Lue*, (Figure 5.7.3) or Seven Abstracts. It was also during this time that a court astrologer named Sima Qian compiled the *Records of the Grand Historian* and made revisions to the *Taichu Calendar*. (Figure 5.7.4)

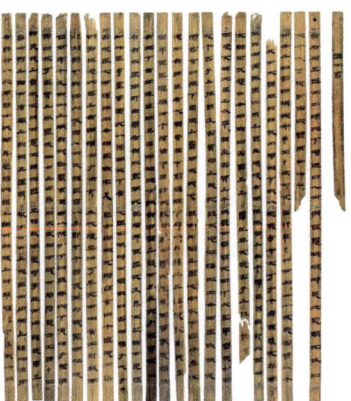

Figure 5.7.2: *Zhao Zhengshu* written on the Han Dynasty wooden strips or bamboo slips, --Xiao He's collection of books, housed in Peking University. (萧何搜书成果的汉简《赵正书》，北京大学收藏)
(http://image.thepaper.cn/wap/image/4/567/148)

七略佚文敘　山陰姚振宗錄
敘七略本末第一
漢書劉向傳向少子歆最知名歆字子駿少以通詩書能屬文召見成帝待詔宦者署為黃門郎河平中受詔與父向領校祕書講六藝傳記諸子詩賦數術方技無所不究向死後歆復為中壘校尉哀帝初卽位大司馬王莽舉歆宗室有材行為侍中太中大夫遷騎都尉奉車光祿大夫貴幸復領五經卒父前業歆乃集六藝羣書種別為七略歆以建平元年改名秀字穎叔云
又傳贊曰七略剖判藝文總百家之緒有意其推本之也師古曰言其究極根本深有意也
荀悅漢紀劉向卒上復使其子歆繼卒父業而歆遂撰羣書而奏七略有輯略有六藝略有諸子略有詩賦略有兵書略有數術略有方技略凡萬三千二百六十九卷
又漢紀論曰孝武皇帝時董仲舒推崇孔氏抑黜百家至劉向父子典校經籍而新義分方九流區別典籍益彰矣
梁阮孝緒七錄敘目曰會向亡哀帝使歆嗣其前業乃徙溫室中書於天祿閣上歆遂總括羣篇奏其七略及後漢蘭臺猶為書部又於東觀及仁壽閣撰集新記校書郎班固傅毅並典秘籍乃因七略之辭為漢書藝文志
又曰劉向校書輒為一錄論其指歸辨其訛謬隨竟奏上皆載在本書時又別集衆錄謂之別

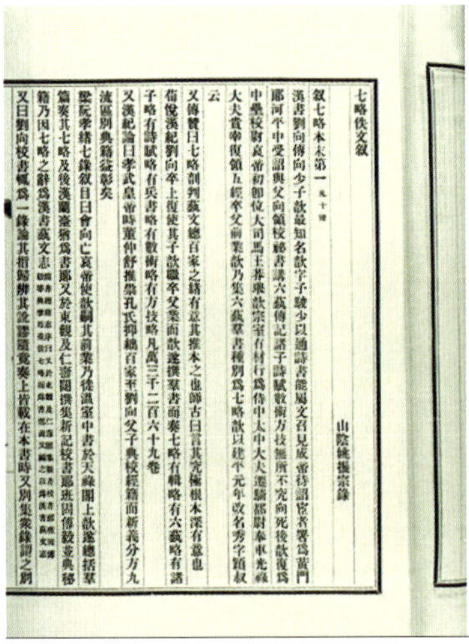

Figure 5.7.3: *Qi Lue* — stereotype edition in the era of the Republic of China by Yao Zhenzong. (清代姚振宗辑《七略》民国铅印本)
(http://book.cssn.cn/ts/ts_slcs/201402/W020140213397400550684)

Figure 5.7.4: *Taichu Calendar* based on the astronomical map drawn by Sima Qian. （根据司马迁《太初历》绘制的天文图表）
(http://c.hiphotos.baidu.com/baike/w%3D268/sign=3d44cbf8442309f7e76faa144a0e0c39/3bf33a87e950352ab452fb645143fbf2b2118baf)

The palace book collection of the Eastern Han Dynasty was better organized and many times larger than its predecessor, more similar in scope and splendor to the palace collections of the Warring States period. Famous halls housed the collection which included a vast range of books, including books from all the major schools of thought, including a collection of Buddhist scripture. During the reign of Emperor Ming, a large number of scholars were ordered to organize, edit and correct the books in the imperial collection. As a result of their efforts the classic histories such as the *Book of Han* and *Dong Han Ji* were compiled. (Figure 5.7.5)

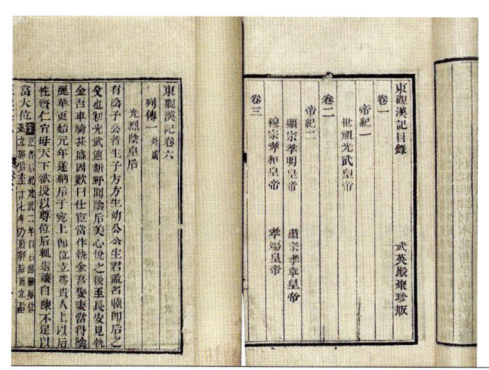

Figure 5.7.5: *Dong Han Ji*—Wuyinydian. （清代武英殿聚珍版《东观汉记》）
(http://www.zgsd.net/userfiles/product/img/20111115/big/1111-244.)

Official or palace book collecting continued into the Wei-Jin periods; it was during this time that the imperial collection began its transition into collecting books made only of paper. The period is especially noted for the organization of its book collections. For instance: the Cao-Wei government not only established a library for housing books on art and literature but also appointed scholars to manage collections and compile bibliographies of titles. The Western Jin Dynasty scholar, Xun Xu, developed a system for the classification of books in his book *Zhong Jing Xin Bu*. The system was based on the Jia, Yi, Bing and Ding characters which represented the Confucian classics, philosophy, history and anthologies, respectively. The Emperor Wu of Jin appointed four officials known as the "Mishu Lang" to manage the Confucian classics, history, philosophy and anthology portions of his collection. In the Eastern Jin Dynasty, Li Chong's *Jin Yuandi Sibu Shulu*, (Figure 5.7.6) set a standard for the classification of books based on Xun Xu's system; this system for categorizing books would be emulated for generations.

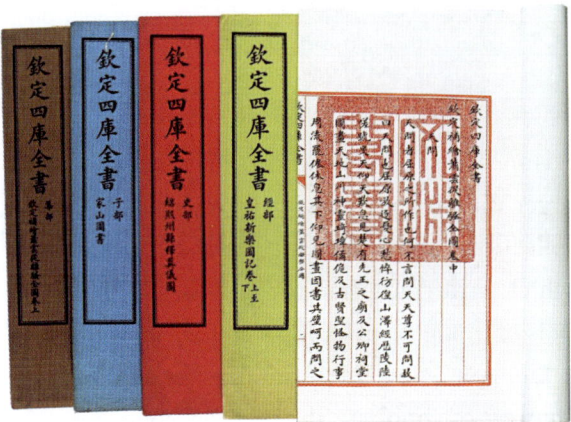

Figure 5.7.6: *Jin Yuandi Sibu Shulu* — part of the *Siku Quanshu* or Complete Library in the Four Branches of Literature of the Pavilion of Literary Profundity, photomechanical printing by the Commercial Press. （源自《晋元帝四部书目》四部分类法的文渊阁本《四库全书》（商务印书馆影印））
(http://www.zgsd.net/userfiles/product/img/20100518/big/1005-272.)

7.3 The interwoven prosperity and decline of book collecting (the Song, Tang and Five Dynasties)

Following the Wei-Jin period, official collecting continued into the Southern Dynasties period. An avid scholar and book collector, Xiao Yan, the Emperor Wu of Liang, increased the palace book collection to over 10,000 scrolls, the largest collection of the Southern Dynasties period. The emperor had the entire collection catalogued on two separate occasions and also established the "Zheng Yu Ben" system of producing hand-copied texts.

Unfortunately, most of the collection of the Southern Dynasties period was destroyed owing to the social turmoil of the Northern Dynasties period. In fact the only notable book collecting effort during the Northern Dynasties period took place in the Northern Wei period when the government implemented four large scale book searches and reorganized the imperial book collection.

From the turmoil of the Northern Dynasties, China entered an era of great prosperity during the Sui, Tang and Five Dynasties periods. Throughout this time, China was strong and prosperous, culture flourished and the imperial examination system continued to develop, all of which resulted in extremely well managed and maintained book collections. Official collections not only benefitted from the importance the emperors placed on them, but also from the advent of woodblock printing. For instance, the Emperor Wen of Sui not only took possession of the book collection of the Northern Zhou, but also ordered the widespread collection of books from the public, as well as the retrieval of books from the Southern Dynasties. He then ordered that all of the books collected be hand-copied and then built a hall to house his collection of over 37,000 scrolls.

It was during the Sui Dynasty that two halls were built in the eastern capital of Luoyang to house the imperial collection. The *Mi Ge*, (Figure 5.7.7) as the imperial collection was known, was home to a large number of scholars who worked on the organization, editing and revision of books. Notable figures from the time include Xu Shanxin and Liu Guyan, who compiled the bibliographies *Seven Forests* and the *Dayezheng Imperial Book Catalogue* (Figure 5.7.8).

Figure 5.7.7: *Mi Ge* — the Pavilion Library for storage of rare books. (北宋宫中与秘阁同样收藏珍本秘籍的藏书楼 —— 太清楼)
(http://img5.duitang.com/uploads/item/201112/16/20111216212751_BMNrz.thumb.700)

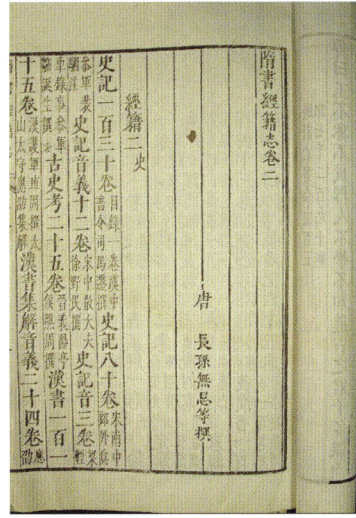

Figure 5.7.8: *Dayezheng Imperial Book Catalogue* printed in Qing Dynasty. (参考《隋大业正御书目录》撰成的《隋书经籍志》清代印本)
(http://pmgs.kongfz.com/data/pre_show_pic/10/24/437)

During the early years of the Tang Dynasty the Imperial Library was headed by such noted scholars as Wei Zheng, Yu Shinan and Yan Shigu. Not only did the library incorporate what remained of the collection from the Sui Dynasty, but it also spent money to acquire texts from private collectors which were then copied and stored.

The Imperial Library of the Tang Dynasty was largest during the reign of Emperor Xuanzong. Interestingly, the library was considered to be an independent organization and was responsible for both its own management and collection of books. Overall the library comprised a number of different halls and pavilions (Figure 5.7.9), with the majority located within the imperial palace itself.

Figure 5.7.9: The Tang Dynasty Pavilion for compiling and editing books. (唐代馆阁学士编校书籍图)

(http://img.itc.cn/x/m_-250x100_1_saa/saapic/t/21264093.jpg_s780)

The halls worked in conjunction with one another although each hall was also assigned a specific set of tasks which were then supervised by the PRIMO minister, leading officials from the court, and on a smaller level, by scholars of varying rank. For instance, the oldest and most influential of the halls, termed the Hongwen Gallery (Figure 5.7.10), was involved in the amendment and production of books, academic research, recruiting students, and teaching and deliberating political affairs, while the Court of the Virtuous focused on editing and publishing classic texts and collecting and composing essays. The Court of the Virtuous was the most important site for book collecting during the Tang Dynasty; to give you an idea of the scope of this hall, as many as 89,000 scrolls were stored there at one time. The scrolls themselves were high quality hand-copied versions which had been expertly checked and amended by one of the over 100 copiers assigned to the task.

Figure 5.7.10: Hongwen Gallery — reconstructed and repaired on the ruins of Tang Daming Palace. (唐代大明宫含元殿遗址附近的弘文馆复原建筑)

(http://img.itc.cn/x/m_-250x100_1_saa/saapic/t/21264092.jpg_s780)

The Tang Dynasty contributed much to the art of book collecting. The court's collection was highly organized and divided into four main sections, including Confucian Classics, history, philosophy and anthologies or collected works. Furthermore, an advanced color coding system was implemented in order to designate the various book categories. You only had to find the right colored ribbons and labels to identify the type of book you possessed.

In large part, the Five Dynasties period continued the practices developed during the Tang Dynasty. Unfortunately, the Five Dynasties period was not as peaceful a time as the Tang Dynasty and due to wars and various conflicts, the palace book collections decreased significantly in size.

7.4 Conclusion

That concludes my lecture on the history of official or government sponsored book collecting. I hope you found it useful to the understanding of how the various dynasties acquired, organized and propagated their collections. Book collecting was an important historical tradition and, along with the invention of printing and paper and the subsequent development of publishing, was the fundamental precondition for the continuation of cultural traditions in ancient China.

It would probably not surprise you to know that people have been collecting books for a long time and this is an extremely good thing because many of these collections have provided us with books that have not only enabled us the opportunity to look into the past, but have also provided us with knowledge that has accumulated over the centuries, and, perhaps most importantly, have allowed for the continuation and cultivation of both regional and national customs and traditions. Perhaps one day you will be in a position to acquire a book of some merit. I hope so, because it would be an item you will not only treasure, but a gift that you can leave to future generations. Let me leave you with a few questions for you to consider and answer perhaps in your online forum. First, who were the two main types of book collectors in ancient China? Secondly, can you give a brief description of official book collecting in the Xia, Shang, and Zhou Dynasties? Thirdly, what was the main contrast in official attitudes towards books between the Qin and the Han Dynasties? Fourthly, when did book collecting reach its peak in ancient China? And fifthly, can you do some research and tell me how far the collecting and buying and selling of rare old books has become big business in China? Good luck with your answers to those questions, and I'll see you all next time.

Task 8 ▶ Join the online forum and write a summary

(Students are required to have an instant and online post-talk discussion)

Irene:	Well, PRIMO group, that was a pretty comprehensive lecture on book collecting in ancient China, wasn't it? What did you think of Professor Richards' questions?
Owen:	I'd like to answer the first one — it was the easiest! There were two main types of collector — official and private. Official collectors were sponsored by the government, and private collectors were… well, everybody else.
Irene:	Well done, Owen — as you said, the easiest of the questions. But who were these official collectors, and why was their work important?
Owen:	Ah, well… the official collectors included the royal family, of course, because they were always among the best educated. And then there would be the organisations designated by the imperial government, civil servants I suppose we would call them today. They played an important role in the collection, editing, and classifying of what became the national archives — the histories, the bibliographies, the encyclopedias. These archives recorded and preserved ancient Chinese culture and traditions.
Irene:	That's better, Owen, a rather more complete answer — I knew you could do it. I wonder if Miriam can show us how to answer a rather more difficult question completely? Can you give a brief description of official book collecting in the Xia, Shang, and Zhou Dynasties?
Miriam:	I'll try, Irene. I'll read from my notes: Official book collecting began as early as the Xia Dynasty. At that time historians were appointed to record what was said in the royal court. These records were then arranged and stored in the ancestral temple of the ruling dynasty. And then in the Shang Dynasty, the royal family collected both oracle bone inscriptions and bamboo scrolls and stored the two separately. In the Zhou

	Dynasty, the storing of records was even more elaborate: books and various documents were stored in a number of different locations by specified organizations, including the Ancestral Temple, the Historical Commission, and the Hall of Treaties. The primary function of these groups was to provide reading material and political advice for the royal family.
Irene:	What do you think of that answer, Owen?
Owen:	Well, it was a bit longer than my first answer — and altogether it was really rather brilliant, Miriam. Great stuff!
Irene:	One thing I have to mention — probably better that I do it. One difficult thing to describe that has to be on our list is the burning of books and the burying of scholars. I'm talking about what happened during the reign of the First Emperor of the Qin Dynasty — he burned hundreds of books and buried Confucian scholars. We lost many philosophical treatises of the Hundred Schools of Thought, not to mention the loss of the intellectuals. It did huge damage to the Chinese intellectual heritage.
Owen:	A great loss, Irene — but it wasn't the first in the history of mankind, and certainly wasn't the last. They're still burning books, even in the 21st century — and not in China.
Miriam:	And besides, the Han Dynasty took the opposite approach to book collecting. Xiao He, the first PRIMO Minister of the Han Dynasty, under orders from the emperor, began to amass a large book collection. It was also in the Han Dynasty that a court astrologer Sima Qian compiled the *Records of the Grand Historian* and made revisions to the *Taichu Calendar*.
Irene:	Quite right, Miriam. And then after that the Han, Wei, and Jin Dynasties saw the popularity of book collecting led by influential officials appointed by the Emperors: Xiao He in the Han Dynasty, Xun Xu in the Wei Dynasty and Li Chong in the Jin Dynasty all amassed large amounts of books through various means for the emperors. And their collections laid the basis for the success of book collecting in the Song and Tang Dynasties.
Owen:	Right! And it was during the Tang and Song Dynasties that book collecting in ancient China reached its peak. Scholar

	officials like Weizheng and Yan Shigu were in charge of official collection, and they not only took over the inheritance from former dynasties, but also purchased important books from private collectors.
Irene:	And that's an important point, Owen — they purchased rare books. And today it's become a huge business — buying and selling old books. Did either of you do any research on that?
Miriam:	Yes, I did, and I was amazed! Do you know how much a scroll by the calligrapher Wang Xizhi sold for in 2010?
Owen:	Wang Xizhi — he was 4th century AD, wasn't he — erm, I don't know, ten million RMB?
Miriam:	Owen, come on! Three hundred and eight million *yuan*!
Owen:	Wow!
Irene:	And the same year, a scroll by Huang Tingjian sold for 436.8 million. What do you think of that?
Owen:	Well, I'm amazed of course — but why so much just for handwriting?
Miriam:	Oh Owen, Chinese calligraphy isn't just handwriting, it's an art form! Most calligraphy expresses a poem or a beautiful saying.
Irene:	And there's often a beautiful water colour as well. Owen, think of those wonderful mediaeval hand-copied versions of the Bible with their beautiful italic script and hand-painted illustrations — how much are they worth today?
Owen:	Oh that's true — tens of millions of dollars. I'm sorry, Irene, I wasn't thinking!
Miriam:	So altogether we can say that the history of publishing in China actually reflects very accurately the history of China itself, and of its culture.
Irene:	Well said, Miriam!

Appendix: Vocabulary for Unit 5

Historical Note
kiln /kɪln/ *n.* 窑炉
picturesque /ˌpɪktʃə'resk/ *adj.* 独特的；生动的；别致的；图画般的
benevolence /bə'nevələns/ *n.* 仁慈；捐赠
incorporation /ɪnˌkɔːpə'reɪʃ(ə)n/ *n.* 公司；合并，编入；团体组织
memoir /'memwɑː(r)/ *n.* 回忆录；自传
envoy /'envɒɪ/ *n.* 使者；全权公使
entourage /'ɒntʊrɑːʒ/ *n.* 随从；周围；环境
unravel /ˌʌn'rævəl/ *vt.* 解开；阐明，解决；拆散
　　　　　　　　　　 vi. 解决；散开

Reading Activity
generic /dʒɪ'nerɪk/ *adj.* 类的；一般的；属的；非商标的
facilitate /fə'sɪlɪteɪt/ *vt.* 促进；帮助；使容易
embellish /ɪm'belɪʃ/ *vt.* 修饰；润色
prevail /prɪ'veɪl/ *vi.* 盛行，流行；战胜，获胜
tablet /'tæblɪt/ *n.* 碑；写字板；小块；药片
manuscript /'mænjʊskrɪpt/ *n.* 手稿；原稿；手写本
codex /'kəʊdeks/ *n.* 法典；古抄本；药典
accordion /ə'kɔːdɪən/ *n.* 手风琴
exterior /ɪk'stɪərɪə/ *adj.* 外部的；表面的；外在的
elevate /'elɪveɪt/ *vt.* 提升；举起；振奋情绪等；提升……的职位
orthography /ɔː'θɒɡrəfɪ/ *n.* 正确拼字；正字法；正字学
equivalent /ɪ'kwɪv(ə)l(ə)nt/ *n.* 等价物，相等物
consort /'kɒnsɔːt/ *n.* 配偶；伙伴
internment /ɪn'tɜːnmənt/ *n.* 拘留；收容
recipient /rɪ'sɪpɪənt/ *n.* 容器，接受者；容纳者

Lecture
fluctuate /'flʌktʃʊeɪt; -tjʊ-/ *vi.* 波动；涨落；动摇
　　　　　　　　　　　　　　 vt. 使波动；使动摇
agenda /ə'dʒendə/ *n.* 议程；日常工作事项
designated /'dezɪɡˌneɪtɪd/ *adj.* 指定的；特指的
amassed /ə'mæst/ *vt.* 积聚，积累

archive /ˈɑrkaɪv/ n. 档案馆；档案文件
pursuant /pəˈsjuːənt/ adj. 依据的；追赶的；随后的
endeavor /ɪnˈdevə/ n. 努力；尽力 (等于endeavour)
overhaul /əʊvəˈhɔːl/ n. 彻底检修；详细检查
astrologer /əˈstrɒlədʒə/ n. 占星家
turmoil /ˈtɜːmɒɪl/ n. 混乱；骚动

Unit 6

Major Accomplishments in the Chinese Publishing Industry

TABLE OF CONTENTS

Warm-up: Be proactive

Task 1 Listen to a historical note: Iconic Book Collectors in Ancient China

Task 2 Discuss the historical note

Task 3 Build up our vocabulary

Task 4 Reading activity: History of Book Illustration

Task 5 Reading comprehension

Task 6 Translation practice

Task 7 Attend a public lecture: The Radical Transitions in the Field of Chinese Publishing

Task 8 Join the online forum and write a summary

Appendix: Vocabulary for Unit 6

Unit 6: Major Accomplishments in the Chinese Publishing Industry

WARM-UP: Be proactive

Irene: Hi, there PRIMO group. How was your weekend? I was so sorry I couldn't come with you to Liulichang — how did you enjoy the visit?

Miriam: We missed you, of course Irene, and needed your help sometimes, but it was a great experience. I just loved all those old stone houses, and the sheer number of Chinese folk art shops rather overwhelmed me, frankly. There was every conceivable form of art and craft — paintings, calligraphy, pottery, carpets, vases, books and scrolls and seals… it was just amazing!

Owen: And you would have been proud of us, Irene — we even went into a bookshop and try to bargain for a really old book. We saw examples of all the old book-binding techniques that we were studying last week.

Irene: Oh, that's great — you saw sutra binding, whirlwind and butterfly?

Miriam: We saw all of those, and it was great to see them in real life as it were. We even saw bamboo-strip scrolls and some beautiful silk scrolls.

Irene: And which category does the book you bought belong to?

Owen: Oh, it's thread-bound — to be frankly we really couldn't afford to buy the older types, but the book-sellers were quite happy to show us some really old books even though they knew we wouldn't be able to afford any of them. Those guys really know their history.

Miriam: Yes, one shopkeeper even sounded as if he'd attended Professor Richard's lecture. He told us about official collections in the Xia Dynasty, and how collection developed from the Qin to the Jin Dynasty and reached its peak in the Tang and Song Dynasties.

Irene: Well, booksellers are usually scholars as well, as we learned from the famous book stores of the Chen and Hua families. And in fact Professor Phillips will be talking about private book collections in his historical note today. It'll be a supplement to Professor Richards' lecture last week.

Owen: That sounds intriguing. But I'm wondering what sort of person managed to collect and preserve books in adverse conditions in ancient China.

Irene: I'm sure Professor Phillips will introduce us to some of the famous collectors from the olden days and describe how they passed on their collections to later generations.

Miriam: I would think that book collection in ancient times would be an extremely expensive and time-consuming occupation. We know from last week that the royal families invested huge amounts of money and time in their collections. Common folk couldn't normally afford books because of the high cost of book production. So how could private individuals collect and preserve books in any great numbers?

Irene: Great collectors were mostly scholars, but not particularly rich. In ancient China, people thought that books were the loftiest of possessions, and therefore book collection was a symbol of spiritual pursuit rather than wealth accumulation. But here's Professor Phillips to tell us more about it.

Major Accomplishments in the Chinese Publishing Industry

Task 1 ▶ Listen to a historical note: Iconic Book Collectors in Ancient China

Philips: Hello there, nice to see you again. So far, we have learned a lot about Chinese publishing including the origin and evolution of Chinese characters, the spreading and translation of Chinese to other languages, the earliest books and their manufacturing operation. We also learned about some influential writers, carvers or engravers, printers and owners of bookshops. We usually give credit to those who contributed to keeping records and preserving the wisdom and knowledge of the past. In my opinion, we should acknowledge the collectors as well, as they promoted the prosperity and development of Chinese culture and publishing. So, in this talk, I'd like to introduce to you several renowned book collectors of ancient China, particularly from the Tang to the Qing Dynasty. (You are required to fill in the blanks with the words and phrases you hear while listening)

In the past, it was traditional for Chinese book collectors to write personal 1) _____ on the books that they collected. This was 2) _____ tradition with roots going back to ancient times. Book inscriptions came in various forms: some voiced the ambitions and 3) _____ of the collector; others were written as a warning to later generations, urging them to take good care of the books. Collector inscriptions were also referred to as collector 4) _____ . Through their style and content, collector inscriptions give us a great deal of insight into the character and feelings of the collector. The inscription of books began in the Tang Dynasty, and continued throughout the Song, Yuan, Ming, and Qing dynasties, with some notable differences in each era. Du Xian, an official and book collector of the Tang Dynasty, wrote an inscription at the end of each scroll he collected (Figure 6.1.1). 5) _____ as a warning, his inscription described how he had bought his books with his 6) _____ as an official and revised them personally, and that it would be 7) _____ if his children and grandchildren ever lent them out or sold them.

Figure 6.1.1: Du Xian — book collector in Tang Dynasty. (将书不外借戒条刻上藏书印的唐代藏书家杜暹)
(http://img.zwbk.org/baike/spic/2015/03/22/20150322101614561_6646.)

In the Yuan Dynasty, the calligrapher and painter Zhao Mengfu left inscriptions at the end of the scrolls he collected (Figure 6.1.2). In his inscriptions, he 8) _____ that a family's book collection did not come easily and that later generations should cherish his books. He called the act of selling an 9) _____ books despicable, and wrote that he would rather see the books given to someone else than ruined.

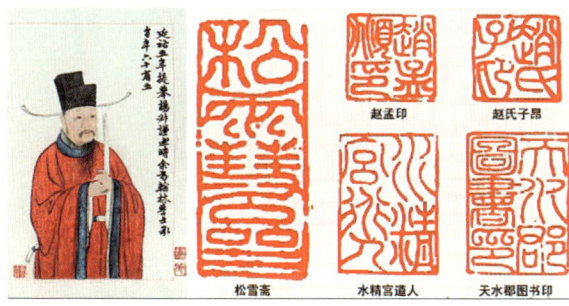

Figure 6.1.2: Zhao Mengfu and his inscription. (赵孟頫和他的藏书印铭文)
(http://image54.360doc.com/DownloadImg/2012/08/2907/26468931_2;
http://image87.360doc.com/DownloadImg/2015/08/1617/57186767_15)

The great Ming Dynasty book collector Mao Jin took Zhao Mengfu's inscription and turned it into a collector's seal, which he stamped on the books in his Jigu Library. In the Ming and Qing Dynasties, the practice of carving seals from book inscriptions was 10) _____. Qian Gu, another Ming book collector, renowned for making thousands of stone inscriptions by hand, produced a collector seal in which he stated that those who borrowed books and never returned them would face divine retribution, and that it would be idiotic for his descendants to sell his books (Figure 6.1.3).

Figure 6.1.3: The Ming book collector Qian Gu's seal for marking his ownership, his social statue, and for protection and management of books. (明朝藏书家钱谷的《悬罄室》藏书印)
(http://img3.doubanio.com/view/photo/photo/public/p192868876.)

The Qing Dynasty book collector Wang Chang, whose collection consisted of 20,000 scrolls, produced a seal that carried a message of warning for his children and grandchildren. According to his inscription, any of his descendants who proved incapable of diligently reading and cherishing his books, or who had the audacity to discard them, were to be lashed like pigs and dogs and driven from the family residence. There are also examples of inscriptions that were more elegant and restrained. For example, Wu Qian, the proprietor of the Bai Jing Library in the Qing Dynasty, carved a collector's seal in which he described the philosophy of the Bai Jing Library (Figure 6.1.4). Quoting an old phrase, he wrote that people could go without clothes in the winter and food when they were hungry, but could not for one day go without books.

Figure 6.1.4: The inscription on the seal of Wu Qian stored in his Worship building. (清代藏书家吴骞拜经楼的藏书印铭文) (http://s4.sinaimg.cn/middle/48be9129n84ca906a47c3&690)

However, looking at the inheritance of privately collected books in ancient China, there are few instances of private book collections remaining fully intact for more than three generations in a row. This was the main reason why book collectors left such stern words of admonishment in their book inscriptions. The late Qing Dynasty book collector Ye Dehui (Figure 6.1.5), noting how the world was changing, lamented that his children and grandchildren cared little for the family's book collection, which after more than three generations had grown to more than 200,000 scrolls. He wished only that the books would not be discarded or destroyed, even if that meant selling the entire collection to someone who would cherish it. An example of a private book collection that was passed down fully intact over many centuries is the Fan family One Sky

Pavilion in Ningbo, which began in the Ming Dynasty and is still intact today (Figure 6.1.6). The admonitions of the One Sky Pavilion were particularly strict. Their practice was to turn the inscriptions and epigraphs of ordinary collectors into strict family rules, which would be recorded on iron strips. These rules included no drinking and smoking in the pavilion, no females or not-family members in the pavilion, no taking books away from the pavilion, and no separation of books. Miraculously, these rules ensured that the collection of more than 70,000 scrolls was able to remain fully intact. The great scholar Huang Zongxi once had the good fortune of being granted access to the One Sky Pavilion. On seeing the collection, he exclaimed: "Reading books is challenging; collecting books is especially challenging; but to keep a collection intact permanently is more challenging still!"

Figure 6.1.5: The Qing book collector Ye Dehui and one of his seals. (清末藏书家叶德辉与其藏书印之一 "叶氏丽楼藏书")

(http://www.hn.xinhuanet.com/115712803_11n; http://www.cidianwang.com/file/zhuanke/2/42278c0a54f)

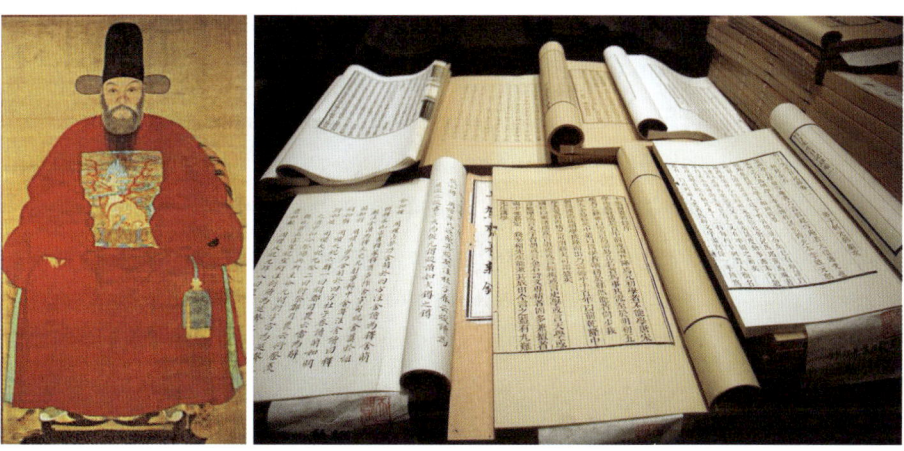

Figure 6.1.6: The Ming book collector Fan Qin and his privately collected books. (明代藏书家范钦和天一阁藏书)

(http://b.hiphotos.baidu.com/baike/w%3D268/sign=519ae8090df3d7ca0cf63870ca1ebe3c/11385343fbf2b2115aab2a79cb8065380cd78e04.)

Task 2 ▶ Discuss the historical note

(Students are required to do role play in groups by imitating the PRIMO's dialogue)

Irene: In his lecture, Professor Phillips introduced us to some distinguished book collectors from all ages in our history. Collectors like Du Xian from the Tang Dynasty, Zhao Mengfu from the Yuan Dynasty, Mao Jin from the Ming Dynasty and Wang Chang from the Qing Dynasty. But did you get a clear idea of what motivated those private individuals to devote themselves to the collection and preservation of books?

Miriam: They certainly were devoted, weren't they — the figures alone show that 20,000 scrolls, 70,000 scrolls, 200,000 scrolls — those are huge numbers for private collections. The motivation is obvious: they were passionate about books, real scholars. And of course they would have earned enormous social respect, because scholarship was always deeply admired by rich and poor alike in Chinese culture — hence the importance attached to the Imperial Examinations that we were discussing before.

Owen: Yes, I agree with you on that, Miriam. A book in ancient China was a symbol of social status. But it wasn't only the individual who got the respect, was it? A private book collection was regarded as a family treasure, to be handed down through the generations.

Irene: That's very good, both of you, you understand the motivation of the great book collectors very well. But what about the inscriptions and seals added to the books, what was their purpose?

Owen: I suppose originally they would be a record of where and when the book was acquired, but it was also a warning for future generations about how important it was to keep the library safe and intact.

Miriam: Yes, they wouldn't want the result of so much hard work and expense to be broken up and sold off. In the Ming Dynasty, they started to make their inscriptions into seals to stamp every book as a kind of identification, and also as a reminder to their descendants to look after the collection.

Irene:	Quite right, Miriam. A book collection would be regarded as a family heirloom.
Owen:	But did the epigraphs really work, though? Just leaving words at the end of a scroll or a book? Does that really ensure that future generations will obey the will of their ancestors?
Irene:	Professor Phillips pointed out that in fact very few collections survived three generations. You can understand that, to a certain extent — keeping 20,000 scrolls could be a very expensive business. But some collections lasted for centuries. The Fan family collection, the One Sky Pavilion, has 70,000 scrolls and has been preserved to this day. Preserving the library became a kind of ethic for the entire family, and that family ethic has ensured its survival.
Miriam:	Yes, and it was the same with the Ye Dehui family, wasn't it? They had family rules for the preservation of their ancestor's collection, and it expanded to 200,000 scrolls after generations of effort.
Owen:	So it wasn't only the government and the royal family that preserved this aspect of Chinese culture, but more ordinary families of scholars and business people who helped to maintain this tradition.
Irene:	Exactly right, Owen. Well put!

Task 3 Build up our vocabulary
(Drag and match exercises)

Match the English words in column A with the Chinese equivalents in column B.

	A		B
1	collotype	A	《康熙字典》
2	"Meihuazi"	B	凹版印刷
3	books with horizontal lines	C	凹雕术
4	large 32 mo	D	碑文；铭文
5	*Kangxi Dictionary*	E	彩色石印术
6	*Charles Darwin's Theory of Evolution*	F	大32开本

7	the government-run publishing houses	G	地图集
8	Westernization Movement	H	官书局
9	professional editors	I	横排本书籍
10	epigraph	J	珂罗版印刷术
11	hieroglyph	K	刻蚀
12	miniature	L	美华字
13	lithography	M	平版印刷术，石印术
14	intaglio	N	《天演论》
15	etch	O	微型画
16	atlas	P	象形文字
17	photogravure	Q	洋务运动
18	chromolithography	R	职业编辑

Task 4 ▶ Reading activity

The following excerpt is recommended to PRIMO. It is about ***The History of Book Illustration.*** Although book illustration becomes so popular nowadays, how, when and where the technique started may still puzzle PRIMO. The excerpt is quite helpful for PRIMO and other learners to explore the origin and development of book illustration.

4.1 The origin of book illustration

Book illustration is said to have evolved from European woodblock printing in the early 1400s from playing cards, in fact, which were created using block printing, which was the first use of prints in a sequenced and logical order. "The first known European block printings with a communications function were devotional prints of saints" (Figure 6.4.1).

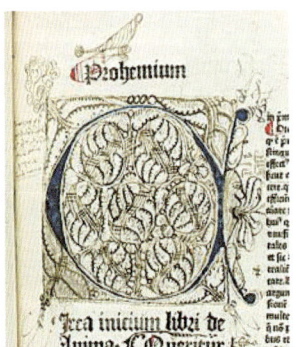

Figure 6.4.1: Illumination with doodles and drawings, including an open-mouthed human profile, with multiple tongues sticking out. Copulata, "De Anima", f. 2a. HMD Collection, WZ 230 M772c 1485.

However, texts accompanied by pictures or graphics have had a long history in China. Books with pictures and an accompanying essay (*Tushu*) are so popular with the Chinese people that they often referred to books as *Tushu* rather than *Shu*. One could even observe that since the earliest Chinese characters were hieroglyphs or pictographs, then illustration was actually built into the writing system. It is well established that the illustration of manuscript books in ancient times, and the tradition of the illuminated manuscript thrived in China. Other parts of the world have comparable traditions of book illustration, such as the Persian miniature, and there are similar traditions in the West. Chinese book illustration dates back to over 2000 years ago. Books with illustrations started with *Jian-bo* (bamboo strips) and silk scrolls. On a Qin Dynasty *Jian* "*Ri Shu*" (秦简《日书》) we find two figures (Figure 6.4.2). Illustrations can also be seen on a Han Dynasty *Jian* (Figure 6.4.3) unearthed from the Han tombs. They are few in number because bamboo strips are really too narrow to be suitable for drawings. Silk scrolls are possibly the finest medium for illustrations. The most famous illustration on a silk scroll is Chu *Boshu Tuxiang* (《帛书图像》) (Figure 6.4.4) from the Warring States period . This is also known as a silk manuscript where the characters and images are written or drawn on silk. This method of illustration was popular from the Eastern Zhou Dynasty to the Wei and Jin Dynasties, much earlier than Qin Jian.

Figure 6.4.2: The Qin illustrated edition with animals carved on the bamboo strip in *Rishu* housed in the Gansu Research Institute of Archaeology. (秦简《日书》中的动物插图)（图见甘肃省考古文物研究所《天水放马滩秦简》，中华书局 2009 年，第 8 页）

Figure 6.4.3: Han Dynasty *Jian* — bamboo script unearthed in Mawangdui Changsha. (长沙马王堆出土的汉代竹简)
(http://p3.so.qhimg.com/t01d888cb3281cb4518.)

Figure 6.4.4: The silk painting — *A Dragon and Phoenix Lady*, unearthed in Chu tomb of Warring States Period. (战国楚墓的帛画《龙凤仕女图》)
(http://www.artx.cn/artx/huihua/161276.html)

As printing technology took off and books became more common, printers began to use woodcuts to illustrate them. Hence, the centers for woodblock playing-card and religious-print production became centers for illustrated books. The Tang Dynasty witnessed the prosperity of woodblock-based illustration from its early period. The merits and advantages of this advance appealed to the Buddhists and monks. They engraved and inserted images of the Buddha in their Sutra manuscripts with the aim of enhancing the preaching of the doctrine and increasing the number of converts. For instance, when Xuan Zang and his disciples went back to Chang'an from their pilgrimage to India to obtain Buddhist scriptures, they engraved the image of Samantabhadra (印普贤像) on a woodblock for distribution to the public.

Woodblock-based illustration further flourished in the Five Dynasties Period. The Royal or Imperial Court organized the carving of classics of Buddhism, and Jiedushi (military governors) in the border area also involved themselves in similar projects. The image of Arya Avalokiteshvara (观世音菩萨像) exemplifies the development of illustration at that time.

Inserting a single illustration or a series of illustrations in Sutra scriptures characterizes the Song version of illustration. Various versions with the picture above, or below the text, — on the left or the right of the text, with the text around the picture, or just irregular insertion — enriched the format of book illustration. Whatever the format, all shared the similar aim of visually and vividly illustrating the story.

With the introduction of western science and culture to China during the Ming and Qing Dynasties, great changes took place in the drawing, content, and craftsmanship of Chinese book illustration. Western technology exerted an enormous impact on the traditional Chinese view, thus leading to the decline and fall of woodblock-based illustration and the rise of new technologies for book illustration.

4.2 The development of illustration technology

Modern book illustration originates from 15th-century European woodcut illustrations. In fact, whole books would be produced by the block printing method, including linearly printed books in China. Later different techniques of illustration, such as engraving, etching, lithography and various kinds of color printing expanded the possibilities and would become widely used (Figure 6.4.5).

Figure 6.4.5: Illustration from "The House that Jack Built" in The Complete Collection of Pictures & Songs; engraving and printing by Edmund Evans, illustration by Randolph Caldecott (1887).

Western printers of large early books used and reused their settings, and also had detachable "plugs" of figures, or the attributes of saints, which they could rearrange within a larger image to make several variations. Luxury books were, for a few decades, often printed with blank spaces for manual illuminations to be made in the traditional way.

Western printers of large early books used and reused their settings, and also had detachable "plugs" of figures, or the attributes of saints, which they could rearrange within a larger image to make several variations. Luxury books were, for a few decades, often printed with blank spaces for manual illuminations to be made in the traditional way.

Unlike later techniques, a woodcut used relief printing just as metal moveable type did, pages including both text and illustration could be set up and printed together. However, the technique either gave rather crude results or was expensive if a high-quality block-cutter was used, and could only manage fine detail on atypically large pages. It was not suitable for the level of detail required for maps. For example, the 1477 Bolognese edition of Ptolemy's Cosmographia (托勒密的世界志) (Figure 6.4.6) was both the first book to contain printed maps and the first to be illustrated by engravings by Taddeo Crivelli, an Italian painter of illuminated manuscripts, rather than woodcuts (Figure 6.4.7). However, hardly any further engraved illustrations were produced for several decades after about 1490. Instead, a style of expensive book, mostly religious in content, was produced using metal cut, a form of relief print making. This method seems to have originated in the Cologne area but books were produced in France, the Low Countries, Switzerland, and were a popular luxury product between about 1480 and 1540. In the middle of the 16th century, woodcut was gradually overtaken by the intaglio printing techniques of engraving and etching which became dominant by about 1560-1590, first in Antwerp, then Germany, Switzerland and Italy, the important publishing centers. The method required the illustrations to be printed separately, on a different type of printing press, so encouraging illustrations that took a whole page, which became the norm.

dolore ad inferos. Ca.XLIII.
Iterim fames omnes
terrā vehemēter pmebat: ɔsūptis
q3 cibis q̄s ex egipto detulerāt di
xit Jacob ad filios suos. Reuertimini: et
emite nob̄ pauxillū escarū. Rn̄dit Judas.
Denūciauit nobis vir ille sub attestatōne
iurisiurādi: dicens. Non videbitis faciem
meā: nisi fratrē vestx minimū adduxeritis
vobiscū. Si ḡ vis eum mittere nobiscum
pgemus pitēr et emem⁹ tibi cibaria. si aūt
non vis: non ibimus. vir eñi (vt sepe dixi-
m⁹) denunciauit nob̄ dicens. Non videbi-

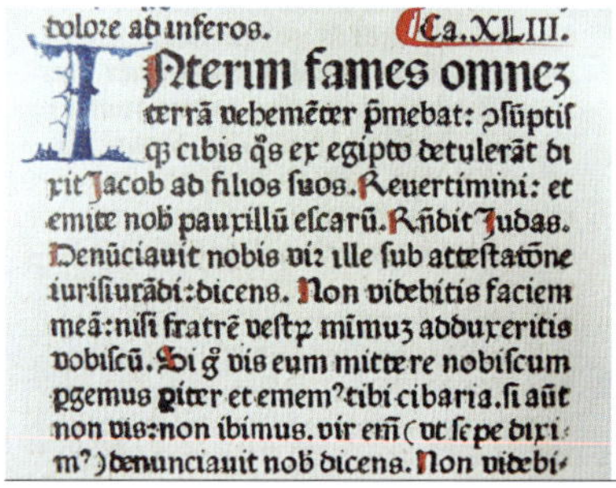

Figure 6.4.6: Incunable Leaf Biblla Latina Nuremberg 1478 Bible.

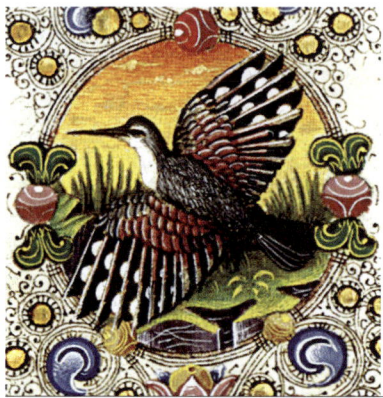

Figure 6.4.7: Taddeo Crivelli
http://www.bollettinodarte.beniculturali.it/opencms/export/(BollettinoArteIt/sito-BollettinoArteIt/Contributi/Editoria/BollettinoArte/Fotogallery/visualizza_asset.html_1662173773.html. CRIVELLI, Taddeo Bible of Borso d'Este Illumination on parchment Biblioteca Estense, Modena)

Engraving and etching gave sharper definition and finer detail to the illustrations, and were dominant by the late 15th century, often with the two techniques used in a single plate. A wide range of books were now illustrated, initially only on a few pages, but the number of illustrations gradually increased over the period, and tended towards etching rather than engraving. Particular kinds of books, such as scientific and technical works, children's books, and atlases, now became very heavily illustrated, and from the mid-18th century many of the new form, the novel, also had a small number of illustrations.

Luxury books on geographical topics and natural history, and some children's books, had printed illustrations which were then colored by hand, but in Europe none of the experimental techniques for true colour printing were widely used before the mid-19th century, when several different techniques became successful. Lithography, (石印；平版印刷术) invented by Alois Senefelder in 1819 (Figure 6.4.8), allowed for more textual variety and accuracy. This is because the artist could now draw directly onto the printing plate itself.

Figure 6.4.8: Lithograph, Portrait of Alois Senefelder （石版画）
(https://en.wikipedia.org/wiki/Alois_Senefelder#/media/File:Senefelder.jpg)

New techniques developed in the nineteenth and twentieth centuries revolutionized book illustration and put new resources at the disposal of artists and designers. In the early 19th century, the photogravure process allowed for photographs to be reproduced in books. In this process, light-sensitive gelatin was used to transfer the image to a metal plate, which would then be etched. Another process, chromolithography, developed in France in the mid-19th century, permitted color printing. This process was labor-intensive and expensive as the artist would have to prepare a separate plate for each color used. In the late 20th century, the process known as offset lithography made color printing cheaper and less-time consuming for the artist. The process used a chemical process to transfer a photographic negative to a rubber surface before printing. There were various artistic movements and their proponents in the 19th and 20th centuries, who took an interest in the enrichment of book design and illustration.

Task 5 ▶ Reading comprehension

(Students are required to launch a discussion to pose new questions and answer all the questions raised in the dialogue, and do the role play based on the following)

Irene: Well, PRIMO team, what's that reading passage all about?

Miriam: That's easy — it's about the origins of book illustration and the development of illustration technology in China and the West.

Owen; Yeah, I got that, but I'm a bit confused about the actual origins. Where exactly was the birthplace of book illustration?

Irene: Well, I think it depends on how you define the word "illustration". If you mean the technology of providing pictures or other graphics in printed works, then book illustration originated in Europe in the early 1400s with woodblock illustrations. They printed playing cards like that, for example, and block books were woodcuts which had the illustration on the same block as the words.

Owen: But there were pictures in some of the earlier hand-written books and scrolls in China, weren't there?

Miriam: You could even say that the earliest Chinese characters were pictures — they were hieroglyphs or pictographs, weren't they, just like Egyptian hieroglyphics?

Irene: That's true, but that wouldn't really count as illustration, would it? Owen is right, though, the earliest actual pictures were discovered on Han Dynasty bamboo strips which can be dated back thousands of years.

Owen: And Professor Phillips pointed out that woodblock prints of the Buddha were common in early Tang manuscripts.

Miriam: Yes, woodblock illustration prospered right up to the Ming and Qing Dynasties, but then began to fade out as the new western illustration technology took over.

Owen: And what exactly were those technologies?

Irene: Well, engraving and etching on to metal plates started during the 16th and 17th centuries and gave much more

	precise images than woodcuts. Then, at the end of the 18th century, lithography allowed even better illustrations to be reproduced. In the 19th century lithography was extended to chromolithography. The first patent was in France, and it allowed color illustrations to be printed. From then on, illustration in Western countries moved into a golden age which had far-reaching effects here in China as well.
Owen:	Thank you, Irene, that progression's much clearer in my mind now. But how does all that fit in with our course?
Miriam:	Oh, that's easy, Owen. The history of illustration is part of the history of publishing. It's a large-scale industrial process and hugely important in today's world.
Owen:	I get it. And of course the adoption of Western technologies in general is very much a part of the story of Modern China, isn't it?
Irene:	Oh, Yeah, to some degree! Let's do more exercise on this topic.

Task 6 ▶ Translation practice
(Students are required to translate the following Chinese paragraph into English individually, in pairs or in group)

Irene:	Hi, PRIMO members! Our next task is a translation passage on exactly the theme: Yangwu Yundong. Do you know what that means?
Miriam:	I've read a bit about that — wasn't it a political reform movement at the end of the Qing Dynasty?
Owen:	Oh yeah, I remember it from Modern Chinese History class. It was the Self-Strengthening Movement, wasn't it? I mean a reaction to a series of military defeats and concessions to foreign powers.
Irene:	That's right. The movement advocated the adoption of western military and industrial science and technology. They

	set up new colleges, a diplomatic office, and — what's relevant to us — publication institutions to spread the modern technology and ways of thinking of the West.
Owen:	So we'll be translating a text about the final great transition of the Chinese publishing industry from its traditional origins to its modern fully international status.
Miriam:	Come on then, let's get down to it!

清代同治和光绪年间，随着洋务运动的展开，各地官书局与新式学校、工厂一同兴起，清代官刻活动由中央出版机构垄断的格局被打破，转为官书局、民间书坊 (或书肆)、私刻、外资出版机构、新式民营出版机构五分天下的局面。在19世纪60年代后，清代官刻有政府独大演变至无中心的多点散处格局。此间，洋务大员倡办官办出版机构蔚然成风，出现了一大批影响较大的书局。清代中前期，皇城的国子监、官城的武英殿和翻译房都是官刻的主要机构。在鸦片战争到甲午战争的近60年间，传统官刻逐渐沉寂，运用传统雕版和活字印刷技术、有官方主持的大规模古籍出版活动基本结束。地方官书局本着洋务派"中体西用"的思想，出版书籍以各种古籍、丛书图志为主，间或有零星的西学翻译书籍。因为刊刻古籍为主，其印刷技术在前期基本演进了传统雕版和活字印刷工艺，直到在19世纪70年代后才逐渐引进一些西方新技术，其底本、校勘的质量在近代古籍出版史上都可圈可点。传统出版业和近代出版因素在"西学东渐"的过程中不断地互相渗透，近代出版因素萌芽并缓慢发展。维新运动后，中国出版业真正走向近代化。

Task 7 ▶ Attend Professor Richards's public lecture

Lecture 6

The Radical Transitions in the Field of Chinese Publishing

Professor Richards

Hello, everybody. As you no doubt remember, in my last lecture I talked to you about book collecting, addressing not only the organization of books but also the scope of the official collections in ancient China. This time, I will address the advances made in the publishing industry during the Qing Dynasty, and then concentrate on the changes which took place in the field of printing and publishing at the turn of the 20th century. First, I'll talk about the Impact of Western technology and its Ethos on Chinese Publishing; Second, I'd like to talk about the outcome of the Western influence, i.e. new publications; and finally I'll elaborate a bit further on the great transformations in Chinese publishing during that time.

7.1 The impact of Western technology and its Ethos on Chinese publishing

One of the watershed moments in the field of Chinese publishing took place in the remaining decades of the Qing Dynasty. It was during this time that Chinese publishing entered the modern era and began to adopt more advanced and efficient modes of printing. Granted the transition was not as clean or as clearly delineated as the change in government but it was nevertheless a time of transformation in both the printing and publishing industries and it would see changes not only in the content of the books which were produced, but also in the way that the publishing industry operated.

During the latter years of the Qing Dynasty, missionaries were the first to introduce Western printing techniques to China. The introduction of this technology prompted changes in the way books were produced and formatted. In 1807, in Guangzhou, the Anglo-Chinese College founded by the missionary Robert Morrison (Figure 6.7.1) began to manufacture lead movable type in Chinese. After a period of 12-years the endeavor culminated in a printed Chinese version of the bible. The printing of this bible encouraged other missionaries to make improvements to Chinese movable type and printing techniques.

Additional changes that affected the printing industry followed: machine made paper and various types of printing machines were imported into China; the printing techniques of lithography and collotype became more widely used; and the *Meihuazi* (Figure 6.7.2) typeface created by American missionaries enjoyed widespread popularity.

Most of the new techniques, machines and supplies were initially imported into Shanghai, where a number of publishers established their operations. These publishers included the London Missionary Society Press, the American Presbyterian Mission Press, the Tushanwan Printing House, the Dianshizhai Studio and the Shen Bao Newspaper Office. (Figure 6.7.3)

Major Accomplishments in the Chinese Publishing Industry

Figure 6.7.1: The British missionary Robert Morrison and the Anglo-Chinese College he built in the Strait of Malacca.（英国传教士罗伯特·马礼逊和他 1807 年在马六甲建立的英华书院）
(http://img1.qq.com/news/pics/3385/3385269.)
(http://yjs.teacher.com.cn/netcourse/tyx003a/zhong/sub/8/003.files/image001.)

Figure 6.7.2: *Meihuazi* designed by Jiang Bieli from Sino-Us Academy.（美华书馆的姜别利创制出的"美华字"）
(http://tieba.baidu.com/p/1100788709)

Figure 6.7.3: Tushanwan Printing House and the Shen Bao Newspaper Office in Shanghai at the end of Qing Dynasty .（清末时期上海的土山湾印书馆和申报馆大楼）
(http://www.chinacatholic.org/news/10546.html)

As a result of the establishment of these printing houses, many changes and improvements followed, including: adopting Japanese modified collotype and multi-color lithographic techniques to produce higher quality duplicates of traditional Chinese calligraphy and paintings; replacing woodblock printing with mechanized lead and lithographic printing techniques; and the use of machine made paper, known as "foreign paper" instead of the traditional hemp, bast, and other hand-made papers.

Over time, the entire form of the traditional book was changed as printing entered a new era. In the 1880s the Dianshizhai Studio (Figure 6.7.4) began printing books with horizontal lines, breaking away from the tradition of vertical lines and right folding pages. Books also began to be divided into deluxe and ordinary editions. By the early 1900s, binding techniques had also changed to reflect mainstream international standards and 32 mo and large 32 mo became the standard specification for books in China. In order to give you an idea of the numbers of books these new publishing houses were producing, in 1883 alone the Dianshizhai Studio issued 100,000 copies of the *Kangxi Dictionary* (Figure 6.7.5) using the lithographic printing process.

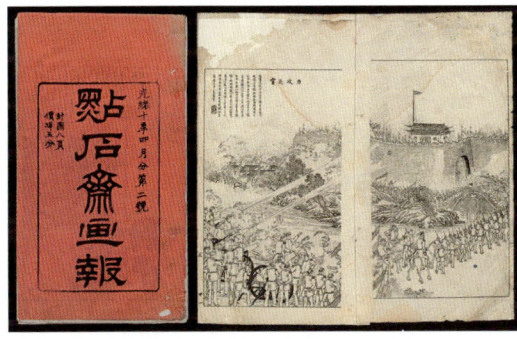

Figure 6.7.4: The Dianshizhai Studio and its main publications — *Dianshizhai Pictorial*. (点石斋书局的主要出版物《点石斋画报》) (http://www.zhuokearts.com/upload/2006/05/17/49eebbaa-7a12-4c3f-b6a1-9fc7603074ea.)

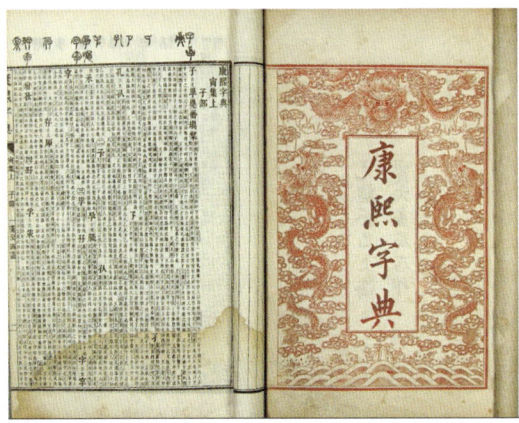

Figure 6.7.5: The *Kangxi Dictionary* published by the Dianshizhai Studio, in 1883. (点石斋书局1883年石印的《康熙字典》) (http://www.zgsd.net/userfiles1/product/img/20090221/big/0903-253.)

7.2 The outcome of the Western influence — new publications

As times changed so did the nature of the books which were being printed. In the final decades of the Qing Dynasty, traditional books were still being produced using woodblock and movable type techniques. These books were made in private workshops, official publishing houses, and by a small number of collectors. However, changes were being introduced by various foreign-based private publishing companies. These developments resulted in a diversity of new publications. From 1860 onwards, Chinese language newspapers established by foreign missionaries and merchants began to appear in cities such as Shanghai and Guangzhou. These publications were the prime source of study, entertainment, and acquisition of information by the general public. Some of the mainstream, commercially operated publications included: *Shen Bao*; *Xin Wen Bao*; *Shang Bao*; *Globe Magazine*; and the *Oriental Magazine* (Figure 6.7.6). The newspaper *Shen Bao*, established by English merchant Ernest Major, would eventually become the largest publisher of news in China.

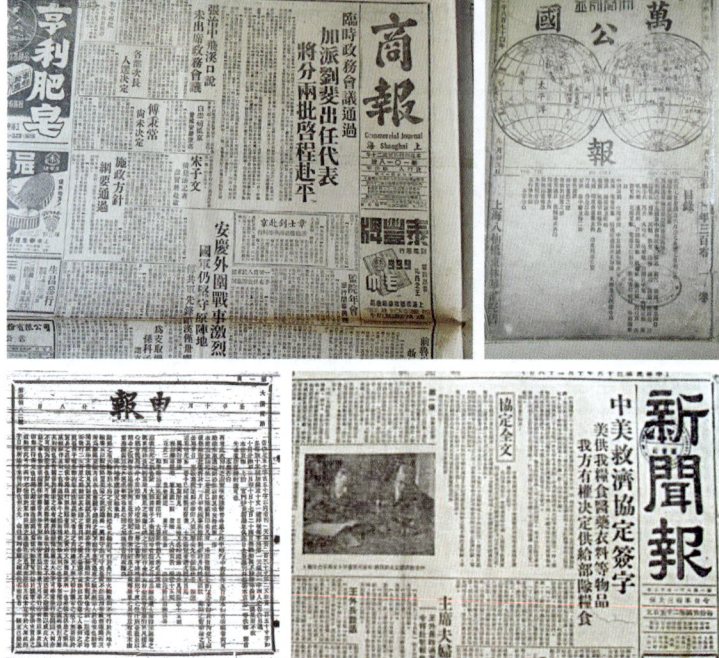

Figure 6.7.6: *Shen Bao; Xin Wen Bao; Shang Bao; Globe Magazine;* and the *Oriental Magazine*. （申报、新闻报、商报、环球报和东方杂志）

Along with the printing of newspapers, other changes took place, including a change in the content of books. Prior to 1895, most translations of Western books were scientific texts in the field of mathematics, chemistry, astronomy, medicine and engineering. However, the defeat of the Beiyang Navy during the first Sino-Japanese War signaled the failure of the "National Prosperity and Military Strength" strategy favored by the Westernization Movement proponents.

The total destruction of Daqing North-Ocean Navy in 1894 verified the fact that the pure economy-oriented Westernization Movement could not lead to Modernization in China. Having taken warning from this movement, some intellectuals represented by Kang Youwei and Liang Qichao from the South part of China initiated the "Gongche Shangshu" movement, which advocated political reform and implementing a constitutional monarchy like Great Britain and Japan. It was "Gongche Shangshu" that directly propelled the first publishing explosion in Modern China.

The failure made it clear that changes were necessary and many believed China needed to understand Western ideology, especially the political beliefs, on which people, parties or countries based their actions. From then on, Western social sciences, literature, history, and philosophy began to appear in different publications in China. For example, in 1895 publishers did this by expanding the scope and content of the books which were being produced in that year. New academic association, publishing houses and newspapers were also established and began printing different content. Consequently, Western books on philosophy, law, history, geography and politics soon became popular, with books on law and politics being the most popular, and amongst which the four works translated by Yan Fu were the most influential: Charles Darwin's *Theory of Evolution*, (Figure 6.7.7); Adam Smith's *Wealth of Nations* (Figure 6.7.8); Herbert Spencer's *The Study of Sociology*, and Montesquieu's *The Spirit of Laws*. These four are considered by many to be the finest examples of social science translations from that period. Interestingly, the change in direction regarding publishing Western material also prompted a change in government-run publishing houses which began using the new translations of Western books to promote reforms and education. Reformers and revolutionaries also began using the new forms of printing technology as a means of ideological enlightenment. The short publishing cycles and rapid transmission of the papers made them ideal for dispersing information.

Figure 6.7.7: Yan Fu and his translation — *Charles Darwin's Theory of Evolution*. (严复与其翻译的《天演论》)
(http://image80.360doc.com/DownloadImg/2014/12/3112/48610321_2.)

Figure 6.7.8: Adam Smith's *Wealth of Nations*; Herbert Spencer's *The Study of Sociology*; and Montesquieu's *The Spirit of Laws*. (亚当·斯密的《国富论》;赫伯特·斯宾塞的《社会学研究》;孟德斯鸠的《法的精神》)

Aside from printing newspapers, the expansion of Western book translations, and government and revolutionary propaganda, other changes also took place in the field of publishing during the latter stages of the Qing Dynasty. With the disbandment of the imperial examination system in 1903, a huge demand for textbooks arose from the large numbers of newly established primary and secondary schools. This demand fueled the emergence of publishing houses which focused solely on the editing and publishing of teaching materials. New textbooks included, but were not limited to: scientific reference books; dictionaries; and specialist texts for foreign languages.

7.3 The transition of the Chinese publishing structure

As the new formats and the expansion of content in publications finally prevailed and gains influence. It was, therefore, inevitable that the editing, printing and distribution modes of publishers also underwent comprehensive changes, displaying increased diversity and transitional features. Perhaps the most significant change occurred with the rise to prominence of private publishers.

At the beginning of the Qing Dynasty, the traditional publishing sector in China comprised official printing organizations, private printers and printing workshops. However, by the end of the dynasty publishing had been transformed, in large part due to the transmission of Western thinking, societal changes and the emergence of modern newspapers and publications. In short, a new publishing sector was established which would usher China into the modern era.

In general, four types of publishers existed during the Qing Dynasty: traditional printing workshops, foreign funded publishers, government run publishers and private publishers. Each of the publishers exerted an influence on the others, from both an operational and institutional perspective; I will briefly review each category of publisher in turn:

First, there were the old or traditional printing workshops. These workshops underwent a variety of changes near the end of the Qing Dynasty in order to remain solvent. The Saoye Shanfang Studio (Figure 6.7.9) is a good example. The studio was initially established during the Wanli years of the Ming Dynasty when it printed classical texts. In 1880, the studio moved from Suzhou to Shanghai and began printing not only classic texts, but also modern novels and popular reading materials using the older method of woodblock printing while simultaneously adopting more modern lithography techniques. As a result the studio was able to sell books at both retail and wholesale levels and so stay competitive.

The second category were the foreign funded publishers. Well versed in Western style movable type printing techniques, these publishers came in two forms: church backed and commercial. The church backed publishers were established by missionaries and mainly published religious materials, scientific and technological texts and books dealing with the social sciences. In contrast, the foreign funded commercial publishers tended to be joint stock ventures that published a wide variety of books. The Dianshizhai Studio, Jicheng Press and Shenchang Press (Figure 6.7.10) are all examples of commercial publishers. Each of the publishers I just mentioned were also subsidiaries of *Shen Bao*, and were responsible for printing more than 100 titles during the last 40-years of the Qing Dynasty. The array of subjects included reference books, encyclopedias, anthologies, texts on the classics and historical, literary and current affairs publications.

Figure 6.7.9: The seal of Saoye Shanfang Studio. (扫叶山房印章)

Figure 6.7.10: The *Lithographic* printing by the Dianshizhai Studio and the *Typographic* printing by Ji Cheng Press. (点石斋书局光绪年间石印《国朝诗别裁集》以及图书集成局光绪年间铅印的地理书籍) (http://www.booyee.com.cn/uploadfile/67947502055.)

The third category of publishers were the government-run publishing houses which were products of the Westernization Movement. Applying Western printing techniques, these institutions printed mainly Western academic texts, customs and trade reports, reference books and textbooks. Apart from the larger government sponsored publishers, local governments also established printing houses using proceeds from local business and salt taxes and through the patronage of wealthy individuals. The local government publishers sought to promote the resurgence of traditional printing by producing mainly classical texts using traditional techniques such as woodblock printing. These localized publishers provided support for academies and the imperial examinations.

Last, but in no way least, private printing publishers experienced phenomenal growth during the latter years of the Qing Dynasty, particularly following the end of the first Sino-Japanese War. The expansion of these capitalist ventures was due to a growing desire to save the nation, major changes in education and new government policies which encouraged enterprise. From 1898 to 1902, more than 20 modern publishing houses were established in Shanghai alone. These printing houses employed machine printing and became leaders in the publishing of textbooks, translations, novels, art books and comprehensive journals. Many of the editors who worked at these houses were experts in both Chinese and Western culture, and were open minded and highly creative. The development and expansion of these private publishing companies was directly responsible for the emergence of an independent group of professional editors at the turn of the century.

The four categories of publishers which existed at the end of the Qing Dynasty represent are good example of the period, combining a variety of traditional and modern viewpoints which China espoused as it emerged into the 20th Century.

7.4 Conclusion

The latter years of the Qing Dynasty represent a turning point in the field of publishing in China. New printing techniques, different formats for publications, varied contents and vast changes to the way publishing houses operated all reflect the emergence of China into the modern era and there was the never-ending quest to strike a harmonious balance between both traditional and modern ideologies — a balance which is still being sought today.

I'd like to leave you with three questions for you to discuss in your online forum. First, what were the three major transitions that occurred at the end of the Qing Dynasty? Secondly, what were they caused by? And thirdly, what was the effect on the Chinese publishing industry?

Task 8 ▶ Join the online forum and write a summary

(Students are required to have an instant and online post-talk discussion)

Irene:	I think that word "transition" is the most important single word in the whole lecture, don't you? There was the transition in societal and political structure, the transition in the introduction of Western technology into Chinese industries, and the transition in people's ideology and thought processes.
Owen:	Nicely put, Irene. And those three major transitions were all the result of the self-strengthening movement we were discussing previously. After the Qing Dynasty's serious defeats in the First and Second Opium Wars, government officials argued that the only way to defend themselves from the West was to take on Western technology and armaments. And that's how it all started.
Miriam:	Oh, you're quite right, Owen. The Self-Strengthening Movement was the beginning of a massive technological and military modernization process that, when you think of it, has continued right up to today!
Irene:	That's very true. We can see the influence of these transitions in three different areas in Chinese publishing industry: innovations in its technology; changes in the types of publications; and changes in the publishers themselves.
Miriam:	You've got that beautifully organized, Irene. You know what I think would be good? If we thought of examples for each of your categories. What examples can we give of new technology?
Owen:	I've got some good notes on that. During the late Qing, Christian missionaries began to make movable lead characters in China. They also imported machine-made paper and printing presses. Even binding technology was transformed to international standards.
Irene:	Good points, Owen. But don't forget the multi-color lithographic technology, and mechanization of lead type and

181

	lithographic printing. These innovations represented a new era in Chinese printing technology.
Miriam:	And with that new technology came hundreds of translations of all sorts of western literature in every kind of field, plus many more progressive publications like Shen Bao, Sin Wan Pao and Globe magazine. This great sea of new information and ideas must have had an amazing effect on people's thinking.
Owen:	The structure of publishing changed radically, too, didn't it? The long-term monopoly of government publication Qing Dynasty was broken by the emergence of private Chinese publishers and foreign publishers along with Western technology. They were all much more open-minded and took Chinese publishing along new roads.
Miriam:	One thing puzzles me, though. Why did the Qing Government turn a blind eye to all these progressive and possibly subversive institutions?
Irene:	I think it was probably that the Qing Government had been weakened by the Western aggressions and had lost their controlling power over the population. Also, of course, the Self-Strengthening Movement was supported by the Government, and therefore could only encourage innovations in the publishing industry.
Miriam:	And one final point was that treaties with Western powers opened up ports like Shanghai and Tianjin to Western trade. Foreign funded business was legal in China, and so foreign funded publishers could develop with no barriers.
Owen:	So altogether we can say that the publishing industry in the late Qing Dynasty was a mirror, reflecting the struggle of the Chinese at that time to renovate and reform.
Irene:	That sums it up perfectly, Owen.

Appendix: Vocabulary for Unit 6

Historical Note

pristine /ˈprɪstiːn/ *adj.* 原始的，古时的；纯朴的
converge /kənˈvɜːdʒ/ *vt.* 使汇聚
                           vi. 聚集；靠拢；收敛
iconic /aɪˈkɒnɪk/ *adj.* 图标的；形象的
epigraph /ˈepɪɡrɑːf/ *n.* 题词；碑文；铭文
meager /ˈmiːɡə/ *adj.* 贫乏的；不足的；瘦的
retribution /ˌretrɪˈbjuːʃ(ə)n/ *n.* 报应；报答
idiotic /ˌɪdɪˈɒtɪk/ *adj.* 白痴的；愚蠢的
audacity /ɔːˈdæsətɪ/ *n.* 大胆；厚颜无耻
lament /ləˈment/ *vi.* 哀悼；悲叹；悔恨
                   vt. 哀悼；痛惜
admonition /ˌædməˈnɪʃ(ə)n/ *n.* 警告

Reading Activity

hieroglyph /ˈhaɪərəɡlɪf/ *n.* 象形文字；图画文字；秘密符号
illuminate /ɪˈluːməneɪt/ *vt. & vi.* 阐明，说明；照亮；使灿烂；用灯装饰
                         照亮
miniature /ˈmɪnɪtʃə/ *n.* 缩图；微型画
doctrine /ˈdɒktrɪn/ *n.* 主义；学说；教义；信条
pilgrimage /ˈpɪlɡrɪmɪdʒ/ *n.* 漫游；朝圣之行
lithography /lɪˈθɒɡrəfɪ/ *n.* 平版印刷术，石印术
detach /dɪˈtætʃ/ *vt.* 分离；派遣；使超然
intaglio /ɪnˈtælɪəʊ/ *n.* 凹雕；凹雕玉石；凹雕术
etch /etʃ/ *vt.* 蚀刻；鲜明地描述；铭记
      vi. 蚀刻
atlas /ˈætləs/ *n.* 地图集；地图册
photogravure /ˌfəʊtə(ʊ)ɡræˈvjʊə/ *n.* 凹版照相；凹版印刷
chromolithography /ˌkrəʊməʊlɪˈθɒɡrəfɪ/ *n.* 石版或锌版套色印刷术；彩色石印术
proponent /prəˈpəʊnənt/ *n.* 提倡者；拥护者

Lecture

watershed /ˈwɔːtəʃed/ *n.* 流域；分水岭；集水区；转折点
lieu /luː/ *n.* 代替；场所，处所
delineate /dɪˈlɪnɪeɪt/ *vt.* 描绘；描写；画……的轮廓

culminate /ˈkʌlmɪneɪt/ *vt.* 使结束；使达到高潮
　　　　　　　　　　　　 vi. 到绝顶；达到高潮；达到顶点
collotype /ˈkɒlətaɪp/ *n.* 珂罗版；重铬酸盐制版法
deluxe /dəˈlʌks/ *adj.* 豪华的；高级的
influx /ˈɪnflʌks/ *n.* 流入；汇集；河流的汇集处
mainstream /ˈmeɪnstriːm/ *n.* 主流
ideological /ˌaɪdɪəʊˈlɒdʒɪɪkəl/ *adj.* 思想的；意识形态的
disperse /dɪˈspɜːs/ *vt.* 分散；使散开；传播
　　　　　　　　　　　 vi. 分散
propaganda /ˌprɒpəˈɡændə/ *n.* 宣传；传道总会
disband /dɪsˈbænd/ *vt. & vi.* 解散；遣散
prominence /ˈprɒmɪnəns/ *n.* 突出；显著；卓越；突出物
patronage /ˈpeɪtrənɪdʒ/ *n.* 赞助；光顾；任免权

Unit 7

Published Output: From Rare Ancient Books to Modern Magazines

TABLE OF CONTENTS

Warm-up: Be proactive

Task 1 Listen to a historical note: The Rise of Magazines and Periodicals

Task 2 Discuss the historical note

Task 3 Build up our vocabulary

Task 4 Reading activity: Aspects of Rare Chinese books

Task 5 Reading comprehension

Task 6 Translation practice

Task 7 Attend a public lecture: Publishing during the Republic Period in China: The Commercial Press as a Case

Task 8 Join the online forum and write a summary

Appendix: Vocabulary for Unit 7

Unit 7 Published Output: From Rare Ancient Books to Modern Magazines

WARM-UP: Be proactive

Irene: Welcome back, PRIMO team! We're starting a new leg of our journey through Chinese publishing today, the Republic of China period. That's about 1912 to 1949. But before we do that, can we still remember the main points from last week's study?

Miriam: Oh, easily! Professor Phillips gave us a great lecture on private book collectors from the ancient Tang Dynasty up to the Qing Dynasty. What really struck me were the inscriptions and family seals that they added to their books or scrolls. They were warnings to their families to look after the collections carefully and pass them down to future generations.

Owen: That's right — I took down their names in my notes. There was Duxian in the Tang Dynasty — all his inscriptions were on scrolls of course. Then Zhao Mengfu in the Yuan Dynasty. Mao Jin was from the Ming Dynasty, and he was the first one to turn the inscription into a seal. And then there was Wang Chang in the Qing Dynasty — he said any of his family who didn't respect his collection should be whipped like pigs and dogs. I loved that bit!

Irene: Great notes, Owen! Then in the reading passage we read about the history of book illustration in China and in the West. What I thought was interesting was how the different cultures interacted with each other even in ancient and medieval times, from the Qin Dynasty all the way up to the Qing period. What did you think of Professor Richards' lecture?

Miriam: Oh, that was massive! He talked about the great

	transformations that took place through Western influence — he called them the great transitions, and they involved new technologies as well as new ways of thinking.
Owen:	Yes, and he gave some practical examples to show how those changes took place, things like the introduction of lead movable type and machine-made paper. As a result, lots of new publications sprang up, like *Shen Bao*, *Shang Bao*, and *Global Magazine*.
Irene:	I like the points you both make. That idea of transition, Miriam, is exactly what the Republic of China was — a transitional stage between Imperial China and the People's Republic of China. And the strong sense of political reform that had been awakened in China was expressed in a number of progressive publications like the ones you mentioned, Owen.
Miriam:	So the earlier westernization movement gave rise to new publications and ways of thinking, and that led to the new wave of the enlightenment movement.
Owen:	The enlightenment movement — hey that's really exciting, is that what Professor Phillips is going to be talking about?,
Irene:	You'll soon know, Owen, here's the Professor himself!

Published Output: From Rare Ancient Books to Modern Magazines

Task 1 ▸ Listen to a historical note: The Rise of Magazines and Periodicals

Philips: Hello again everybody. In today's historical note I want to take you on to another stage of Chinese publishing history. As you all know, the Qing Dynasty was replaced by the Republic of China after the success of the Northern Movement led by Sun Yat-sen, which was also viewed as the start of modern China. With the foundation of a new government, new thoughts and ideologies began to spread , among which the pursuit of freedom and democracy took hold all over the country. New publications and magazines sprang up to popularize the new thinking. This wide spread reformation of the publication industry and political thought is also called the enlightenment in Modern China. I therefore want to begin our new chapter with an introduction to new publications in Modern China. (You are required to fill in the blanks with the words and phrases you hear while listening)

After the 19th century, with the rise of modern publishing, the content and type of publications in China changed greatly. Magazines and periodicals 1) _____ between the 2) _____ and before the adoption of new 3) _____ in 1949, which were 4) _____ by the desire to rebuild the country and to adjust the Chinese tradition in the light of the new ways of thinking and scientific approaches imported from the Western countries of Europe, Russia, and America. *Science* was one of the most symbolic magazines. It was a 5) _____ science publication founded in Tianjin in 1915 and later 6) _____ Beijing, and the first magazine of its kind to be established by Chinese scientists. Together with *New Youth*, which was founded in the same year, *Science* magazine (Figure 7.1.1) helped to set in motion the 7) _____ trends of "science" and 8) "_____" in China's publishing industry. As an official publication of the Science Society of China, *Science* was founded with the goals of 9) "_____ the nature and uses of science" and 10) "_____ the latest scientific knowledge from around the world."

188

Figure 7.1.1: *Science* — A journal, inaugural issue in 1915. (《科学》杂志创刊号，1915 年)
(http://2011.hnzqw.com/attachments/month_1108/11081711082603d673633c5eb1.)

The magazine was distinguished first by its extraordinary team of editors and authors, and second by its contributions. The founders, Hu Mingfu, Zhao Yuanren, Zhou Ren, Bing Zhi, Zhang Yuanshan, Guo Tanxian, Jin Bangzheng, Yang Xingfo, and Ren Hongjun (Figure 7.1.2), were all alumni of Cornell University in the United States. I will focus here on Ren Hongjun, the initial editor-in-chief of the magazine. Ren Hongjun was a mathematician whose strong grasp of logic enabled him to offer detailed explanations of the relationship between science and culture, the definition of science, and the spirit of science. Moreover, Ren Hongjun's theory of "scientific culture" helped to make *Science* an important launching platform for the view that life should be treated scientifically. Besides the editor-in-chief, it is worthwhile to mention that its authors and readers were all practising professionals or enthusiasts in the field of science. This was a congregation of experts and elite individuals.

Figure 7.1.2: The founders of *Science* included Zhou Ren and Ren Hongjun the second and the third from the left etc.《科学》杂志编委：前排左二周仁，左三任鸿隽，左五赵元任，左六杨杏佛；中排左二秉志，左三胡明复，左四金邦正）

http://www.kaiwind.com/culture/hot/201506/15/W020150615715851091074)

Thanks to those talents, *Science* magazine contributed hugely to Modern China through its comprehensive introduction of scientific concepts and methodologies. For almost without exception, the pioneering figures of each modern scientific discipline in China were published in *Science*, fields such as modern mathematics, physics, chemistry, geology, astronomy, agriculture, and forestry. At its outset, the introduction of the most cutting-edge developments in science at that time predominated. X-rays, the radioactivity of radium, the structure of the atom, the theory of relativity, and quantum mechanics and other newest scientific developments of the early 20th century were, without fail, transmitted through the medium of *Science*, though it was not the product of original research. It also initiated penetrating discussions on a wide range of cultural topics such as the activities of the Science Society of China, the definition of science, the methods of scientific research, the traits of scientists, the unification of scientific terms, and the relationship between science and society (views on life, industry, art, and lifestyles). Many of its articles can be regarded as classic pieces of foundation literature in China's modern sciences. These included *Why There is No Science in China*, *The Outlook of Modern Science on the Universe*, *War and Science*, *Discovery and Invention*, *Classification in Science*, *Science and Industry*, and *Science and Education*. In the 1920s, in a bid to enable the Chinese people to understand the fundamental question of what science was, the magazine engaged in constant attempts to explore and explain science from a range of different angles, such as the composition of scientific knowledge, the traits of scientific spirit, the notion of scientists, and the means of scientific thinking. Much of this effort appeared in other scholarly journals as well. These can be classified either as secondary sources or as primary sources. Leading scholarly journals included the *Quarterly Review of Social Science* (*Shehui Kexue Zazhi* 社会科学杂志, academia Sinica, 1930-1937) and the *Critical Review* (*Xueshu* 学术, Shanghai, Monthly, 1922-1926) (Figure 7.1.3.1-2). At the same, periodicals flourished. *Minbao* (民报), Chinese privately owned and managed newspapers took the lead, followed by new types of official gazette (*Guanbao* 官报), reflecting new organizations. Then institutional periodicals (*Jiguan Bao* 机关报), political parties (*Dangbao* 党报)，professional journals (Zhuanye Bao 专业报) and the like came into being. Foreign periodicals (*Waibao* 外报) and Learned journals (*Xuebao* 学报) (Figure 7.1.4-1-2-3) continued to thrive. All those represented the first systematic attempt to spread both modern natural scientific and social scientific concepts in China's cultural domain.

Figure 7.1.3-1: *Journal of Social Science* edited by Tao Menghe and Zeng Bingjun, stored in China National Library (photocopy) (陶孟和、曾炳钧主编的《社会科学杂志》影印本，国家图书馆，2011 年)

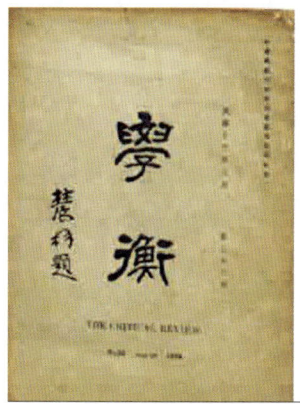

Figure 7.1.3-2: The journal —*Xueheng* edited by Wu Mi, stored in China National Library (photocopy). (吴宓主编的《学衡》杂志影印本，国家图书馆，2011 年)

Figure 7.1.4-1: Newspaper — *Minbao* , the symbolic party newspaper in late Qing Dynasty, inaugural issue in 1905 in Tokyo. (晚清党报代表——同盟会《民报》创刊号，1905 年 11 月 26 日创刊于东京)
(http://photocdn.sohu.com/20111010/Img321706492)

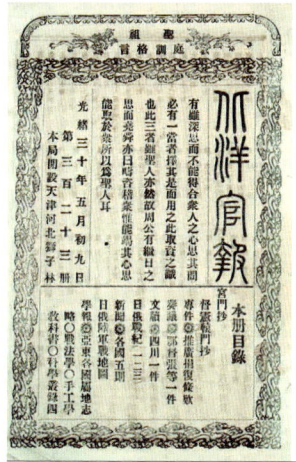

Figure 7.1.4-2: The first Local Government newspaper — *Beiyang Guanbao*, inaugural issue in 1901 in Tianjin. (中国第一份地方政府官报《北洋官报》，1901 年 12 月 25 日创刊于天津)
(http://img.lishijintian.com/201502/27205256886)

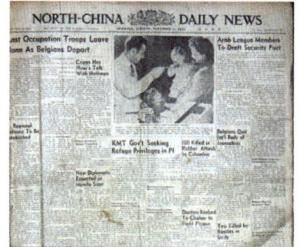

Figure 7.1.4-3: *North China Daily News* — the earliest English newspaper issued in China, inaugural issue in 1850 in Shanghai. (中国最早的英文报《字林西报》，1850 年 8 月 3 日创刊于上海)
(http://jds.cass.cn/UploadFiles/ywzl/2013/11/201311211431452113.)

Task 2 ▶ Discuss the historical note
(Students are required to do role play in groups by imitating the PRIMO's dialogue)

Irene: The historical note goes into the background of the transformation of publishing in Modern China. Professor Phillips gave examples of the huge number of the new publications that emerged, and he linked them to what he called the enlightenment movement. What do you think were the main causes of this new movement?

Miriam: I think one key point was mentioned at the beginning of the lecture: the imperial censor was abolished. This new freedom naturally encouraged new publications. Another trigger for reform was the new foundation of government led by Sun Yat-sen. His government's new policies encouraged citizens to believe in the power of democracy and freedom. They liberated minds of the people, whose thoughts had been enslaved by imperial China.

Owen: Wow, that's beautifully expressed, Miriam — two really good points. I'd like to add a couple of my own. The first one is the influence of western technology. The introduction of lead movable type, for example, made cheap mass production of publications possible. The second one, though, is perhaps even more important: those great minds who left China to Cornell University to study western thoughts and technology, and came back to spread the new ideas and techniques. They founded magazines like *Science* and the *Quarterly Review of Social Sciences* which helped to bring China into the 20th century with the power of science and technology.

Irene: Yes, men like Hu Mingfu, Zhao Yuanren, Zhou Ren and so on, what brilliant minds they were. You obviously got a lot from the historical note, but I'd like to make one last point that Professor Phillips didn't touch on about those great men: they were great patriots as well as great scholars. They worked unceasingly to save their motherland through spreading these new ideas.

Miriam: Yes, that's clearly true. And what's impressive, is the sheer range of disciplines covered by their publications — politics,

		culture, technology.
Owen:		*Science and the Quarterly Review of Social Sciences* obviously dealt with natural and social sciences, while the *Critical Review* dealt with academic topics.
Miriam:		Social issues were covered in privately-owned periodicals — *Minbao* — as well as officially owned *Guanbo* while institutional periodicals and party journals were concerned with politics.
Irene:		That's a really good analysis of the enlightenment movement and its publications. Isn't it interesting how when we put all our ideas together, we get a much better understanding of any topic?
Owen:		As you said before, Irene, that's the advantage of working as a team.

Task 3 ▶ Build up our vocabulary
(Drag and match exercises)

Match the English words in column A with the Chinese equivalents in column B.

	A		B
1	The Commercial Press	A	主编
2	Commercial Press textbooks	B	现代文化普及丛书
3	collections of modern literature	C	商务印书馆
4	Classical texts	D	商务版教科书
5	*Collectaneum of the Four Categories and the Complete Twenty-Four Histories*	E	民国出版界与学术界
6	category of books	F	跨学科
7	the commercial and academic worlds of the Republic of China era	G	古籍丛书
8	cross-disciplinary	H	工具书
9	etymology	I	方法论
10	editor-in-chief	J	词源学
11	the *Critical Review*	K	《中国伪书综考》
12	*Comprehensive Study of Forged Books in China*	L	《学衡》
13	methodology	M	《四部丛刊》
14	botany [ˈbɒt(ə)nɪ]	N	植物学

Task 4 ▶ Reading activity

*The following excerpt is recommended to PRIMO. It is about **Aspects of Chinese Rare Books.** Defining what rare books are is not that easy. After reading the excerpt, PRIMO can learn a lot of concepts concerning the ancient Chinese rare books and their origin, evolvement and preservation.*

Chinese rare books generally refer to pre-twentieth century Chinese books, and are defined as "rare" s (*shanben* (善本) and *zhenben* (珍本)) if they are fine editions printed or hand-copied in the Ming Dynasty or earlier. A recent tendency is to include in the definition fine early Qing editions, in other words, to the end of Qianlong's reign. The criteria used to define rare 20th century books and source materials are of necessity different. Five such criteria are used by the Yenching Library at Harvard University. Among them are signed copies of important political figures, limited edition publications that may never have been put on sale, or rare border publications. For China itself, there is a union catalogue of 60,000 pre-20th century rare books held by 781 public libraries and institutions according to *The Comprehensive Catalogue of Chinese Rare Books* (中国古籍善本总目——翁连溪) (Figure 7.4.1). It includes rare, beautifully printed works, works of a historic or academic interest or handwritten works by a famous personality. The holdings of 791 public and 67 private collections have been catalogued. There are indexes indicating which institutions hold each item. The different categories are classics (*jingbu* 经部), histories (*shibu* 史部), philosophy (*zibu* 子部), literature (*jibu* 集部), and series (*congbu* 丛部) . This is easily searchable online. The largest collection is probably held by the National Library of China.

Figure 7.4.1: *The Comprehensive Catalogue of Chinese Rare Books*, Chief editor: Weng Lianxi, 2005. (翁连溪主编的《中国古籍善本总目》,（2005 年）

(http://shopimg.kongfz.com.cn/20130727/1299080/12990805jpbS0_b.)

4.1 Shanben and Zhenben

China is a country with a long history and great civilization, comparable to that of ancient Egypt and Mesopotamia. Its civilization has been passed down through various media marked with trace of the era. Prior to the invention of paper, rock, stone and bronze inscription, bamboo and wood script and silk scroll were all employed as media, equivalent to books to record and preserve the achievements of civilization. However, the constant substitution of one new regime for the old, coupled with natural disasters and catastrophes made it difficult to maintain and preserve ancient Chinese books — *Shanben & Zhenben,* (Figure 7.4.2) which become rarer and more precious. Hitherto, historically speaking, *Shanben & Zhenben* were real carved or written documentation materials with which to study all aspects of the age including political affairs, the economy, military affairs, and culture. The production process went through the stages of fine annotation and calibration, then experienced refinement of the scripts ink color, examination of the paper, carving skills, the design of the layout and binding, testing the printing technology and so forth. Among *Shanben* were *Zhenben* whose extreme value lay not in their accuracy but in their rarity. No cultural relics or publications produced before Qianlong the 6th could be exported in accordance with the Law of the PRC Governing Cultural Relics. That clause fully highlights and emphasizes the importance of Chinese ancient books — *Shanben & Zhenben*.

Figure 7.4.2: The autumn night lamp records (*Ye Yu Qiu Deng Lu*) — one of the symbolic *Zhenben* (rare books) after the collection of bizarre stories by Pu Songling of the Qing Dynasty (*Liao Zhai Zhi Yi*). (晚清申报馆聚珍本《夜雨秋灯录》) (http://shopimg.kongfz.com.cn/20130319/1749765/1749765Etbxf3_b.)

4.2 Recovered books

When mentioning rare books, collectors naturally come to mind. Have you ever thought about how to recover partially destroyed rare books? Over the centuries many books were lost for numerous reasons. Obviously, poor storage accompanied by the depredations of mice, worms, and mildew were all key reasons. In addition, catastrophes, such as fire, flood, or pillage added to more destruction. Beyond that, other human factors also played a big part. Some books were banned politically, or simply because fashions and interests changed and a book was no longer copied or collected and so was not transmitted. This often happened when a newer version of a work was endorsed by a famous scholar or by an emperor. An example would be the emergence in the Tang Dynasty of Fanye's (范晔) (Figure 7.4.3). Hou-Hanshu (后汉书) (Figure 7.4.4) as the history of the Later Han, after which previous histories of the later Han, including ones that had been popular for centuries, were gradually lost. Hence, it is small wonder that only 85 of the 600 works in the Han book catalogue have survived, some of them only in part. Likewise, 86 percent of the titles in the *Suishu* book catalogue have been lost. The losses declined after printing became more widespread in the Song Dynasty and more copies were made. But those works that continued to be produced only in one or two manuscript copies, such as the veritable records of all dynasties between the *Jin* and the *Yuan* or the *Yongle Dadian* (永乐大典) (Figure 7.4.5) had a low survival rate.

Figure 7.4.3: Fanye — the honorary scholar in Tang Dynasty. (范晔)
(http://i5.qhimg.com/dr/200__/t019d5f179f01601440)

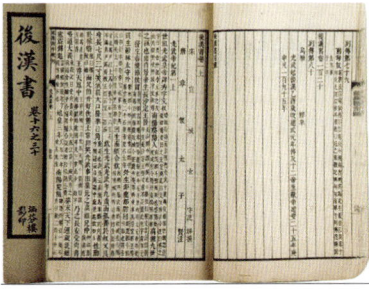

Figure 7.4.4: *History of the Later Han Dynasty* (*Hou-hanshu*) — Wuyingdian photocopy Version in Qing Dynasty published by Commercial Press in the Republic of China. (民国商务印书馆影印清武英殿本《后汉书》)
(http://pmgs.kfzimg.com/data/pre_show_pic/7/466/376.)

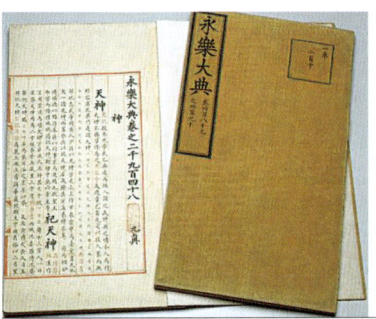

Figure 7.4.5: The original manuscript of *The Yongle Canon* (*Yongle Dadian*). (《永乐大典》原本)
(http://img.jiaodong.net/pic/0/11/87/33/11873331_423596.)

In view of the above, starting in the late Ming and accelerating in the Qing Dynasty, scholars used much ingenuity in trying to recover lost texts (*Yishu* 佚书), often excerpt by excerpt or quotation by quotation from *Leishu*. The practice is known as *jiyi* (辑佚). Sometimes they succeeded in recovering the whole text. An outstanding occasion was during the collection of books for possible inclusion in the *Siku Quanshu* (四库全书) (Figure 7.4.6) in the late eighteenth century. A total of 516 complete works were recovered from the *Yongle Dadian* at that time. Of these 388 were copied into the *Siku Quanshu*, and 128 were noted, but not included, i.e. placed in the *Cunmu* (存目) of the *Siku Catalogue*. The *Yongle Dadian* continued to be a gold mine albeit a diminishing one for recovering lost works or parts of lost works during the 19th century until it itself was almost entirely lost by the end of that century.

Figure 7.4.6: Complete Collection in Four Treasuries (*Siku Quanshu*), stored in China National Library. (文津阁的《四库全书》，现存国家图书馆新馆)
(http://imgreader.gmw.cn/attachement/jpg/site2/20120718/b8ac6f402e5b1170c05c07.)

The scholar whose name is credited with the recovery of a lost text did not do the actual copying, of course. What he did was to mark the pages that he wished to be copied with slips of paper and then let paid copyists do their work. Once they handed him a draft, he would then do the final editing. Such recovered, recompiled, or reconstituted texts are called *Jiyiben* (辑佚本). (Figure 7.4.7) (中国古籍佚书辑本总目— *Comprehensive Catalogue of Ancient Chinese Recovered Books*).

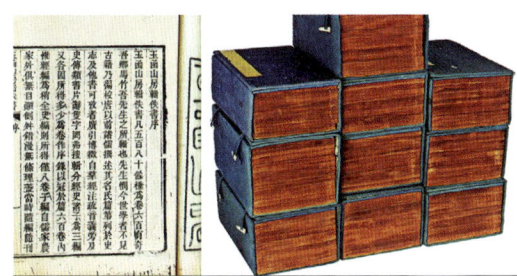

Figure 7.4.7: *Comprehensive Catalogue of Ancient Chinese Recovered Books — Yuhanshan Jiyiben*. (清代马国翰编录的辑佚本丛书《玉函山房辑佚书》)
(http://pmgs.kongfz.com/data/pre_show_pic/6/1002/800.)

4.3 Forged books

Controversy between the supporters of each version of classic texts had long been a major intellectual debate from the Han Dynasty to the Qing

Dynasty and early Republic with accusations of forgery, some justified, freely exchanged. Plenty of other kinds of forgery took place and continue to this day. In some cases, the term forged books is probably too strong a term, because some were simply attributed to the wrong author. The techniques for proving a forgery were referred to as distinguishing the spurious (*Bianwei* 辩伪). The key work on forgery was by the Ming scholar Hu Yingling (胡应麟 1551-1602), *Sibu Zheng'e* (四部正讹) (Figure 7.4.8). Hu formulates nine rules for detecting forgery in his *Complete Study of Forgery* (1586), for example, if there is a misfit between the facts described in the book and the period in which the author lived; and if the number of *pian* or *jian* (篇 or 简) are different from what is known of an old book then the book being examined is a forgery. The latest summary of the many aspects and degrees of forgery, misrepresentation, and misattribution can be found in 1,200 titles in *A Comprehensive Study of Forged Books in China* (中华伪书综考) by Deng Ruiguan and Wang Guanying (1998) (Figure 7.4.9). This, to some extent, replaces earlier studies.

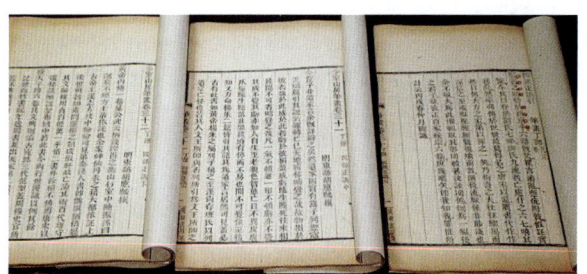

Figure 7.4.8: *Sibu Zheng'e* — the block-printed edition by Hu Yinglin. (胡应麟的《四部正讹》清代刻本) (http://img.kongfz.cn/20131123/3881447/38814477Dp2n0_b.)

Figure 7.4.9: *A Comprehensive Study of Forged Books in China* edited by Deng Ruiquan and Wang Guanying in 1998. (邓瑞全、王冠英主编《中国伪书综考》,1998 年)

4.4 Imperially authored or commissioned works

In the Ming and Qing Dynasties, imperially authored works, paintings, and calligraphy for which the emperor wished to claim authorship were often published with a prefix (*Yuzhi* 御制) in the title. All Ming Taizu's (明太祖) works are prefixed with Yuzhi. His successors rarely used it. The Qing emperor revived the practice, especially Kangxi and Qianlong. Their reasons were no doubt the ever present desire of Manchu (minority) emperors to show their Chinese subjects the extent to which they were personally involved in producing and authorizing works in the classical Chinese tradition. Occasionally *Yuzhi* is used interchangeably with *Qinding or Yuding*. Sometimes one of these terms appears on the cover and one of the others in the preface. They normally mean "by imperial command" or "imperially commissioned". Works that had less imperial involvement in their writing, compilation, editing, or annotating were indicated with the prefixes like *Qinding* (by imperial command or imperially commissioned or authorized). This prefix was not used for book titles until the mid Qing. Between then and the end of the Dynasty, over 200 *Qinding* titles were produced. Most of them are found in the titles of official regulations of boards and departments, for instance, *Qinding Da Qing Huidian* (钦定大清会典) (Figure 7.4.10). Only very occasionally does *Qinding* have the sense of being imperially edited or revised. When the prefix command *Yuding* appeared, it meant imperially edited, reviewed, commissioned or a combination of these. About 25 *Yuding* titles were published in the early Qing, mainly in works checked over or sponsored by Emperor Kangxi. Today, the best remembered of these is the *Yuding Kangxi Dictionary* (Figure 7.4.11). Editorship of such works is often attributed as "compiled or edited at imperial command".

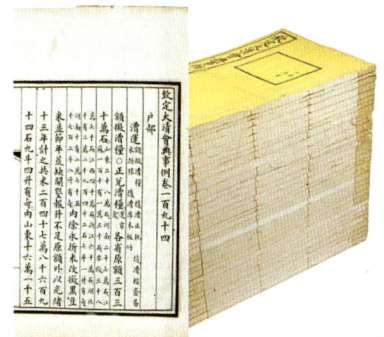

Figure 7.4.10: *Qinding Da Qing Huidian* — the record of laws and systems of Qing Dynasty, the lithographic printing copy. (清代石印本《钦定大清会典》) (http://pmgs.kfzimg.com/data/pre_show_pic/3/223/267.)

Figure 7.4.11: *Yuding Kangxi Dictionary* — the carving version in Qing Dynasty. (清代刻本《御制康熙字典》) (http://pmgs.kongfz.com/data/pre_show_pic/2/41/3508.))

Even before the fall of the Qing Dynasty, in many cases imperially authorized books were printed without the imperial attribution. The *Kangxi Dictionary* was a good example, often simply printed under that title in the 19th century, not as the *Yuding Kangxi Dictionary*. Since the fall of the Qing, titles are often quoted without the imperial prefix or with the prefix in parentheses. It is worth knowing this because some reference works give the full book title without giving a cross reference. And "at imperial command" is now usually dropped.

The title of imperially commissioned works that were published during a ruling dynasty are usually symbolized by Da (大) added before the dynasty name, as in *Da Tang Liudian* (大唐六典), *Da Minglu* (大明律) or *Da Qing Tongyizhi* (大清统一志) (Figure 7.4.12-1-2-3). Superfluous titles such as (*Guochao* 国朝) or (*Huangchao* 皇朝) were also much used in book titles in the later empires, especially in the Ming and Qing Dynasties. In many cases such dynastic indicators were dropped from titles after the dynasty ended. Modern scholarship has almost invariably favored dropping them.

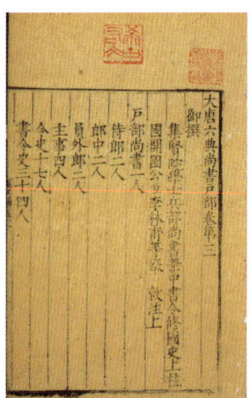

Figure 7.4.12-1: The Six Canon of Tang Dynasty (*Da Tang Liudian*) — the carving version in Qing Dynasty. (明代刻本《大唐六典》)
(http://image.digitalarchives.tw/ImageCache/00/07/97/5d.)

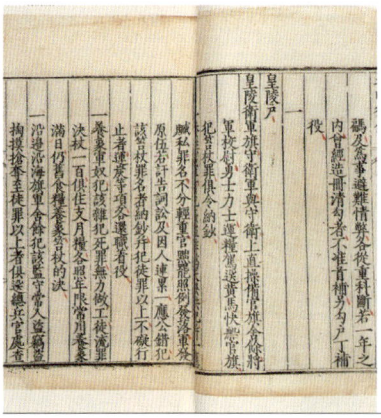

Figure 7.4.12-2: *Da Minglü* — The Criminal Law of the Ming Dynasty, the edition of the Ming book. (明代刊本《大明律》)
(http://pmgs.kongfz.com/data/pre_show_pic/1/982/844.)

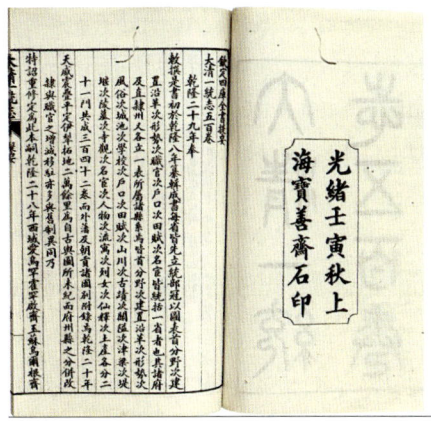

Figure 7.4.12-3: *Da Qing Tongyizhi*—The Chorography of Qing Dynasty. (清代石印本《大清统一志》)
(http://photo.99ys.com/1113/10/367/20110309102136899705.)

Task 5 Reading comprehension

(Students are required to launch a discussion to pose new questions and answer all the questions raised in the dialogue, and do the role play based on the following)

Owen: That's an interesting article about rare Chinese books, but I'm a bit unclear as to what exactly is the meaning of the word "rare". Does it only mean "ancient"?

Irene: Well, the two generally go together of course. The rarest books are usually the most ancient. But there are rare 20th century books, for example, and some definitions of rare ancient Chinese books come up even as far as the end of the Qianlong reign, which is the end of the 18th century. However, most of the rare books — the *shanben* or *zhenben* — mentioned in the text were from the Ming Dynasty or earlier — indeed, much earlier.

Miriam: As you said, Irene, ancient books are usually rare, and rare books are usually ancient. The recovery of ancient books that had been damaged or lost in some way must have been a very difficult job. How did they do that?

Irene: Well, as you can imagine, the recovery work was normally carried out by groups of scholars, usually supported by the imperial families. Take the collection of *Siku Quanshu* for

201

	example — 516 complete works were recovered from the *Yongle Dadian* alone. This work was done under the direction of a famous scholar, Ji Yun. He led a team of more than 360 scholars, and supported by the Emperor of course. They fulfilled the recovery task in 13 years. Can you imagine the workload?
Owen:	It must have been amazing! And of course, every word had to be copied by hand, yes?
Miriam:	Must have been — they didn't have computers in those days. But I don't suppose the scholars did the actual copying, did they?
Irene:	No, they had professional copyists to do that, but they had to edit everything themselves.
Owen:	But how could they be certain that the restoration of the ancient book matched the original book… if the original book didn't exist?
Miriam:	Ah — the article talks about that. Didn't someone from the Ming Dynasty set out a list of rules for judging whether a recovery was accurate or not.
Irene:	Yes, you're talking about Hu Yingling and his book *Sibu Zheng'e*. In his book he pointed out that if the facts described in the recovered book didn't match the period in which the author lived, or if the number of the *pian or jian* were different from the old book, then the recovered book was probably a forgery.
Owen:	One last question, Irene, the *Kangxi Dictionary*. Was it really written by the Emperor?
Irene:	No, it was commissioned by the Emperor and so had the prefix *Yuding*. Many books had prefixes showing they were imperially commissioned or authorized, but prefixes are mostly dropped by modern scholars.
Miriam:	You can understand why rare books are priceless, can't you? Let's start to prepare for the following translation practice!
Owen & Irene:	Sure.

Task 6 ▶ Translation practice

(Students are required to translate the following Chinese paragraph into English individually, in pairs or in group)

Owen: Hi, everybody! I've had a quick look at the translation passage, and it appears to be an introduction to the modern period — the People's Republic of China. But I am going to need your help, Irene. There are some terms that I really can't understand — what does *Jihuajingji* (计划经济) mean?

Irene: Ah yes, the planned economy! There are quite a few terms like that that you need help with. There's also "the Third Plenary Session of the 11th Central Committee of the Chinese Communist Party" and "Cultural Revolution". Once the People's Republic of China was founded, all the aspects of economy — including publishing of course — came under the regulation of government, and that's more or less where it is today.

Miriam: So this translation passage will introduce us to the basic government economic policy of the PRC.

Irene: You've got it, Miriam — shall we begin?

Owen & Miriam: Okay.

中华人民共和国成立后建立了高度集中的计划经济体制，出版工作也被纳入到计划经济的轨道中运行。"十一届三中全会"之后，国家致力于改革过于僵化的出版体制，出版行政部门修订和制定了一系列法律法规和政策法令，以健全和完善在"文化大革命"中被摧毁的出版法规政策。在出版社工作制度方面，当时的国家出版事业管理局颁布了《出版社工作暂行条例》，在稿酬制度方面，国家出版局对恢复稿酬办法进行了修订，提高了稿酬标准，恢复印数稿酬；在版权保护制度方面，把著作权作为公民的民事权利，列入知识产权中，第一次以法律的形式确认了著作权，还制定了相关行政规定。1986年10月，国家出版局和国家版权局脱离文化部。1987年1月，成立了国家新闻出版总署（现为国家新闻出版广电总局），隶属国务院领导。我国也于1992年加入了两个主要的版权国际保护公约——伯尔尼公约和世界版权公约；在对违法违禁出版物的管理方面，国务院发布法规条例，把非法出版物的制造、销售和传播而获利的行为定为投机倒把，并对如何应用刑法条款惩处非法出版犯罪活动作了明确规定，为查处非法出版提供了法律依据。此外国家还在期刊管理、图书定价、对外合作出版等方面制订了不少的法规和政策文件，其目的就是调动出版机构和出版工作者的积极性，提高出版能力。

Task 7 ▶ Attend Professor Richards's public lecture

Lecture 7

Publishing during the Republic Period in China: The Commercial Press as a Case
Professor Richards

Hello again. In this lecture I want to outline for you how the field of publishing changed during the Republic of China period, which lasted from 1912-1949. I hope to accomplish this by taking the Commercial Press — the most influential publishers operating during the time period as an example of publishing as a whole and will discuss the topic from the following four aspects.

7.1 The background of publishing development

1933 to 1936 witnessed the rapid expansion of Chinese publications. It is estimated that roughly 100,000 different titles were printed during the Republic of China period, with the majority of them being produced during the capitalist golden age. Although the content of the books which were being printed remained diverse, much like those printed at the end of the Qing Dynasty, a definite shift toward printing social science texts took place during the Republic of China era. In fact, besides Confucian classics, many books on history, philosophy literature, many natural sciences, applied science, philosophy and social science were published and many new disciplines established. More than 120,000 different books in 18 categories were published, although approximately only ten percent of the books dealt with science and technology. At the same time, many translated books were published to spread the new knowledge, which led to fundamental changes in the content and structure of publications. Scholars believe that the dominance of the humanities texts reflected a growing national awareness and widespread concern surrounding Chinese national culture during a time of social unrest and political turbulence.

7.2 The influential publishers at that time

Due to their publishing of humanities texts, three Chinese-owned publishers were able to distinguish themselves from their peers during the

Republic of China period. The three were the Commercial Press (Figure 7.7.1-1), the Zhonghua Book Company (Figure 7.7.1-2) and Joint Publishing. Of the three, the Commercial Press was noted for its ability to merge commercial interests with a humanistic spirit; it was also responsible for printing almost half of the books during this era. The cultural values of the press, along with its cultivation of specialized personnel, influenced the entire publishing industry; the evolution of the company is also representative of the wider changes which were taking place in China's private publishing industry at the time.

Figure 7.7.1-1: The Commercial Press in 1930. (1930 年的商务印书馆)
(http://photocdn.sohu.com/20120926/Img353961240.)

Figure 7.7.1-2: Zhonghua Book Company in the period of the Republic of China. (民国时期的中华书局)
(http://www.pep.com.cn/zt/zhdsb/2012/8/201206/W0201 20621381039307447.)

The Commercial Press was founded in Shanghai in 1897, by four people (Figure 7.7.2-1-2-3). The organization began as a small printing house that specialized in printing commercial notebooks. The Press later became a joint-stock company following the introduction of new investors in 1901, and in 1902 opened new printing, translation, editing and distribution offices. Editing and publishing textbooks for primary and secondary schools and universities became the company's area of expertise and over time Commercial Press textbooks became the standard for schools in China. Aside from printing textbooks, the Commercial Press also engaged in other activities, from running bookstores and organizing activities for students to providing vocational training and manufacturing teaching equipment. The Press was also involved in a number of other pursuits, such as insurance, filmmaking and charitable work. At its peak, the company employed almost 5,000 people, running 36 subsidiaries and over 1,000 agencies located both in and outside China. By 1932, the Commercial Press was by far the largest publisher in Asia and along with Peking University was considered as one of the two cultural powerhouses of China.

Figure 7.7.2-1: Xia Ruifang — one of the founder of the Commercial Press. (夏瑞芳)
(http://www.todayonhistory.com/upic/201002/4/6A173832282.)

Figure 7.7.2-2: Baoxian En and Baoxian Chang — brothers as well as the founders of the Commercial Press. (鮑咸恩、鮑咸昌兄弟)
(http://culture.people.com.cn/mediafile/200508/30/F2005083019160000000.)

Figure 7.7.2-3: Gao Fengchi — one of the founder of the Commercial Press. (高凤池)
(http://img226.poco.cn/mypoco/myphoto/20131124/13/55446216201311241356021519916642577_061.)

7.3 Publications by the Commercial Press

Books printed by the Commercial Press during the Republic of China period fell into one of five different categories.

First, there were textbooks, compiled by the company and then printed for primary and secondary schools and universities. The textbooks covered such subjects as Chinese literature, history, geography and self cultivation. The books were of high quality, well written, well edited and considered to be very progressive.

The second category of books printed were collections of modern cultural popularization. The *Wanyou Wenku*, (Figure 7.7.3) published in 1929, was a collection which consisted of 4,000 booklets belonging with 1,710 titles. This collection was an anthology of other collections the press had previously printed and covered a wide range of subjects. The collection was designed to be easily accessible, systematic and compiled with the intent of placing an emphasis on new knowledge. A separate textbook, titled *The University Collection*, was published in 1933, after first having been edited by a committee of more than 50 employees and scholars.

Figure 7.7.3: The fifth category of *Wanyou Wenku* — a series of books.（《万有文库》丛书中之五种）
(http://pmgs.kfzimg.com/data/pre_show_pic/7/422/995.)

Next were the Classical texts. From 1911 to 1946, the Commercial Press printed a total of 58 classical collections, 17 of which numbered more than 100 booklets, or titles, in length. Each of the collections was compiled using high quality copies from the company's own library as well as books located both in and outside of China. One of the stockholders of the company and the head of the translation and editing offices, Zhang Yuanji (Figure 7.7.4), made seven trips to Mt. Lushan from 1929 to 1935, where he personally checked and revised the *Collectaneum of the Four Categories* and the *Complete Twenty-Four Histories*.

Figure 7.7.4: Zhang Yuanji — the stockholders of the company and the head of the translation and editing offices.（张元济）
(http://barb.sznews.com/res/1/21/2015-04/07/B07/res01_attpic_brief.)

The fourth category of books published by the company was reference books, including dictionaries. The *Ciyuan — Etymology* (Figure 7.7.5), published in 1915, was the first modern Chinese dictionary to list large amounts of composite words from single character headers. The book was considered comprehensive for the reason that it incorporated encyclopedic elements into a word based format. The company also published other reference works based on subjects ranging from botany, zoology, medicine and mineralogy to philosophy, business and law. The press even published reference books regarding noteworthy people and places. Excellent brief articles on the main periodicals, newspapers, magazines, editors, journalists, printers, and publishers, plus reproductions of the front pages of all leading periodicals acted as a good starting point for references. There was a phonetic transcription (*pinyin* 拼音) index, a Chinese-English glossary of standard printing terminology, and a chronology of main events in the development of Chinese newspapers and publishing. Its coverage was worldwide.

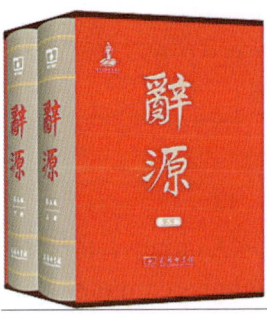

Figure 7.7.5: The *Ciyuan* — the *Etymology*, revised version in 2015. (2015 年第三版修订本《辞源》) (http://www.qz828.com/pic/0/10/85/13/10851377_242012.))

The fifth category of books published at Commercial Press was periodical publications, or magazines. The Press established more than a dozen popular publications, some dating from the late Qing Dynasty. The titles of some of the more popular publications include: *Oriental Magazine, Short Story Monthly, The Education Magazine, Youth Magazine, English Magazine, Student's Magazine, Women's Magazine, Children's World* and *Children's Pictorial*. The publications were very popular and influential; *Oriental Magazine* itself ran from 1904 to 1948 with a total of 811 issues published over the course of 44 volumes. At first the magazine had a conservative orientation, placing emphasis on scientific knowledge, but following the May Fourth Movement it began to address world trends and contemporary political issues, over time becoming one of the most influential publications printed during the Republic of China era.

7.4 The operation of publishing in this period

Of course, the Commercial Press is just one example of how the commercial and academic worlds of the Republic of China era were able to complement one another. I hope this makes sense to you. The publishing house was not only a place to work, but also to study and conduct research. During its years of operation the press was able to assemble a large collection of books and resource materials. The collection of books and the academic atmosphere espoused by the company appealed to scholars; as a result the press was able to hire a number of noted academics and encouraged them to author, revise and edit various publications. On the other hand, the academics were able to draw on the reputation of the publisher to further their own careers and have their work published, or alternatively, work on projects that interested them.

By bringing together the two worlds, commercial and academic, the Commercial Press gathered an exceptional group of editors and authors to work on its collections, classical texts and periodicals. Renowned authors such as Yan Fu, Lu Xun, Cai Yuanpei, Chen Duxiu and Hu Shi (Figure 7.7.6-1-5) all had works published by the company, or conversely, were involved in either the editing of texts or administration of the company. By fostering a collegial and academic atmosphere the Commercial Press became one of the most important platforms for the transmission of academic and cultural knowledge during the Republic of China era.

Figure 7.7.6-1: Yan Fu — one of the renowned Chinese authors and translators. (严复，1854年1月8日—1921年10月27日)

Figure 7.7.6-2: Lu Xun — one of the renowned Chinese authors. (鲁迅，1881.9.25—1936.10.19)

Figure 7.7.6-3: Cai Yuanpei — one of the renowned Chinese educators and statesman. (蔡元培，1868年1月11日—1940年3月5日)

Figure 7.7.6-4: Chen Duxiu— one of the renowned Chinese revolutionaries, reformers and political thinkers. (陈独秀，1879年10月9日—1942年5月27日)

Published Output: From Rare Ancient Books to Modern Magazines

Figure 7.7.6-5: Hu Shi—one of the renowned Chinese thinkers and philosophers. (胡适，1891 年 12 月 17 日 —1962 年 2 月 24 日)

7.5 Conclusion

The Republic of China era was a tumultuous time in China's history. It can be argued that the books which were published during this period were indicative of a growing national consciousness and widespread reflection on the part of Chinese citizens over the salvation of the country against a backdrop of social unrest and political upheaval. By first specializing in printing books in the field of humanities which the public craved, Commercial Press was later able to expand its operations to become not only a model of success, but also one of the most influential cultural and political voices of the period. I will leave you with two questions which I think will assist your online discussion of the topic of my lecture. Firstly, how was it that the publishing industry was able to prosper during the Republic of China era, which was known for its social unrest and political instability? Secondly, although I didn't characterize it in precisely this way, my description of the Commercial Press dealt with three different sorts of expansion. What were those three expansions? Good luck with your discussions!

Task 8 ▶ Join the online forum and write a summary

(Students are required to have an instant and online post-talk discussion)

Irene: The Republic of China era was so short, and yet so many new things happened during it. It really was a tumultuous age. What do you think the answer is to Professor Richards' first question: How did publishing manage to prosper in such unstable times?

Miriam:	I think it was because publishing was central to what was happening in Chinese society. The old feudal control of thought had been thrown off. People were seeking their own values, their own criteria. And to do that they needed information. There was no radio, no television. Information could only come from publications — newspapers, magazines, books.
Owen:	You are absolutely right, Miriam. The publishers were simply responding to the demand of the market. The people wanted knowledge, and the publishers provided it.
Irene:	Good points, both of you. And of course a lot of that knowledge came from the West. Science and technology, social sciences, politics, they all had to develop in the new China.
Miriam:	I'm a bit puzzled by Professor Richards' second question, though. What did he mean by the three expansions of the Commercial Press?
Owen:	Oh, the first expansion was obviously in the product line. It started out in Shanghai in 1897 as a small printing house that produced school textbooks. It expanded its product line over the years to literary collections, company reference books, classics, modern periodicals and magazines — the company took over the market share of the Press at that time.
Irene:	Yes, it wasn't only an expansion of its product line. It actually expanded its market, not just domestic but overseas business as well. According to the statistics, the Commercial Press ran 36 subsidiaries and over 1,000 agencies all over the world. This expansion into the international market made the small publishing house a cross-border giant.
Miriam:	Yes. And the third expansion was into the academic world. The Commercial Press employed the most distinguished scholars as authors, editor, and researchers. This ensured the quality of their publications, and also made them a center for study and research — almost like a university, really!
Irene:	That's a really good analysis, team. It'll be interesting to see how the Commercial Press compares with the contemporary

publishing after the foundation of the People's Republic of China, which of course will be the subject of the last unit in this series.

Appendix: Vocabulary for Unit 7

Historical Note

censor /ˈsensə/ *n.* 检查员；[心理] 潜意识压抑力；信件检查员
orthodoxy /ˈɔːθədɒksɪ/ *n.* 正统；正教；正统说法
cross-disciplinary /ˈkrɒsˈdɪsɪplɪnərɪ/ *adj.* 跨学科的；交叉学科的
contemporary /kənˈtemprərɪ/ *adj.* 当代的；同时代的；同属一时期的
congregation /kɒŋgrɪˈgeɪʃ(ə)n/ *n.* 集会；集合；圣会
methodology /meθəˈdɒlədʒɪ/ *n.* 方法学，方法论
quantum /ˈkwɒntəm/ *n.* 量子；量子论；定量
transmit /trænzˈmɪt/ *vt.* 传输；传播；发射；传达；遗传
   vi. 传输；发射信号

Reading Activity

Mesopotamia /ˌmesəpəˈteɪmɪə/ *n.* 美索不达米亚 (亚洲西南部)
substitution /sʌbstɪˈtjuːʃ(ə)n/ *n.* 代替；[数] 置换；代替物
regime /reɪˈʒiːm/ *n.* 政权，政体；社会制度；管理体制
catastrophe /kəˈtæstrəfɪ/ *n.* 大灾难；大祸；惨败
calibration /kælɪˈbreɪʃ(ə)n/ *n.* 校准；刻度；标度
mildew /ˈmɪldjuː/ *n.* 霉；霉病
pillage /ˈpɪlɪdʒ/ *n.* 掠夺；掠夺物
endorse /ɪnˈdɔːs/ *vt.* 背书；认可；签署；赞同；在背面签名
veritable /ˈverɪtəb(ə)l/ *adj.* 真正的；名副其实的
albeit /ɔːlˈbiːɪt/ *conj.* 虽然；即使
forgery /ˈfɔːdʒərɪ/ *n.* 伪造；伪造罪；伪造物
spurious /ˈspjʊərɪəs/ *adj.* 假的；伪造的；欺骗的
superfluous /suːˈpɜːfluəs/ *adj.* 多余的；不必要的
parentheses /pəˈrenθəsɪz/ *n.* 括号；圆括号
circumlocution /ˌsɜːkəmləˈkjuːʃ(ə)n/ *n.* 婉转曲折的说法，累赘的陈述；托词

Lecture

turbulence /ˈtɜːbjʊləns/ *n.* 骚乱，动荡；[流] 湍流；（天气等）狂暴

accessible /əkˈsesɪbl/ *adj.* 易接近的；可进入的；可理解的
booklet /ˈbʊklɪt/ *n.* 小册子
botany /ˈbɒtənɪ/ *n.* 植物学；地区植物总称
mineralogy /ˌmɪnəˈrælədʒɪ/ *n.* 矿物学；矿物学书籍
complement /ˈkɒmplɪmənt/ *vt.* 补足；补助
collegial /kəˈliːdʒɪəl/ *adj.* 学院的；社团的；大学生的
backdrop /ˈbækdrɒp/ *n.* 背景；背景幕；交流声
upheaval /ʌpˈhiːv(ə)l/ *n.* 剧变；隆起；举起
videlicet /vɪˈdiːlɪset/ *adv.* 换言之，即；就是说
etymology /ˌetɪˈmɒlədʒɪ/ *n.* 语源，[语] 语源学
tumultuous /tjuːˈmʌltʃʊəs/ *adj.* 吵闹的；骚乱的；狂暴的
salvation /sælˈveɪʃ(ə)n/ *n.* 拯救；救助

Unit

The Evolution and Diversification of Publishing in China in Modern Times

TABLE OF CONTENTS

Warm-up: Be proactive

Task 1 Listen to a historical note: Fan Yong — Curator of Literary History

Task 2 Discuss the historical note

Task 3 Build up our vocabulary

Task 4 Reading activity: The history of Chinese Libraries

Task 5 Reading comprehension

Task 6 Translation practice

Task 7 Attend a public lecture: Diversification of Publishing in the New Era

Task 8 Join the online forum and write a summary

Appendix: Vocabulary for Unit 8

The Evolution and Diversification of Publishing in China in Modern Times

Unit 8 The Evolution and Diversification of Publishing in China in Modern Times

WARM-UP: Be proactive

Irene: Welcome back team PRIMO! We've been working hard for the past 7 units, but I'm sure we're all as keen as ever, starting this final unit.

Miriam: Absolutely right, as usual, Irene. I'm sure there's still so much to learn and say about Chinese publishing. In the last unit we learned about famous private book collectors, and we also got an overview of the situation from 1912 to 1942, which was fascinating. Now I'm looking forward to learning about how book distribution has grown into a huge industry supported by things like libraries and bookstores.

Owen: I think you'll be fully satisfied by this unit, Miriam. I've been working on questions about just that topic to challenge our professors with — and to challenge the pair of you as well.

Irene: I really like your attitude, Owen. You always have such fresh ideas, and your questions always get to the heart of the matter. Are you going to give us some of your thoughts here and now?

Miriam: Chronologically speaking our exploration of the subject has to enter a new era, doesn't it? I've been doing some preparatory research into the birth and evolution of libraries and bookstores in Modern China. I think that's what Professor Phillips will be focusing on.

Owen: Great minds think alike, Miriam. I think we have cooperated really well as a team. I agree with you about libraries and bookstores, but I also think this unit will have a close look at diversification in publishing.

Irene: I think you're both right. This unit is going to be inclusive, it'll look at modern publishing as a whole. Our two supervisors will provide an overall framework that will help us to join together all of our fragmented pieces of knowledge.

Miriam: I can't wait!

The Evolution and Diversification of Publishing in China in Modern Times

Task 1 ▶ Listen to a historical note: Fan Yong—Curator of Literary History

Irene: Professor Philips suggested that we should discuss the relationship between libraries and bookstores. Which of you would like to make a distinction between the two and see where that takes us?

Miriam: Good idea, let me kick off. My understanding is that bookstores developed from libraries, and that libraries originated from both official and private collections. But I'm not entirely certain about this.

Owen: I see what you mean, but what about publishing houses? How did they come into being? And are they also within the remit of our discussion?

Irene: Good question, Owen. I think you're going to be able to answer that question yourself from the historical note, isn't that so Professor Phillips?

Philips: Partially right, Irene. On the one hand, I believe you have acquired a lot of information, and on the other hand, just as you said, I will help you combing and connecting your piecemeal knowledge. However, you know I can just highlight several famous Publishing Presses today and leave other issues for Professor Richards and for your later reading and discussion. I am sure that every one of you must know the Joint Publishing Press, but I wonder whether you know what "Joint" refers to and why this Press is so celebrated. (You are required to fill in the blanks with the words and phrases you hear while listening)

Actually, the Joint Publishing House grew out of three famous book stores: the *Shenghuo* Bookstore (生活书店), the *Xinzhi* Bookstore (新知书店), and the *Dushu* Publishing House (读书出版社) (Figure 8.1.1-2-3-4).

Figure 8.1.1-1: Chongqing Branch of *Shenghuo* Bookstore in the Republic period.（民国时期生活书店重庆分店）
(http://photocdn.sohu.com/20130626/Img379895690.)

Figure 8.1.1-2: The publishing logo of *Xinzhi* Bookstore.（新知书店的出版标记）
(http://a0.att.hudong.com/64/34/01300000361874124581342516554.)

Figure 8.1.1-3: The Periodical published by *Dushu* Publishing House growing from the Periodical office.《读书生活》杂志社是读书出版社的前身
(http://p0.so.qhimg.com/t01fa23debe498eb02f.)

Figure 8.1.1-4: The Joint Publishing House, founded in 1948 in Hong Kong. (1948 年在香港成立的生活·读书·新知三联书店）
(http://p0.so.qhimg.com/t01fa23debe498eb02f.)

It was in 1948 when the three were merged into one. From onwards, this Publishing House has been of great influence in the publishing field in China. Today I will just focus on one important figure in the contemporary age: Fan Yong (Figure 8.1.2), the famous publisher who was undoubtedly the soul of Joint Publishing House during the 1980's.

Figure 8.1.2: Fan Yong — the famous publisher in the Joint Publishing House. (范用，三联书店著名出版家)
(http://img1.gtimg.com/cul/pics/hv1/45/194/1923/125092590.)

With his trademark dark 1) _____, red sweater and scarf, and black-rimmed glasses, Fan Yong had a pronounced western air and a strong scholarly 2) _____. Everyone who knew him knew of his 3) _____ sentiments and 4) _____, qualities that were rare among literary men. For this reason, Fan Yong came to be known respectfully as "Boss Fan" among the literary circles of Beijing. Fan Yong also went by the name of "Mr. Three Many", which was a reference to the fact he owned lots of books, drank lots of alcohol, and had lots of friends. At Joint Publishing, Fan Yong was known by another name: the 5)"_____", which was a pun derived from an old in-joke started by Fan Yong's colleagues at Joint Publishing, with Fan acquiring the name because his office on the fifth floor happened to face the 6) _____ (In Chinese, the words for "Literary History" and 7) "_____" have exactly the same pronunciation). But in the end, Fan Yong really did become the "The Curator of Literary History". It was from that small, unpleasant smelling office that Fan Yong frequently 8) _____ high-spirited literary conversations, receiving visits from such great cultural figures as Wang Shixiang (Figure 8.1.3-1), Fei Xiaotong (Figure 8.1.3-2), Li Shu, Wang Yunsheng, Xiao Qian, Wu Zuguang, Feng Yidai, Huang Miaozi, Yu Feng, Ai Wu, and Ge Baoquan.

Figure 8.1.3-1: Wang Shixiang — one of the great Chinese cultural figures (王世襄，中国的文化人物之一)
(http://szb.ch365.com.cn/dsck/res/1/20080924/65501222188383625.)

Figure 8.1.3-2: Fei Xiaotong — one of the great Chinese cultural figures（费孝通，中国伟大的文化人物之一）

(http://wj.js.xinhuanet.com/2010-10/26/xinsrc_423100726144104681248.)

The 9) _____ poet Bian Zhilin once stopped off at Fan's office on the fifth floor while on the way to Dongsi (a place downtown) to post a letter. Upon arriving at the office, he extended to Fan Yong a casual greeting: "Don't let me bother you; I'm just here for a smoke." In an article he wrote, Fan Yong once recalled an 10) _____ he had with Qi Gong (Figure 8.1.3): "One day, the real Curator of Literary History came."

Figure 8.1.3-3: Qi Gong — Educator, Calligrapher, Painter, Poet, Connoisseur, and master of Chinese culture.（启功，教育家、古典文献学家、鉴定家、红学家、诗人，国学大师）

http://9610.com/qigong/xiang10.

To my surprise, the old fellow came upstairs and gave me a book and a painting. I never had the nerve to ask people for their calligraphy or paintings (with the exception of Wang Shixiang and Yu Feng), and certainly never dared to ask Mr. Qi. Seeing the lengths he had gone to, I was totally lost for words. Fan Yong was well known as a sentimental person. Reveling in conversation, he often insisted that visitors to his office stayed behind for dinner and wine when discussions became lively. Sometimes these discussions would continue from the restaurant downstairs to the "Fan Family Restaurant" (a humorous reference to the Fan family home). Fan Yong even received a painting from Huang Yongyu especially for this reason. The inscription on the painting read: "There is nothing that should distract a man from his duties, with the exception of borrowing books and enjoying wine."

The "Hall of Literary History" was also the scene of an amusing episode in which Fan Yong "interrogated" a book thief. The Joint Publishing Bookshop was once visited by a hard-up university student who stole books from the shelves and hid them in his clothes as he went. The student was eventually discovered by the shop assistants, who escorted him straight to Fan Yong's office. It didn't take Fan Yong long to see that the student, who had shame written all over his face, was genuinely infatuated with books. Waving his hand with a smile, Fan Yong said: "I'll let you off this time. The books are yours. But next time you want a book, come and find me. Under no circumstances can you go stealing again!" With this, "Boss Fan" had made himself another good friend, this time a student who was years younger than him.

Such was Fan Yong, outwardly a layman; however, in essence, he made a great contribution not only to the publishing industry, but also to its the magazines and periodicals. He was the founder of *Dushu* and *Xinhua* Digest. I think that is all for today's topic. If you still hope to explore more, please log in to wapbaike.baidu.com for more information. I look forward to seeing you again next time.

Task 2 ▶ Discuss the historical note
(Students are required to do role play in groups by imitating the PRIMO's dialogue)

Irene:	Hi, Miriam! Hi, Owen! Let's get down to business and discuss Professor Phillips historical note.
Miriam:	How should we structure our discussion, Irene?
Irene:	Why don't we each raise one question, and the other two try to answer it. We can all give assessment and feedback.
Miriam:	Sounds good. I propose Owen as the most appropriate person to start the ball rolling — he's always full of questions.
Owen:	Okay Miriam, here's my question for you two girls: Can you explain the "joint" in the name Joint Publishing Press?
Miriam:	Oh that's easy! In the 20s and 30s there were three vibrant organisations in the publishing field: Shenghuo Bookstore, Xinzhi Bookstore, and Dushu Publishing House. They were merged in 1948 to become the Joint Publishing Press.
Irene:	It's important to remember that those three organisations were quite distinct from each other before 1948, and they themselves had developed from other entities, for example

	the Shenghuo Bookstore grew out of the *Shenghuo Journal*, while the *Dushu* Publishing House had previously been the *Dushu Shenghuo*, a semimonthly journal.
Miriam:	Okay, time for my question. I wonder why Professor Phillips chose this press as an example — I mean, why did the Joint Publishing House become so famous?
Owen:	As I understand it, its reputation came from two sources. On the one hand you had the aspect of multiple development — one large company derived from the amalgamation of three smaller entities. But on the other hand, the larger company managed to preserve the creative features of its predecessors. And if you need a third factor, it was probably the company's insistence on being an honest recorder of the times — hence its reputation.
Irene:	That's a really impressive analysis, Owen, I like it very much. But I'm still not sure that we've totally explained the relationship between bookstores and publishing houses.
Miriam:	Isn't that because the histories of the two are interwoven with each other? In ancient times bookstores themselves compiled and edited books, then they printed and sold them. But as the market grew, so it became necessary to separate the different functions.
Owen:	That's a good point, Miriam. But what about that Fan Yong guy, the "Curator of Literary History". Don't you think we should introduce that character in class?
Irene:	Great idea, Owen — let's make it a group task. We'll work together to find a novel way of introducing Fan Yong and the work he did at Joint Publishing.
Miriam:	Fabulous idea! Let's get going.

The Evolution and Diversification of Publishing in China in Modern Times

Task 3 ▶ Build up our vocabulary
(Drag and match exercises)

Match the English words in column A with the Chinese equivalents in column B.

	A		B
1	Twentieth Century Literary Collection edited	A	中国出版集团
2	*Principles of Aesthetics*	B	数字出版
3	"light reading"	C	上海世纪出版集团
4	Essay Collection published	D	青春文学作品
5	"The new realism"	E	伯尔尼公约和世界版权公约
6	*Berne Convention and the Universal Copyright Convention*	F	编年史
7	Beijing Publishing Group	G	北京出版集团
8	Shanghai Century Publishing Group	H	《品三国》
9	"going global" strategy	I	《美学原理》
10	*A Taste of the Three Kingdoms*	J	"二十世纪文库"
11	Teenage literature	K	"百花散文书系"
12	China Publishing Group	L	"走出去"战略
13	digital publishing	M	"新写实"
14	chronicle	N	"轻阅读"

Task 4 ▶ Reading activity

The following excerpt is recommended to PRIMO. It is about *The History of Chinese Libraries.* People are so accustomed to reading in libraries that they usually take it for granted. But how do libraries start? PRIMO will invite anyone who are interested in publishing to join them to explore the origins and development of libraries.

Chinese libraries have existed for at least 2500 years. They evolved from collections and collectors and book markets. A review of their developmental history may assist in further clarifying Chinese publishing history, because the accumulated collections are actually a part of the evolution of publishing.

Book collections can be traced back to the Han Dynasty, when various book classification schemes were used, the most influential being the ones elaborated for the emperor's collections. Book catalogues are included, among which are catalogues of many privately compiled collections. Basically, books and documents in China were collected by the royal court and government offices, academies, temples and private individuals. Owners of libraries in the later empire allowed selective access to their collections to scholars and other books collectors. Officials, too, were sometimes granted access to the imperial collections. However, books were rarely lent out. Instead scholars usually copied books by hand or, if they could afford it, employed copyists to do the copying for them. Modern public lending libraries were opened for the first time at the beginning of the twentieth century. The history of libraries encompasses the following stages.

4.1 Imperial libraries

The earliest document repositories may have been those of the royal ancestral temple. The first libraries for which there is any evidence date from the Spring and Autumn period. Not much is known about them except that they were primarily archives of official documents possibly including divination records and depositories of state papers (*cefu* 册府, or generically, *gufu* 故府). Their contents were regarded as secret. The scribes attached to them served in various functions, including confidential secretary to the ruler and court chronicler. Divination records, if kept at all, were probably stored separately in the palace or in cult centers. For instance, the first imperial library as such was established in the palace of Han like the Lan Tai (兰台) — orchid Terrace, where Ban Gu (班固) (Figure 8.4.1) worked for much of his life. A step was taken to separate the functions of the librarian from the court secretariat with the appointment of a Mishu Jian (祕书监) — literally, director of written secrets; Mishu was the term frequently used for the palace library. The library and archives were separated from the secretariat in the third century. Later dynasties up to 1380 continued the tradition of calling the imperial government library and archives Mishu Sheng (祕书省) (Figure 8.4.2). Individual collections in the library were most often named after the halls or departments (*ge* 阁 or *bu* 部) in which they were housed or after the names of the famous Han palace library buildings.

Figure 8.4.1: Ban Gu ever in *Lan Tai*（兰台）— orchid Terrace（曾在兰台任兰台令史的班固）
(http://pic.baike.soso.com/p/20130620/20130620155521-1655758793.)

Figure 8.4.2: The relics of Mishu sheng — Imperial Library in Xian, Tang Dynasty.（西安的唐代秘书省遗址）
(http://image.cnwest.com/attachement/jpg/site1/20080820/001372d8a0ba0a15baf20d.)

Large imperial libraries housing full sets of the Classics and the other branches of orthodox learning symbolized the prosperity of an age and the emperor's role as the foremost patron of orthodox scholarship, and their possession conferred legitimacy on a dynasty. As the saying goes, a kingdom can be destroyed, but history cannot be lost. Thereafter, almost every dynasty made great efforts to protect its rare books as well as documents and archives. The Tang Dynasty saw a prosperous period of cultural development and preservation of all the heritages. The Song Dynasty had 16 rulers and held the empire for more than 300 years. Despite the chaos and war in the later Song, the records of its grand scribes are all in the history office. Even when the Jin captured Kaifeng in 1127, the minority not only took the imperial art collections as loot, but took the books as well, which were transported north to the Jin capital of Nanjing (present day — Beijing). It was no exception when Zhu Yuanzhang took Dadu in 1368, he instructed that the imperial book collections be well kept and shipped to the new capital — Yingtian (应天, present day Nanjing) via the Grand Canal.

The last major displacements of the imperial collections were in the 1930s and 1940s, when a careful selection of the Palace Museum collections was put into crates and shipped to Shanghai (1933–1936), briefly to Nanjing, and then in July 1937 to the Upper *Yanzi* valley for safekeeping. They were held in temples and shrines in Sichuan until 1947. In 1948–1949, 1538 crates of rare books and documents were shipped to Taibei along with the cream of the museum's art objects. In 1966, the Library of Congress sent the 200 Song editions from the National Library of Beiping that it had been requested to hold for safekeeping in 1941 along with 1500 other rare editions from the same library to the museum. What was left of the Northern Song book and painting collections had been on the move the most — in the course of 500 years they had been shipped back and forth across the country and to America and Taiwan on no fewer than eleven occasions, thus demonstrating that imperial libraries have remained an important place for storage.

4.2 Buddhist temple libraries

The imperial libraries took keeping the Classics and the other branches of orthodox learning as a major mission. It is not surprising, therefore, to find that Buddhist monks and lay believers were at the forefront in the search for ways to produce large quantities of texts to memorize, recite, and copy in order to gain merit. Nor is it surprising to find the huge efforts that went into translating and commenting on the doctrines of Buddhism and preserving these in an enormous scriptural canon, Tibetan editions, the core elements of which were disseminated to every major Buddhist temple in China, and as a consequence of which, Temple libraries also came into being.

Temple libraries were called *Cangjingge* (藏经阁) or *Cangjinglou* (藏经楼) (Figure 8.4.3-1-2) — hall for storing the sutras. The sutras were usually placed on the second usually the top floor of the library. In the Tang Dynasty the largest collections were in the temple of Luoyang that also acted as translation centers. Unique evidence of what a Buddhist library had accumulated by the early Song Dynasty comes from the cave library at Dunhuang. Publicly sponsored printings of *Tripitakeu* (the three collections of books making up the Buddhist canon of scriptures 嘉兴藏) were distributed to major temples from the Song Dynasty. Many of the sutra catalogues were based on temple collections. Occasionally, there is some evidence that temples stored Daoist or secular works, such as the collected writings of a famous poet.

Figure 8.4.3-1: *Cangjingge* — the Tripitaka Sutra Pavilion in Luoyang White Horse Temple. (洛阳白马寺藏经阁)
(http://www.pctowap.com/doimg/img3.laibafile.cn/p/m/200730337.)

Figure 8.4.3-2: *Cangjinglou* — the normal Depository of Buddhist Sutras. (藏经楼)

In the Ming and Qing Dynasties, temples served as printing centers for the Tibetan edition. In one notable case at the end of the Ming Dynasty, the Jiaxing Tibetan was edited and printed in one temple and bound and distributed in another in the same province. The huge collection of stone-carved sutras at the Yunjusi (云居寺) (Figure 8.4.4) was not strictly speaking a library, but more a merit-making exercise.

Figure 8.4.4: *Yunjusi*— Yunju Temple located in Fangshan District, Beijing. (北京房山的云居寺) (http://www.csw333.com/upload_files/qibosoft_news_/135/83557_20141013161003_ugnim.)

Over the centuries many scholars found temple libraries and halls a peaceful environment for study. One example that comes to mind is the 28-year-old Wan Sitong (万斯同) — a famous historian in the Qing Dynasty and his young friend Huang Baijia (黄百家), who closeted themselves in their local Buddhist temple during the year 1666-1667 to read the "21 Histories" and other historical works (Figure 8.4.5).

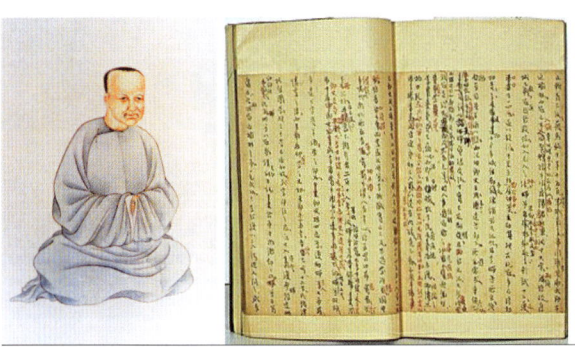

Figure 8.4.5: Wan Sitong, a famous historian and his works — the manuscript of the *Ming History*. (万斯同和他的《明史稿》抄本) (http://m.aikangguoji.com/pic/21828062524.233078361810.thumb.)

4.3 Academy libraries

Academy Libraries refer to academies or schools in China with another name *Shuyuan* 书院. The term dates from the Tang Dynasty, and was used for schools since the Han Dynasty, including *Xueguan* (学官), *Xuegong* (学宫), and *Xuetang* (学堂). It was the name of an official office for collecting and collating books. In the Tang Dynasty, some 47 *shuyuan* are known to have been established. Most were private. There was a surge in their numbers in the Song and Yuan Dynasties, of which two thirds were private, sometimes situated in lineage schools. Thereafter, the numbers grew enormously: 1699 in the Ming Dynasty and 3868 in the Qing Dynasty. Unlike in previous ages, about 60 percent of the Ming and Qing *Shuyuan* were under official auspices and some of them were famous centers for the teaching of *Lixue* (理学) — Neo-Confucianism. Their libraries held anything from a few dozen to several hundred works, which came from various sources, including public and private donations. During the golden age of the *Shuyuan*, their collections grew, and catalogues of individual *Shuyuan* libraries were published. The Ming Dynasty also saw the extension of officially sponsored libraries from prefectures to counties. Typically, such local libraries were called *Zunjingge* (尊经阁). It is said that the largest Qing *Shuyuan* library — *Wenkai Shuyuan* (文開书院) (Figure 8.4.6). It claimed 20,000 titles in over 300,000 *ce* (册). The smallest Qing *Shuyuan* library, that of the *Longhe Shuyuan* (龙河书院) in Jiangxi, had only one title, the *Shisan Jing Zhushu* (《十三经注疏》) (Figure 8.4.7).

Figure 8.4.6: *Wenkai Shuyuan* — the academy of classical learning in Taiwan. (台湾彰化的文开书院)
http://img1.gtimg.com/rushidao/pics/hv1/53/134/1456/94710623.

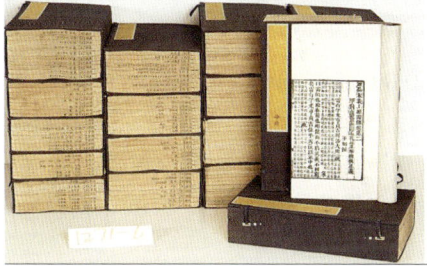

Figure 8.4.7: *Shisan Jing Zhushu* — The Thirteen Classics with Collation Attached published in Jiangxi Publishing House in Qing Dynasty. (清代江西书局重刊宋本《十三经注疏》附校勘记)
http://pmgs.kongfz.com/data/pre_show_pic/3/69/276.

In the late Qing educational reforms (1901), *shuyuan* were renamed with the old term *xuetang* or *xuefang* in many of the southern dialects. *Daxue Tang* — universities were established in Beijing and in the provincial capitals. After the 1911 revolution, the *xuetang* gained their modern name *xuexiao* — school, and *Daxue Tang* was abbreviated to *daxue* — university, henceforward the modern name for university.

4.4 Private libraries

The first detailed evidence giving a hint as to the contents of ancient Chinese private libraries comes from the books buried alongside individuals in tombs during the Warring States and Han Dynasties.

In the centuries after the invention of paper in the Han Dynasty, private collections grew in size, for example, the biography of Fan Ping (范平) (215-284) in the *Jinshu* mentions that he owned so many books that large numbers of people came from far and near to read and copy them and his grandson provided them with food and drink. But he had only 7,000 scroll, amounting to not more than a few hundred titles. Two centuries later, we know that the collection of the famous writer and bibliophile Zhang Mian (张缅) numbered over 10,000 *juan* and was considered large. Even more impressive was that of the scholar and historian, Shenyue (沈约, 441-513), who also worked at the Liang court. His is said to have numbered 20,000 *juan* — possibly over 1,000 titles. Emperor Yuan of the Liang claims to have had a collection of 80,000 rolls.

The size and number of private collections grew after the spread of printing during the Song (the names and in a few cases, the details, survive of some 700 collections). Two collectors in the Dynasty were said to have had libraries of 100,000 *juan* about 6,000 titles. One was that of the influential early Southern Song official Ye Mengde (叶孟德, 1077-1148) and another large collection was that of the minister, Chen Zhensun (陈振孙, 1183-1262), the catalogue of whose library, the *Zhizhaishulu Jieti* (《直斋书录解题》) (Figure 8.4.8) lists 3,069 titles in 51,180 *juan*. By the end of the Ming, in addition to the *Tianyi Ge*, perhaps the largest, was that of Qi Chenghan (祁乘汉, 1562-1628) Shanyin, Shaoxing (绍兴). His collection is said to have contained some 10,000 works between 140-150 thousand *juan*.

The first mention of special buildings to house private book collections come in the fourth century AD. They were called *shucang* (书藏). Starting in the Tang, but especially in the Song Dynasty, other terms appear, such as *Shulou* (书楼), *Cangshulou* (藏书楼), *Shuzhai* (书斋). Whatever names were used, they actually functioned as private libraries.

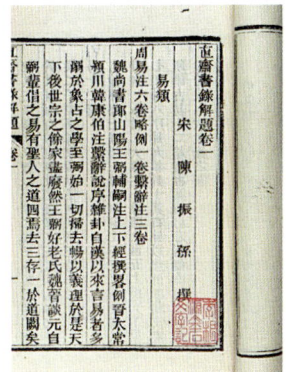

Figure 8.4.8: *Zhizhaishulu Jieti* — the annotated bibliography of book categories stored in Qing Wuying Dian. (清代武英殿聚珍版《直斋书录解题》)

http://pmgs.kongfz.com/data/pre_show_pic/105/571/1469.

4.5 Lending and public libraries

In general, collectors did not open their collections to the public, although some notable exceptions are occasionally recorded. In the later empire several private collectors advocated giving wider access to their collections. Cao Rong (曹溶, 1613-1685) in his *Liutong Gushu Yue* (《流通古书约》) Figure 8.4.9), which was a compact regarding the circulation of old books, recommended that copying and block printing should be used to give book collections a wider circulation. In the eighteenth century, Zhou Yongnian's (周永年 (1730-1791), *Jieshu Yuan* (籍书园) (Figure 8.4.10) — *ji* 籍 is a loan character for *jie* 借, was opened to a certain extent to scholars. That initiated the early lending library in China. Zhou was a scholarly bibliophile, who began collecting books as student and later worked as an assistant compiler at the *Siku* office. While in Beijing, he accumulated a collection of 100,000 *juan* from the book stores at Beijing's most famous book and antiques street, *Liuli Chang* (琉璃厂). In the preface to the catalogue of his library Zhou makes the case for *Rucang* (儒藏) (Figure 8.4.11) — a Confucian series, along the lines of the great Daoist and Buddhist collections, the *Daozang* (道藏) and *Shizang* (释藏 or 大藏经) (Figure 8.4.12-1-2). The idea had surfaced previously and has resurfaced on several occasions since. Zhou also sets out his view that collections should be open to readers and advocates the establishment of public libraries, one of whose duties would be the exchange of their catalogues.

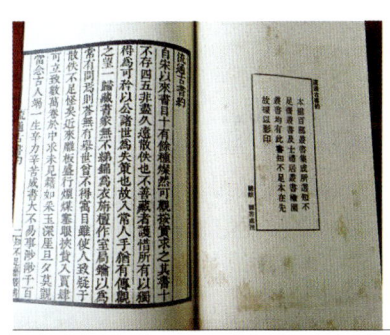

Figure 8.4.9: *Liutong Gushu Yue* — the Ancient Book circulation protocol by Cao Rong, published by Taiwan Yiwen Publishing Press in 1964. (曹溶撰《流通古书约》(台湾艺文印书馆，1964 年出版)

http://img.kongfz.cn/20140616/2829727/2829727tatwS0_b.)

Figure 8.4.10: The original site of *Jieshu Yuan* nearby Wulong Lake in Jinan — a library for scholar to borrow books.（藉书园最初所在地 —— 济南五龙湖畔）
http://img1.ph.126.net/wpDdB07x5pddHx0kwhsR
tw==/2097270051571772890.

Figure 8.4.11: *Rucang* — a Confucian series by Tang Yijie (photocopy version), published by the Peking University Press.（汤一介主编的影印《儒藏》精华编，（北京大学出版社出版）
(http://y3.ifengimg.com/cmpp/2014/09/12/14/bc694956-f42a-4ea4-bb20-12f7957d3bc1.)

Figure 8.4.12-1: *Daozang* — a Taoism series (photocopy version) published by Shanghai Book Store in 1988.（影印本《道藏》（上海书店等，1988 年出版）
(http://www.jieti.com/admin/editor/uploadfile/2011925205559670.)

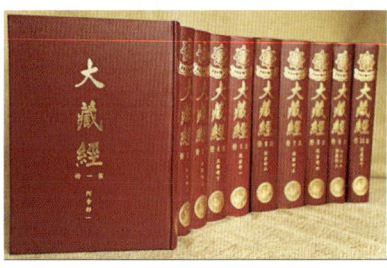

Figure 8.4.12-2: *Shizang or Dazangjing* — The confluence of Buddhist Classics edited by A Japanese published by a Japanese Press in 1934.（日本高楠顺次郎主编的《大正新修大藏经》，即《大正藏》，大正一切经刊行会，1934 年出版）

Zhou was ahead of his time in many respects. Public libraries came to China about a century after his day and the idea of *Ruzang* came to fruition only over 200 years after his death. The first modern public libraries were established at the initiative of the provincial governors Zhang Zhidong (张之洞) and Zhao Erxun (赵尔巽) at Wuchang and Changsha in 1904. They were named Hubei Public Library and Hunan Public Library respectively. The Qing court called for the establishment of public libraries in all the remaining provincial capitals in 1907 and many were set up in the following years. The nearest to a national public library in the Qing Dynasty and Republic era was the *Jingshi* library (京师图书馆) (Figure 8.4.13) established in Beijing in 1909. It was officially opened to the public in 1912. The collections were based on the holdings of *Guozi Jian* (国子监) and *Hanlin Yuan* (翰林院, Figure 8.4.14-1-2).

Despite the upheavals of the warlord period and of the Japanese invasion and the subsequent civil war, a considerable number of public libraries were established in the Republic and existing ones were enlarged.

Figure 8.4.13: Jingshi library established in Beijing in 1917. (1917 年京师图书馆开馆纪念摄影)
http://images.china.cn/attachement/jpg/site1000/20140619/c03fd54abc3e150cb9c344.

Figure 8.4.14-1: *Guozi Jian* — the Directorate of Imperial Academy of Three Dynasties *Yuan*, *Ming* and *Qing*. (历经元、明、清三代的国子监)
http://pic20.nipic.com/20120409/7336507_163415690000_2.

Figure 8.4.14-2: *Hanlin Yuan* — the Imperial Academy established since Tang Dynasty for cultivating officials. (《翰林院》图)
http://www.people.com.cn/mediafile/200403/23/F20040323082 42100000.

Task 5 ▶ Reading comprehension

(Students are required to launch a discussion to pose new questions and answer all the questions raised in the dialogue, and do the role play based on the following)

Irene: Hello, PRIMO team, that was a really long reading passage, wasn't it? But it was just what I wanted, because it answered so many questions for me. Was it the same for you, Miriam?

	Did it help you to distinguish between libraries and bookstores and their evolution?
Miriam:	Oh, it did, absolutely! I've now got the whole question clear in my mind and can classify the evolution of libraries into several different categories.
Philips:	I admire your pursuit of the truth, Miriam. That's what learning is all about, and I want to be involved in your discussion and share ideas and opinions with you.
Richards:	I've also come along to join in your discussion. This is the last unit, and I value the chance to accompany you in your learning.
Irene:	It's a privilege to have our two teachers with us. I'd like to kick off the discussion with a general question: Who can specify the characteristics of each type of library mentioned in the reading passage?
Miriam:	Oh, please let me start — I've made lots of notes! Modern Chinese libraries evolved originally from collectors who were either real book-lovers or book sellers or owners of bookstores. And of course there were imperial libraries which were housed in royal temples dating back to the Spring and Autumn Period. The books kept there were mostly archives of official documents and sometimes divination records. They think the first library was established in the Han Dynasty and was called *Lantai*. In later Dynasties the term used for the palace library was *Mishu*, and in the Ming Dynasty it became *Mishu Sheng*.
Owen:	Can I interrupt here, Miriam? You mentioned royal temples as storage places for imperial libraries, but there were also temple libraries, weren't there? How did they start? And why is Dunhuang so closely connected with various sutras and other scriptures?
Richards:	Perhaps I can help out here, Owen. Religion has probably existed since *homo sapiens* first walked the earth — possibly even before. One of the earliest religions in China was Buddhism, and Buddhists believed that the larger their collection of scriptures, or sutras to be memorized and

recited, the more merit they would gain. This accounts for why so many monks were eager to collect and copy sutra and other related items like paintings and statues. Now, to get on to the Dunhuang Caves or Mogao Grottoes as they are also called. Carving out the caves started in AD 366 and the complex of hundreds of cave temples became the most magnificent treasury for Buddhist religious art works, where generations of monks have gathered for over 1600 years. It is a major Buddhist pilgrimage site, and also for other religious people, and of course for tourists. It probably reached its peak during the Tang Dynasty, and became the biggest collection of sutra in the world, despite having suffered 9 disasters caused by wars and political upheavals. It is also a mural library, because many artists, including Zhang Daqian, engraved, carved, and painted many murals recording both culture, customs, and landscapes. In 1987, the Mogao Grottoes were registered in the World Heritage List. I hope you can see how Dunhuang is a perfect example of how temple libraries came into existence.

Owen: A wonderful example, Professor Richards, thank you so much.

Irene: But what about lending libraries. After all, that's what we mean by a library today, isn't it?

philips: Yes indeed. But that is a very recent development in the evolution of the Chinese library. As you read in the text, modern libraries developed through many stages, from Imperial libraries, Temple libraries, Academy libraries, private and public libraries, all of which originated from both private and official collectors. Now, in ancient times, hardly any kind of library would provide access to the public. Reading, after all, was the privilege of the rich and powerful. Sometime during the Emperor Wanli reign, a bookstore owner, Cao Rong, initiated the circulation of old books and recommended that copying and block printing should be used to give book collections a wider circulation. In the eighteenth century, Zhou Yongnian also opened his book collection or library to scholars. Those two great scholars

	were the inaugurators of the modern lending library, and we all owe them a great debt of thanks because of the benefit they brought to ordinary people. My final recommendation to you is that you spend a little more time researching Academy Libraries. Can you do that?
Owen:	No problem, Professor Phillips. I can see why you leave us with this task, because in fact none of us has concentrated on the topic, so there's a bit of a gap in our understanding.
Miriam:	I suggest we treat this as a joint task, like we did with Fan Yong, don't you think so, Irene?
Irene:	I couldn't agree more. Let's do it before we start the translation task.

Task 6　Translation practice

(Students are required to translate the following Chinese paragraph into English individually, in pairs or in group)

Owen:	Hi, everybody! I'm really looking forward to this translation task. Do you know why?
Miriam:	I think it's because you know all about the subject — digital publishing and data-based business. Don't you think so, Irene?
Irene:	I don't think it's just that. I think you both like these translation tasks because you're translating into your mother tongue, but from a good command of Chinese. It's different for me — I'm translating into a second language, which is always harder.
Owen:	That's true, but your English is terrific, Irene, much better than our Chinese. And anyway, that's where teamwork comes in, isn't it?
Miriam:	Of course it is! You help us with the Chinese, and we help you with any English problems there may be.
Irene:	You're right, teamwork is the answer. Now here are some terms that I have difficulty with: "数字汇聚", "二进制代

	码"、"印刷模拟出版物"、"博客出版"、"网络游戏出版", and "产业价值链".
Owen:	I'm pretty confident about those terms. "数字汇聚" is "digital convergence", "二进制代码" is "binary code format".
Miriam:	And the others are "simulated publications", "blog publishing", "online computer game" and "well-defined value chain" in that order. Any other problem terms?
Irene:	No, that's great, both of you. Now that's all sorted, we can start.
Owen:	Okay, let's begin!

在互联网大数据时代，出版产业面临巨大挑战，即来自技术进步引发的"数字汇聚"——数字化时代的市场化和全球化。数字技术发展不断地颠覆传统的出版概念，在数字化环境下诞生的电子书、报、刊和交互行为使"出版"的概念越来越模糊，大数据不断地改写传统出版规则。所谓数字出版，是指在整个出版过程中，从编辑、制作到发行，所有信息都以统一的二进制代码的数字化形式存储于光、磁等介质中，信息的处理与传递必须借助计算机或类似设备来进行的一种出版形式，也指利用数字技术从事图书、期刊和报纸等印刷模拟出版物的制作和生产。数字出版作为一种新兴的出版形态，包含手机出版、博客出版、网络学术出版、网络游戏出版、软件、网络杂志、网络广告、网络音乐、影视出版、动漫产品等多种形式。数字出版呈现出产品内容丰富、类型齐全的特点。此外，先进的出版经营理念和商业模式，产业价值链比较完整清晰，市场规模不断地扩大，涌现出一批具有良好经济效益和社会效益、技术力量雄厚、用户数量剧增、在国内外知名的数字出版企业。随着我国数字出版在技术创新能力和管理能力方面的提升，我国必将从出版大国发展为出版强国。

Task 7　Attend Professor Richards's public lecture

Lecture 8

Diversification of Publishing in the New Era
Professor Richards

Hello, PRIMO members. How time flies! Our series of lectures is coming to an end. Today I will present the eighth and final lecture in our series and

I will address the topic of modern publishing in China. In my last lecture I reviewed the state of publishing during the Republic of China era by focusing on the development and success of one particular publisher, the Commercial Press. In this lecture I will review the state of Chinese publishing in the modern era by focusing on the development of the publishing industry from the 1980s onwards. It was then that Chinese publishing turned a new page and moved forward.

At the conclusion of the "Cultural Revolution" in 1978, a new era began in China. The government introduced new policies regarding intellectuals, there was a shift towards economic development and an effort to develop socialism. This new direction directly affected the publishing industry. Many of the publishing organizations that had been curtailed or shut down were restored, transformed and became very active as China made the transition from a planned economy to a socialist-featured market economy. I will elaborate on the topic in chronological order.

7.1 Features of publishing in the 1980s

The 1980s not only saw the rapid recovery and development of the publishing industry, but also a diversification in the content of the books which were being published. The diversification was symptomatic of the cultural shift which had taken place and which served to promote the social progress of the time. Examples of this change can be seen in the scope and content of the books published during the period: Changes in novel publishing preceded others. Full length novels began to be serialized and the publishing of book collections became a popular trend. Titles such as *A Collection of Modern Chinese Novels* and *A Collection of Contemporary Novels*, led a wave of literary publishing efforts that afforded many talented young writers the opportunity to be read. Comprehensive book collections became the speciality of some publishing houses. The Liaoning People's Publishing House introduced the *Collection of Translations on Aesthetics*, and the *Collection of Books on Psychology, People and Culture*. The Shanghai People's Publishing House printed the Collection of New Subjects and the Collection of Books on the History of Chinese Culture. The titles I have just mentioned not only had a widespread influence on the culture of the 1980s, but also played an important role in the field of education.

Next, books concerning the humanities, social sciences, natural sciences and technology appeared in large numbers. Interestingly, more than 46,000 books dealing with the subject of philosophy and social science were published;

38,000 of these were new titles. During the decade, the introduction of Western philosophical and social science texts also became an important cultural trend. These titles were usually published in the form of collections, among which three titles are especially noteworthy: the paper *Walking Toward the Future* chose three knowledge groups in the "culture fever" as study cases, they are "Toward Future Series" editorial committee represented by Jin Guantao (金观涛), *China and the World* edited by Gan Yang (甘阳) (Figure 8.7.1), and *Twentieth Century Literary Collection* edited by Li Shengping (李盛平) (Figure 8.7.2). These three publications are credited with having had a large influence on Chinese cultural values and the shaping of modern ideas among the intellectuals of the time.

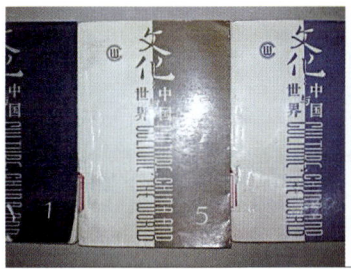

Figure 8.7.1: *China and the World Series* edited by Gan Yang published by SDX Joint Publishing Company in 2014. （甘阳等主编的《文化：中国与世界丛书》之一，三联书店，2014 年出版）

https://book.douban.com/subject/4002320/

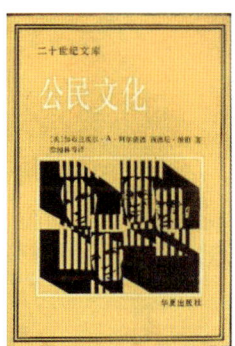

Figure 8.7.2: *Twentieth Century Literary Collection* edited by Li Shengping published by Huaxia Publishing House in 1989. （李盛平等主编的《二十世纪文库》之一，华夏出版社，1989 年出版）

https://book.douban.com/subject/4002320/

Complementing the surge of publishing new and old titles in the fields of philosophy and social science, another popular type of book printed during the 1980s dealt with traditional Chinese culture. To name a few: *The History of Chinese Philosophy* written by Ren Jiyu (Figure 8.7.3), *A Study of Confucian Dialectics* by Pang Pu (Figure 8.7.4), *Principles of Aesthetics* written by Cai Yi, (Figure 8.7.5) and *The History of Aesthetics in the West* written by Zhu Guangqian (Figure 8.7.6) were all published in the 1980s. These books provided both the public and scholars with the opportunity to reflect over the history and development of traditional Chinese culture.

Figure 8.7.3: *The History of Chinese Philosophy* written by Ren Jiyu, published by People's Publishing House in 1996.（任继愈著《中国哲学史》，人民出版社，1996 年出版）

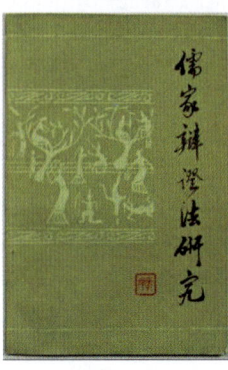

Figure 8.7.4: *A Study of Confucian Dialectics*—written by Pang Pu, published by Zhonghua Book Company in 1984.（庞朴著《儒家辩证法研究》，中华书局，1984 年出版）

Figure 8.7.5: *Principles of Aesthetics* written by Cai Yi, published by Hunan People's Publishing House in 1985.（蔡仪著《美学原理》，湖南人民出版社，1985 年出版）

Figure 8.7.6: *The History of Aesthetics in the West* written by Zhu Guangqian, published by People's Literature Publishing House in 1982.（朱光潜著《西方美学史》，人民文学出版社，1982 年出版）

Other popular books published in the 1980s dealt with the subject of economics. Xue Muqiao's *China's Socialist Economy* (Figure 8.7.7), Sun Zhifang's *Critique of Socialist Economics* (Figure 8.7.8) and Xu Dixin's *On*

Socialist Production (Figure 8.7.9), Circulation and Distribution, all laid down the foundations for the exploration of theories concerning economic reform.

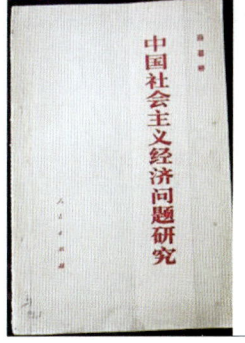

Figure 8.7.7: *China's Socialist Economy* — written by Xue Muqiao, published by People's Publishing House in 1979.（薛暮桥著《中国社会主义经济问题研究》，人民出版社，1979 年出版）

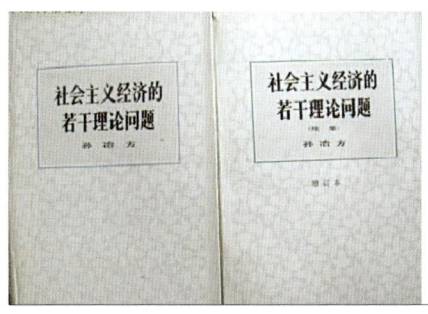

Figure 8.7.8: *Critique of Socialist Economics* written by Sun Zhifang, published by People's Publishing House in 1984.（孙冶方著《社会主义经济的若干理论问题》，人民出版社，1984 年出版）

Figure 8.7.9: *On Socialist Production* written by Xu Dixin, published by People's Publishing House in 2003.（许涤新等著《中国资本主义的萌芽》，人民出版社，2003 年出版）

Additionally, the government's new outlook and the idea that science and technology would lead the way to a brighter future brought about significant progress in both scientific and technological research. Close to 87,000 titles concerning science and technology were published in the 1980s, with more than 2 billion individual copies being printed. The texts covered a wide array of scientific and technologically related subjects.

Aside from the proliferation of the academic and scientific oriented books which were being printed, popular literary titles from Hong Kong and Taiwan were also published in large numbers. Bestsellers included martial arts novels by Jin Yong, Gu Long, Ling Yusheng and Wen Rui'an, as well as romantic novels by Qiong Yao and Yi Shu (Figure 8.7.10-1-2). The printing of these books not only reflects the diversity of the material which was being published at the time, but also is indicative of the direction the publishing industry would take as China moved into the 1990s.

Figure 8.7.10-1: *Martial Arts Novels* by Jin Yong published by SDX Joint Publishing Company in 1994. (《金庸作品集》，三联书店，1994 年出版)

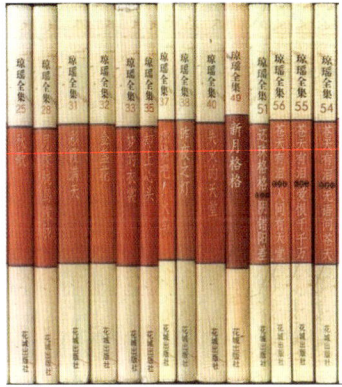

Figure 8.7.10-2: *The Whole Collection of Romantic Novels* by Qiong Yao published by Huacheng Publishing House in 1996. (《琼瑶全集》，花城出版社，1996 年出版)

7.2 Features of publishing in the 1990s

The publishing sector continued to flourish in the 1990s with commercialization replacing cultural demand as the driving force behind growth. The emergence of a more sophisticated and diverse audience resulted in an increasingly strong market in the area of literature and a decline in the demand for academic texts. Specialty or niche markets grew, fueling a demand for nostalgic, leisurely, consumer and avant-garde reading materials. Wang Shuo's novels were very popular and were soon followed by the avant-garde novels of Su Tong and Yu Hua. These authors were in turn followed by the publishing of other popular writers such as Zhang Ailing, Lin Yutang, Liang

Shiqiu, Wang Xiaobo and Zhou Zuoren(Figure 8.7.11-1-2-3-4-5). The books these authors produced became favorites of the publishing industry and their success served as a guide for publishers.

Figure 8.7.11-1: *The Whole Collection of Zhang Ailing's Works* published by Huacheng Publishing House in 1997.（《张爱玲作品集》之一，花城出版社，1997 年出版）

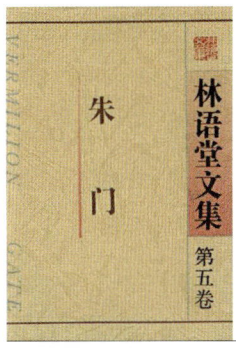

Figure 8.7.11-2: One of published by Writers Publishing House in 1995. *the Collected Works by Lin Yutang* （《林语堂文集》之一，作家出版社，1995 年出版）

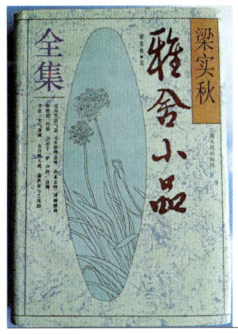

Figure 8.7.11-3: *The Writer Yashe Essay Works* edited by Liang Shiqiu published by Shanghai People's Publishing House in 1993.（梁实秋《雅舍小品全集》，上海人民出版社，1993 年出版）

Figure 8.7.11-4: *The Great Silent Majority* by Wang Xiaobo published by China Youth Publishing House in 1997.（王小波《沉默的大多数》，中国青年出版社，1997 年出版）

Figure 8.7.11-5: *The Collected Lyric Prose by Zhou Zuoren* published by Culture and Art Publishing House in 1992.（《周作人抒情散文》，文化艺术出版社，1992 年出版）

The trend toward "light reading" also spurred an increase in the publication of essays in sets and collections. Local publishing houses dominated the publishing of essay collections. A fine example of an essay collection printed in the 1990s is *The Hundred Flowers Essay Collection* (Figure 8.7.12) published by Baihua Literature and Art Publishing House. The set was divided into three separate series: contemporary, modern and classical and included more than 100 titles in total.

Figure 8.7.12: One of *the Hundred Flowers Essay Collection* published by Flowers Literature and Art Publishing House in 1990.（《百花散文书系》之一，百花文艺出版社，1990 年出版）

With the rapid development of the economy and the media, the 1990s also saw the population begin to be fascinated by public figures, such as movie, television and sports stars. As a result, the decade saw a rise in the number of publications concerning celebrities. The "new realism" novels by Chi Li also became very popular and themselves were turned into movies and television programs.

What is more, One of the major changes which affected the publishing industry during the 1990s was the introduction and adoption of copyright law. In 1992, China also entered the Berne Convention and the Universal Copyright Convention. These developments not only protected authors and publishing houses from infringement, but also led to the gradual increase in copyright trading with foreign countries. By 1999, China was trading copyrights on a large scale with other developed countries such as the Unites States, the United

Kingdom and Japan. Along with the introduction of copyright law, another major shift in the 1990s which took place in the publishing industry was the consolidation of some of the existing publishing houses. Internal restructuring within publishing houses, the management of resources and the building of publishing brands into corporations were all encouraged by the government. In 1999, approval for the establishment of several large scale publishing houses was granted and both the Beijing Publishing Group and the Shanghai Century Publishing Group were formed. The formation and influence of these larger publishing groups in the 1990s is evidenced by the corporate atmosphere which currently pervades the industry.

7.3 Features of publishing in the 2000s

Diversification in the publishing industry has continued into the 21st Century. Publishing as a whole is prosperous and digital publishing is steadily changing the composition and future of the industry. Digital publishing falls mainly into two categories: the first is digital works presented through display devices and tangible electronic publications in the form of CD-ROMs, CD-Is, DVD-ROMs, etc; the second is online publications like the electronic books and magazines mediated through the Internet, excluding news content such as online newspapers. Improvement in government legislation and China's "going global" strategy have also provided for a more open and standardized industry.

The current model of digital publishing in China is such that digital publishing operators, mostly IT firms, obtain copyright from traditional publishing houses or other copyright owners, digitalize the authorized works and supply them to end readers. Under this model, traditional publishing houses become simply providers of original works. It may also make it possible for the public to gain access to both digitalized works and celebrities through the Internet or other media like corresponding television broadcasts. Some authors have even gained celebrity status more easily. For instance, University lecturers Yi Zhongtian and Yu Dan now enjoy success in multiple fields after appearing on CCTV show *The Lecture Hall*. Yi Zhongtian's *A Taste of the Three Kingdoms* sold 650,000 copies in 2006 alone and his book *Five Great Ancient People* was also widely accessible both in paper form and over the Internet. Moreover, the development of education and the Internet has additionally created another active reader group in today's society; children and teen literature is a viable new market that has become popular in the publishing industry. Contemporary children's books have done a great deal to breathe life into a sector of the publishing industry that once lay dormant. Teenage literature is geared towards attracting middle school and university aged readers. Many books have been particularly popular in urban areas and boast a great deal of content relevant to their audience. Notable examples include: Han Han's *Triple Door*, Chun Shu's *Beijing Doll*, Guo Jingming's *River of Sorrow* and Cai Jun's *Secret* (Figure 8.7.13-1-4). These and other novels have helped establish teenage novels as a viable publishing genre.

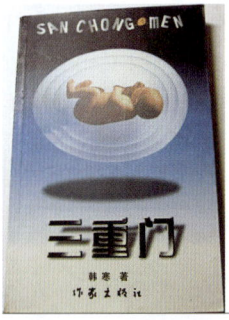

Figure 8.7.13-1: *Triple Door* by Han Han published by Writers Publishing House in 2000.（韩寒《三重门》，作家出版社，2000 年出版）

Figure 8.7.13-2: *Beijing Doll* by Chun Shun published by Yuanfang Publishing House in 2002.（春树《北京娃娃》，远方出版社，2002 年出版）

Figure 8.7.13-3: *River of Sorrow* by Guo Jingming published by Changjiang Literature & Art Press in 2007.（郭敬明《悲伤逆流成河》，长江文艺出版社，2007 年出版）

Figure 8.7.13-4: *Margaret's Secret* by Cai Jun published by Jieli Publishing House in 2006.（蔡骏《玛格丽特的秘密》，接力出版社，2006 年出版）

Aside from historically based material, children's and teenage literature, a third category of book, perhaps more unique to modern times, is also being published. I am talking about books dealing with health related issues and that address healthy living and dietary themes coupled with various digitalized versions such as DVD or online versions. In 2006, Hong Zhaoguang's *On the Highway to Health at 40* and Wu Qingzhong's *Instruction Manual for the Human Body* (Figure 8.7.14-1-2) rapidly climbed the bestseller lists and were commercially successful. Other books have followed this trend as the population becomes ever more concerned and vigilant about their health and health related issues.

Figure 8.7.14-1: *On the Highway to Health at 40* by Hong Shaoguang, published by Lijiang Publishing House in 2006.（洪昭光《40岁登上健康快车》，漓江出版社，2006年出版）

Figure 8.7.14-2: *Instruction Manual for the Human Body* by Wu Qingzhong published by Huacheng Publishing House in 2005.（吴清忠《人体使用手册》，花城出版社，2005年出版）

Chinese books are also finding overseas audiences. With China's entry into the World Trade Organization, the development of digital technology and an ever evolving contemporary social landscape, Chinese publishing has gone global. By participating in international book fairs, international cooperation and exchanges and through the establishment of publishing houses overseas, publishers have made it possible for Chinese titles to find audiences abroad. To date over 1,000 titles have been translated and distributed in foreign countries. Copyright trading on a global scale also continues to increase, although from an international perspective, China's activity level is low considering the size of its economy.

One of the ongoing problems facing the publishing industry in this new century is piracy. Books by non-existent authors or that include fabricated content are common. This makes it difficult for readers to distinguish between legitimate and phony titles; biographies, teaching materials and books on finance and the economy are the most common books copied. The Copyright Law introduced in 2000, along with a number of subsequent regulations have strengthened legislation geared towards protecting publishers and the public, although infringement is still a large concern.

In addition to the laws introduced to protect publishers from copyright infringement, corresponding legislation has also been adopted that has affected the publishing industry… Specifically I am talking about the laws which made it possible for large publishing groups to be established. I mentioned this previously when speaking of the shift towards the consolidation of publishing houses and the corporate atmosphere of the 1990s. This trend has continued into the present century. Companies such as the China Publishing Group, founded in 2001, operate on such a large scale that it is difficult for other Chinese publishers to compete. Some publishers such as Commercial Press, Zhonghua Book Company and Joint Publishing are able to rely on brand familiarity and traditional market positions to stay competitive. Other publishers have been financially successful and so stay competitive. However, the majority of publishers cannot compete for the reasons that they are not large enough, are not well situated in the market or have failed to take advantage of the opportunities presented by digital publishing.

As the publishing industry moves forward publishers will need to continue to be culturally innovative and to embrace the growing trend of digital and "all-media" publishing in order to be successful. The success of the industry will be determined by a number of factors, including, but not limited to: the quality of education provided in the schools that teach printing and publishing, the quality of the students or future employees of the publishing companies, the adequacy of government related laws addressing the industry, and the publishers themselves, who will need to embrace both technological and cultural trends in order to stay competitive.

7.4 Conclusion

To wrap up my lecture, I can't help eulogizing the publishing accomplishment in China. For more than 30-years the Chinese publishing industry has experienced phenomenal growth. The growth coincides with and is partially responsible for the country's successful reforms. The unmitigated success of the industry should come as no surprise given China's long history and extensive cultural connection to the fields of printing and publishing. The Chinese publishing industry not only has the ability to reference one of the most profound civilizations and extensive cultures in the world, but also has the ability to reflect the present and become a barometer for social change and the evolution of values in society. There is no doubt that the publishing industry will continue to thrive in the future as it embraces themes of progress and innovation and there is certainly no doubt that it will continue to play a vital role in the rejuvenation of the Chinese nation.

Finally, I hope the end of this series of lectures does not mean the end of our discussion and exploration. You are welcome to contact me whenever and wherever you are thanks to digitalization and the Internet. Now I must say good-bye.

Task 8 ▶ Join the online forum and write a summary

(Students are required to have an instant and online post-talk discussion)

Richards: Hello again everybody, finally we come to the last task of the last unit. So welcome everybody to Forum 8. The theme of this forum is The Diversification of Publishing in the New Era. I am privileged to invite guest professor Phillips to attend our follow-up debate. These are the discussion questions that I propose for the forum:

1) Try to summarize the unique features of Chinese publishing from the 1980s to the present time;

2) Try to name and describe as many influential publishing houses as possible and determine their contribution to the field of publishing in China.

3) Try to compare modern publications with the ancient publications in terms of content, and methods of publishing and distribution.

	4) What impact has digital publishing had on traditional publishing and why?
Philips:	I must thank my respected colleague for his kind invitation to the forum. Professor Richards' speech was of course wide-ranging and most thought-provoking. If I may, I would like to add a question to his very comprehensive list. You are all majoring in publishing, and looking at the most recent contributions to publishing in China, I can't help thinking about Wang Xuan. I don't know if you know the name, but he invented the computerized laser photo composition system for Chinese character typesetting. His contribution to Chinese publishing can't be exaggerated. So I suggest you research his invention and discuss its importance. I know this is a rather rigorous demand, but I really think it is worthy of your consideration.
Irene:	Thank you so much for all your suggestions, dear supervisors. I promise you we won't let you down — will we, PRIMO group?
Owen:	We surely won't, Irene. We're a good team, and there's nothing we can't do when we work together. I'm going to work on enrolling more members for our forum and finding answers to some of those questions. How about you, Miriam?
Miriam:	Oh, I volunteer to collect materials on Wang Xuan and his wonderful invention to share with whoever joins us on the forum.
Richards:	Well, I'd just like to say what a pleasure it has been to share this learning experience with all of you. Let me repeat on behalf of my colleague Professor Phillips and myself, that as we drop the curtain on this first period of our exploration of Chinese publishing, we hope that you will free to contact either of us for further information in this field. To the future!
All:	To the future!

Appendix: Vocabulary for Unit 8

Historical Note
beret /ˈbereɪ/ n. 贝雷帽
demeanor /dɪˈmiːnə/ n. 风度；举止；行为
chivalrous /ˈʃɪvəlrəs/ adj. 侠义的；骑士的；有武士风度的
forthrightness /ˈfɔːθraɪtnɪs/ n. 直率；率真；正直
curator /kjʊ(ə)ˈreɪtə/ n. 馆长；监护人；管理者
pun /pʌn/ n. 双关语；俏皮话
revel /ˈrev(ə)l/ vi. 狂欢；陶醉
infatuate /ɪnˈfætjʊeɪt/ vt. 使糊涂；使冲昏头脑；使迷恋
layfolk / ˈleɪfəʊk/ n. 俗人，普通人

Reading Activity
repository /rɪˈpɒzɪt(ə)rɪ/ n. 贮藏室，仓库；知识库；智囊团
archive /ˈɑːkaɪv/ n. 档案馆；档案文件
divination /ˌdɪvɪˈneɪʃ(ə)n/ n. 预测；占卜
confidential /kɒnfɪˈdenʃ(ə)l/ adj. 机密的；表示信任的；获信任的
chronicler /ˈkrɒnɪklə/ n. 记录者；年代史编者
cult /kʌlt/ n. (尤其指宗教上的) 祭仪；礼拜；狂热信徒
secretariat /ˌsekrɪˈteərɪət/ n. 秘书处；书记处；秘书 (书记，部长等) 之职
orthodox /ˈɔːθədɒks/ n. 正统的人；正统的事物
adj. 正统的；传统的；惯常的；
legitimacy /lɪˈdʒɪtɪməsɪ/ n. 合法；合理；正统
shrine /ʃraɪn/ n. 圣地；神殿；神龛；圣祠
crate /kreɪt/ n. 板条箱；篓
sutra /ˈsuːtrɑ/ n. 佛经；经典
collate /kəˈleɪt/ vt. 核对，校对；校勘
lineage /ˈlɪnɪɪdʒ/ n. 血统；家系，[遗] 世系
abbreviate /əˈbriːvɪeɪt/ vt. 缩写，使省略；使简短
vi. 使用缩写词
bibliophile /ˈbɪblɪəfaɪl/ n. 藏书家；爱书的人
warlord /ˈwɔːlɔːd/ n. 军阀

Lecture
curtail /kɜːˈteɪl/ vt. 缩减；剪短；剥夺……特权等
diversification /daɪˌvɜːsɪfɪˈkeɪʃ(ə)n/ n. 多样化；变化

symptomatic /ˌsɪmptəˈmætɪk/ *adj.* 有症状的；症候的
serialize /ˈsɪrɪəlaɪz/ *vt.* 连载；使连续
humanity /hjʊˈmænɪtɪ/ *n.* 人类；人道；仁慈；人文学科
array /əˈreɪ/ *n.* 数组，阵列；排列，列阵；大批，一系列
indicative /ɪnˈdɪkətɪv/ *adj.* 象征的；指示的；表示……的
infringement /ɪnˈfrɪndʒmənt/ *n.* 侵犯；违反
pervades /pəːˈveɪd/ *vt.* 遍及；弥漫
gear /ˈgɪə/ *vt.* 使适应；用齿轮连接
vigilant /ˈvɪdʒɪl(ə)nt/ *adj.* 警惕的；警醒的；注意的；警戒的
fabricate /ˈfæbrɪkeɪt/ *vt.* 制造；伪造；装配

主要参考文献

Brokaw, Cynthia J., & Chow, Kai-Wing, eds. *On the History of the book in China* Studies on China, Volume 27: Printing and Book Culture in Late Imperial China. Berkeley, CA, USA: University of California Press, 2005. ProQuest ebrary. Web. 17 August 2015. Copyright © 2005. University of California Press. All rights reserved.

Shah, Angilee, and Wasserstrom, Jeffrey. *Chinese Characters : Profiles of Fast-Changing Lives in a Fast-Changing Land*. Berkeley, CA, USA: University of California Press, 2012. ProQuest ebrary. Web. 11 August 2015. Copyright © 2012. University of California Press. All rights reserved.

Eugene Wu. *Recent Developments in Chinese Publishing.* Source from The China Quarterly, No. 53 (Jan.-Mar., 1973), pp. 134–138, Published by Cambridge University Press on behalf of the School of Oriental and African Studies Stable. (URL: http://www.jstor.org/stable/652510)

Endymion Wikinson. *Chinese History,* Harvard University Asia Center, Boston, Untied States, 2013.

Brokaw, Cynthia J., & Chow, Kai-Wing, eds. *On the History of the Book in China, Studies on China, Volume 27: Printing and Book Culture in Late Imperial China.* Berkeley, CA, USA: University of California Press, 2005. ProQuest ebrary. Web. 17 August 2015. Copyright © 2005. University of California Press. All rights reserved.

肖东发. 中国编辑出版史（上下册）[M]. 沈阳：辽海出版社. 2005.

李瑞良. 中国出版编年史（上下册）[M]. 福州：福建人民出版社. 2006.

张树栋，庞多益，郑如斯.《简明中华印刷通史》[M]. 桂林：广西师范大学出版社. 2004.

宿白.《唐宋时期的雕版印刷》[M]. 北京：文物出版社. 1999.

叶树声，余敏辉.《明清江南私人刻书史略》[M]. 合肥：安徽大学出版社. 2000.

杨玲. 宋代出版文化 [M]. 北京：文物出版社. 2012.

叶德辉.《书林清话》（插图本）[M]. 上海：上海古籍出版社. 2008.

查猛济，陈彬龢. 中国书史[M]. 北京：知识产权出版社. 2012.

郭孟良. 晚明商业出版 [M]. 北京：中国书籍出版社. 2011.

李常庆. "四库全书"出版研究 [M]. 郑州：中州古籍出版社. 2008.

翁连溪. 清代内府刻书研究（上下册）[M]. 北京：故宫出版社. 2013.

徐宗泽. 明清间耶稣会士译著提要 [M]. 上海：上海世纪出版集团. 2010.

元青主编.《中国近代出版史稿》[M]. 天津：南开大学出版社. 2011.

吴永贵.《民国出版史》[M]. 福州：福建人民出版社. 2011.

陈矩弘.《新中国出版史研究（1949-1965）》[M]. 上海：上海交通大学出版社.

2012.
[美] 伊丽莎白·爱森斯坦. 作为变革动因的印刷机 [M]. 北京：北京大学出版社. 2010.
范继忠. 文化比较视角下的中国出版文明 [J]. 北京印刷学院学报，2013（5）.
潘吉星. 印刷术的起源地:韩国还是中国 [J]. 自然科学史研究，1997（1）.
薛伟明. 宋版书的艺术风格和魅力 [J]. 苏州工艺美术职业技术学院学报，2008（3）.
宋缨. 商务印书馆与中国现代出版文化 [J]. 出版科学，2004（5）.